THE EXPOS
INSIDE OUT

THE EXPOS
INSIDE OUT

DAN TURNER

McClelland and Stewart

The Canadian Publishers
McClelland and Stewart Limited
25 Hollinger Road
Toronto M4B 3G2

Canadian Cataloguing in Publication Data
Turner, Dan.
    The Expos inside out

   ISBN 0-7710-8640-7

   1. Montreal Expos (Baseball team).   I. Title.

GV875.M6T87   796.357′64′09714281   C83-094120-7

Every reasonable attempt has been made to attribute copyright
material used in this publication. Information regarding
inadvertent errors or omissions of copyright information would
be appreciated, and efforts will be made to correct same in
future editions.

"Hard Core Support" by John E. Maxfield originally appeared
in *Baseball I Gave You All the Best Years of My Life*, edited by
Kevin Kerrane and Richard Grossinger, published by North
Atlantic Books. It appears by permission of the publisher.

"Anthem" by William "Sugar" Wallace is from *The Ultimate
Baseball Book*, edited by Daniel Okrent and Harris Lewine.
Copyright © 1979 by Eisenberg, McCall and Okrent, Inc., and
Harris Lewine. Reprinted by permission of Houghton-Mifflin
Company.

Photos of Lee, Rogers, Fryman, Tito and Terry Francona by
Terry Vollum. All other photos by Dan Turner.

Printed and bound in Canada by
T. H. Best Printing Company Limited

To the real Ted Turner,
sponsor,
Sarnia Moore Paint Midgets,
1952–1954

Acknowledgements

Jim Fanning, Brian Kappler, Nancy Southam, Charis Wahl and Lynne Reilly were instrumental in the completion of this book. Each in turn proved to be the salvation of what was a dicey project at best, and I hope I have at least partially rewarded them with a good read.

Which isn't to mention: Duke Snider, Gayle Turner, Dave Van Horne, Terry Vollum, Bryn Smith, Anne McCaffrey, Bob Elliott, Doug Weir, Ian MacDonald, Ted Blackman, Serge Touchette, Doug Camilli, Toivo Kiil, David McDonald, Shorty Turner, Sandy Rubin, Rich Griffin, Duncan Macintyre, Richard Tallman, Michael Bate, Jean-Paul Sarault, Carl Mollins, Del Mackenzie, Monique Giroux, James E. Turner, Dave McIntosh, Michael Farber, Brodie Snyder, Gerry McNeil, Annette Leung, Ara Egoyan, Mildred and Clayton Harris, Doug Smith, Howard Watson, Herb Linder, Ronald Timms, Lew Gleeson, and Dylan.

I would like to thank the members of the Baseball Writers' Association of America (Montreal Chapter) and other citizens of the press box for making me feel welcome, and of course franchise holders in the Ottawa Dead Ball Baseball Association, who in collaboration with the tireless workers of Ottawa Glebe Little League sustained me throughout. And most obviously, Charles Bronfman, Rodney Scott, and the scores of other people who agreed to be interviewed to make this book possible. That's a lot of helpful people.

Contents

Mondo Carne

*About the only thing most people know me for is the
knack I have for getting in front of pitched balls. But it
could be worse. They might not know me for anything.*
—Ron Hunt
   July 1974

"Hut one! Hut two!" The big man in knee socks barks it out,
drops back, and lofts a soft, perfect spiral, hitting a red-headed
twelve-year-old in the hands at the goal line.

"Attago Red!" he shouts in a gravelly, down-home voice. "You
faked him right out of his jock."

They spring forward in succession—about three dozen of
Missouri's aspiring little-league footballers—and each time they
get thirty yards out they're greeted by a football, falling like a
feather in a dream.

The man throwing the ball, with the Sunoco cap on backward,
weighs 230. A lot of it's in the shoulders, arms and barbecue-sized
thighs, but some of it's in the paunch. Too heavy for a 5'11"
quarterback, he admits. But he likes his beer and there are no
$100-a-day fines any more to keep him lean.

Ron Hunt is 41 now. When he played quarterback at high
school he weighed 172. "They killed me—I was too small.
Wrenched my neck. Broke my finger. I had some college offers,
but when I got down there and saw the steers they had for linemen,
I came back home. I liked the physical contact of football, but
there are limits to being stupid."

When Ron Hunt played second base for the Montreal Expos he
weighed 184, and nobody thought he had any limits to the physical
punishment he could absorb. Hunt wasn't just from the old school
of ballplayers that Jim Fanning misses so much. He was the
valedictorian.

He came to the Expos from the Giants, shaking his head that
Horace Stoneham must have been drunk to have traded him for a
minor-league first baseman named Dave McDonald. Fanning's
stint as Expos' general manager is best remembered for his trading

away of Ken Singleton and Mike Torrez for nothing. But he also engineered some good deals, and Hunt for McDonald was one of them.

While Hunt came over from the Giants and played a year with the Dodgers, he simply wasn't a west-coast ballplayer. He broke in with the Mets when they were only a year old and came to the Expos when they were two years old, and it's doubtful that any player in baseball history did more for two expansion franchises. He was the guts of both teams.

The Mets brought him up because Casey liked him. "It was Stengelese logic," he remembers. "I had a sore foot at the end of spring training. Casey said—"Hey kid, I know you can't run, but can you hit? I said, 'yeah.' So he said, 'Okay, go and hit, and if you can make it to first base I'll put a runner in for you.' So I got a base hit and he put in a runner for me, and then he says, 'Hey kid—you're making me look good.' And that was it."

A hard-nosed, young second baseman with a brush cut, Hunt not only played on the 1964 National League All-Star Team in his second season, the fans elected him to the starting line-up. He was named as a back-up player in 1966. He was featured in a 1964 *Sports Illustrated* article as the one Met with a future; the article ended by talking about his aspirations to stay with the club until it was finally a contender. No dice. He was traded away in 1967, with the Mets coming off a 66–95 season and two years away from glory.

By the time he arrived in Montreal he had a reputation as a gamer—a guy who came to play and would do anything to win. He didn't have much speed, range, or power. But he played with brains and heart. His talent was his ability to get on base, with a hit placed deftly between fielders with his choked-up bat, a bunt, a walk—any way he could. The more he slowed in the field, the more hungry he got at the plate. He'd always crowded the plate and, not surprisingly, been hit now and then. When he was with San Francisco it occurred to him that he didn't mind getting hit that much. Or at least the pleasure of getting to first base outweighed the pain of getting hit. In most cases.

So he started absorbing baseballs. He stood so close to the plate, sometimes tilted over it, that there was no leeway for the pitcher on the inside corner. To throw it there and miss inside by an inch was to put the lead-off man on first. The battle between pitcher and batter comes down to who owns the plate. Hunt had built a bunker on the inside chunk of it, so there wasn't much left to fight over. And what did remain—a narrow corridor from the middle of the plate out—became the focus of his bat's attention.

It was simple. "If they threw it inside, it hit me. If they threw it outside, I hit them."

"Pitching," said the great Sandy Koufax, "is the art of instilling fear by making a man flinch." In a game in which most young men are weeded out early because they can't conquer their fear of the ball, nobody flinched less than Hunt did.

But even a man who has learned calm in the eye of terror has limits. If a ball was coming at him at less than 90 mph he wouldn't get out of the way. If it was faster he might or might not try, but sometimes there was no time to bail out. In the days before tight-fitting, double-knit uniforms he wore his top as loose as he could, the better to get hit in the nothing.

"I tried to catch the slow ones, but every now and then they'd drill me."

He was also a pretty good hunt-and-peck hitter (over .300 twice) and had amazing bat control. In 520 at-bats in 1971 he hit into only one double play. Omar Moreno did the same thing in 434 at-bats in 1981; but Omar Moreno could run.

In 1971 Hunt batted a modest .279 for the Expos—fair enough, but easily forgotten. But his on-base percentage was .403—the kind of mark you'd expect from Al Oliver or Rickey Henderson in a good year.

The secret, of course, was that Hunt was hit by 50 pitches that year, breaking the record of 49 set by Hugh Jennings of the Baltimore Orioles in 1896. Nobody has come close since. In 12 years he was hit 241 times, and his record may be eternal. His "take one for the team" attitude was the essence of the tough, un-complaining old-school creed.

The fans would roar in appreciation when he'd roll the ball back to the pitcher, spitting contemptuously after taking one in the ribs. If Lou Brock brought the race track to the baseball stadium, Ron Hunt brought the bull ring. Here was a matador who worked on the horns.

And like many brave men, he was funny.

"It ain't my record," he'd drawl for reporters. "It belongs to the guys who hit me. I'm not hitting them, am I?"

And when he finally paid the price—a Tom Seaver fastball off the helmet, a concussion, and a hospital bed, he took it all with a smile. "Well whaddya know," he chuckled. "They finally found my weak spot."

His body, tattooed with bruises and spike marks, was said to carry more of Chub Feeney's autographs than did the league president's own chequing account. One writer suggested that he simply outfit himself in one big poultice instead of a uniform.

"I swear he likes it," said coach Jerry Zimmerman after Hunt had been hit once by Steve Renko, again by Gene Mauch, and three times by the pitching machine in the same day at spring training.

But Hunt didn't like it. He liked the tough-guy image. Underneath it all, he knew as well as anybody that he was gambling to stretch his career.

"My ability isn't that great," he said. "When you lack something you try to make up for it in other ways."

"This guy gets paid for getting on base," said Mauch. "That's all he knows, and he knows it very well."

Mauch had grown up in a game in which fear plays as much of a role in determining who can hit as talent does, and his appreciation of Hunt was profound. "He understands you can get the shit beat out of you and it's not the end of the world. He understands pain. Few people do."

But pain, as any child knows, is nature's way of telling you there's something wrong with your body.

On August 6, 1973, the Expos were in the middle of their first pennant race, with four teams—the Mets, Cards, Pirates, and Expos—hovering around the .500 mark. None of them were able to play respectable baseball consistently enough to pull away. Hunt was leading the team in hitting—he would finish with a .309 average and an astounding .419 on-base percentage.

On this particular day the Expos were losing by a run to the Giants late in the game, with Hunt on second, when third-base coach Dave Bristol went for the bundle and waved him home on a hit to left. Gary Matthews was up to the challenge. He threw a perfect strike to catcher Dave Rader, who was blocking home plate with the ball in his mitt and Hunt still twenty feet out.

Hunt slid hard, trying to knock the ball out of Rader's glove. He missed, but his spikes were high enough that the left one got caught in Rader's shin guard. When the dust cleared, Hunt lay rolling on the ground, wincing in pain and pounding the dirt with his fists.

He lurched to his feet, went down again, and had to be helped off the field by two team-mates. He was the last out of the inning, so he went to the dugout, staggered back to his position, felt dizzy from the pain when he tried to bend over for a practice grounder, and had to leave the game.

"Everybody knows Hunt's reputation around the league," said Rader in the Giants' dressing room. "I knew he wasn't going to quit when he was obviously dead, so when he tried to kick the ball out I was ready. With a guy like him you've got to be."

Hunt said that, if he had it to do over, he would have tried to knock Rader down instead of kicking the ball loose.

For fifteen days, on the disabled list, he did exercises to try to strengthen the muscles around his knee so he could play in September. But soon after he came back the cartilage, already torn, snapped completely. He was twisting to get out of the way of an oncoming fielder when he fell in a heap and had to be carried off the field.

For the Expos, the race was as much as over. The Mets won the division with an 82–79 record. The Expos were fourth at 79–83 and finished as serious competitors for six long years.

And Hunt was tottering toward the scrap heap, his knee in a cast and time running out. He worked hard over the winter after the cast came off, ready to prove he wasn't washed up. He came back to hit .263 for the Expos in 115 games but was shunted off to the Cardinals toward the end of the year as the Expos rushed wholesale to youth. The day he was traded two new players appeared in the line-up, both up from the Quebec Carnavals. Larry Parrish, 21, played third. Warren Cromartie, 21, was in center. On the same day the club announced that it had purchased the contract of Gary Carter, 20, from its Memphis affiliate.

Hunt was released from the Cardinals after managing only 4 hits in 23 at-bats. He was finished at 33, with legs that looked 70. The next year the Cardinals called him again, asking him to take a pay cut and come to spring training.

He said he wasn't about to take a pay cut. They said he'd make up for it with a World Series cheque. He told them to give him what he was asking for and they could keep their World Series cheque. They never called back.

Football practice is finally over and Ron Hunt, sweating like a pig, trundles toward his car. The odd bruise and spike scar still decorate his legs, but he's not gimpy—he just walks as much like a sailor as he always did.

His face is still leathery and round as a pie, the sideburns remain where he and Elvis always liked them, there's no more space between his blue eyes than there ever was, and he continues to wear that mean-and-friendly grin. And he's thirsty, after three hours of sweating in the semi-permeable vapour that passes for summertime air in Wentzville, Missouri.

Which means a cold quart of one of August A. Busch's malt-and-hops spectaculars, nestled in a brown bag for the drive home. He sips his way past the dreary junk food stores and gas stations that line the highway and service roads. He points to where he used to run his classic good-ol'-boys convenience store—liquor, guns, ammunition, and other sporting equipment. But not any more.

This man's empire is down the road and into the bush now, through a jungle of magnolia trees and other lush vegetation, into a chorus of cicadas, across a small bridge, through fields grazed by Black Angus cattle, and finally to a split-log house, surrounded by woods, meadows, and a pond. And protected by a doberman with a craving for strangers' throats, just where you'd think the welcome mat would be.

"If people are nice," Ron Hunt used to tell the sportswriters, "I can be very nice. If they're not, I can be meaner than anybody." The doberman, a snarling projectile of muscles and teeth, is eventually locked away, making it safe to get out of the car. Where, thankfully enough, the people are very nice.

There is Jackie with the laughing eyes—his wife and high-school sweetheart, of whom he says fondly, "We've been truckin' together for a long time." There is Tracy, 18, slim, attractive, and outspoken like her father. Ronnie, cheerful, responsible, and good looking. And Suncere (Morning Star), 12, part Apache, part Navajo, adopted, beautiful, and quiet.

"Me and the kids raise our own pigs and cattle," says the father, a refugee from the alleys of north St. Louis. "Suncere took number three hog carcass overall at the fair this year and got two dollars a pound for it. The average was sixty-one cents. Ronnie won his class in beef. We started out just raising our own meat. Now we run twenty-three head of hogs, twenty head of beef."

He is bursting proud of these kids, and proud of himself as well for pushing them. Too hard sometimes.

"Ronnie doesn't play baseball—it interferes too much with his fishing," he tells you at first, laughing. The truth, says Tracy, is that dad pushed son too hard. "I told him I didn't care whether he played it, but if he did he was gonna do it right," says dad. "You might say I pushed him too hard."

But the kids all have credit ratings after borrowing from the bank to buy the feeding stock they nourished and sold at auction. He's proud of that.

He's proud of the Black Angus calves in the field—"Look at that one, look at the length on him! He's gonna be my bull when that guy over there's finished."

He's even proud of the four, fly-ridden Black Angus hoofs, cut off at the shank, rotting outside his pig barn. "Slaughtered a steer here last week," he says. "We eat some ourselves and sell the rest at a premium."

And the pig barn itself, where he hangs out when he wants to get away from everybody. When he played ball he looked like Pig Pen in the Peanuts comic strip. Now he spends his idle time in one. "Got to have a place to get away," he says.

The hunting trophies are everywhere—a moose head, a caribou head, an elk head, all of a mallard, all of a grouse, and others.

So are pictures of the kids, posed proudly beside their livestock. He's paid to put several of them in the local newspaper. "It's good for the sponsors who buy the meat," he says. And the kids look good, too.

As for baseball, he's proud of what he did; but it's done. Unlike many players, he always knew it would be. When he was traded to the Expos he had to fill out a questionnaire for the publicity people. "What is your ambition in life?" was one of the questions. A batting title? The Hall of Fame? "To be a good provider for my family," he replied.

And he is. He raises cattle and hogs, runs a collection agency, bales hay, and plows snow. Like Fanning, he grew up to hard work.

"Dad always worked. Mom worked hard. Even when I played,

we always came home and worked in the winter. If I played hard it's because that's what I grew up to. If I work hard, it's the same."

Dozens of awards, trophies, gloves, and other memorabilia clutter a display cabinet behind a living-room bar built out of baseball bats. Among it all rest two gold-plated balls—number 49 and number 50.

Number 49 tied Jennings and was the kind he liked. "The ball just ticked my shirt. I didn't even feel it. It was nice."

No. 50 had a bit more sting to it, but he remembers it more for the humour. "Ernie Broglio got furious. He stomped around the mound claiming I didn't try to get out of the way, the way the rule book says you're supposed to.

"I said I didn't know what he was so mad about. I put him in the record book. There sure as hell wasn't any other way he was going to get there."

He got a three-minute standing ovation at Jarry when he set the record. "That was when the fans were great. They knew we were putting out and appreciated an effort. They've probably changed by now. After they come close to winning something they get a little bloody minded."

He's not into baseball any more, he says. "I don't spend a lot of time talking to guys who are playing now. What are you going to talk about? What it's like to be retired, and what it's like to still be playing?

"I tried playing again about five years ago. I managed a semi-pro team for Sunoco. We came in second in the league. So I'm a hard-assed manager and I played some, too, at second.

"So my brother didn't show up for a game. He said he was hurt. So I went over before the game to see what the situation was. It turned out he had some broad and had gone to the Ozarks to water ski. So I took his uniform from my mother's house and kicked him off the team. My mother's still mad at me.

"So I quit managing. I tried to play on a slow-pitch softball team. I was doing all right—shit, I can still hit—but this guy came in standing up and I was making the double play. And the guy was supposed to slide, right? Well he didn't, and I about took his head off.

"Then I thought—this guy's got to go to work on Monday morning. So I quit. I can't play fun games any more. I don't play right. I like to play for money. I play nasty." He leers with the pleasure of the thought.

He always played nasty. Mauch said, "He's not afraid to make them hate him." And sometimes they played nasty back.

Catchers used to throw dirt on him to distract him.

"Jerry Grote did that," says Jackie, laughing.

"Yeah," Ron says, savouring the image. "But he only did that once. As the ball was coming in I took one quick step back and hit his glove with my bat. The ball ricocheted off his chest. He never touched me again."

One day at Jarry Park Hunt booted a ball when Mike Marshall was pitching. Marshall, a testy personality at best, threw up his arms in disgust. Hunt came over to the mound, apparently to apologize.

"I told him if he ever showed me up like that again I'd knock him on his fanny."

Just like that?

"No. I said on his fucking ass. And I said 'If you're so damned perfect, why don't you get 'em to hit it somewhere else?' "

His Montreal memories are good ones, right up until near the end, after he'd hurt his knee sliding into home.

"Now you've got to remember when I tell you this that you're talking about a guy who'd given his all over the years—namely me. I played hurt, I never backed off, I played to win.

"But when I busted up my knee going into home I can remember Fanning talking to the doctor in the next room and saying, 'Okay, we'll drain it before every game and give him some novocain, and at the end of the season he can have an operation.'

"Now I know they wanted to win. Hell, I wanted to win. You don't see any World Series rings on my fingers, do you?

"But they'd already drained 400 cc of blood off the knee with one of those big needles they stick up inside. And I couldn't put any pressure on it.

"So I looked at Jackie, and Jackie looked at me, and she said 'Ron, you've got to walk on that leg some day.'

And then Fanning told me what we'd do, and I said, "No—I want it fixed now."

But he did want to win and he didn't get it fixed. He went on the disabled list, lifted weights, pumped on an exercise bicycle, and tried to build up the muscles around it so he could come back for the stretch drive. He did, only to go down again, the cartilage tear completed.

It was the winter he changed hair styles because he couldn't get out to a barber for a brush cut. "The team was writing me off. The press was writing me off. But the next year I showed them. I came back and played well. But they were finished with me. They wanted to break in some kid named Jim Cox.

"That was the year they had Willie Davis, and he was making a fool out of them. They were transporting his girl friend and his doberman all over the place—hell, she'd be on the team bus leaving the airport and the dog would be riding in a cage underneath. *Nobody* was supposed to come on the team bus.

"Anyway, it was in our contracts that we could take our families on the team plane going to Montreal in the spring and going home from Montreal in the fall. It was getting near the end of the season so I told them that I was taking Tracy and Ronnie back with me on the last road trip to St. Louis.

"And they told me no. Because Davis had been embarrassing them all year they just decided they weren't transporting anybody any more. But hell, we had all our plans made with the apartment and everything. So I told them 'like shit.' And I said to Mauch, who was passing on their rules, 'Do you think it would help if I was black?'

"Anyway, I took the kids, but the Expos didn't like my attitude. And after one of the games in St. Louis, Mauch told me I was traded. He said he'd help make arrangements for getting Jackie and Suncere back from Montreal—Suncere had a broken leg.

"We're still waitin' for their help."

There's more, says Jackie. "About five years ago Ron wanted to get back into baseball as a coach, so he had a letter hand delivered to Charles Bronfman, the Expos owner, asking if there were any openings.

"They didn't have to say yes—a nice note would have done. But there was nothing."

Ron nods, pushes back from the table, and without the slightest facial movement moves a toothpick all the way from one side of his mouth to the other.

"You know, him saying that about my knee—I'll remember that

for a long time. That's when I realized I was just like a piece of meat, just like at the slaughterhouse."

That evening they're showing cattle at the Lincoln Summer Fair, just a few miles from Wentzville. It's a soft, heavy night and Louise Mandrell is wailing country over at the bandstand.

The steers are lined up on the infield of the ball diamond. Kids no taller than their exhibits tickle the steers' bellies with pointers to make them arch their backs and get the meat up there where it looks good. Back-combed, curly swirls on their rumps, they're tugging, lowing, slobbering, and sometimes looking inscrutable.

Around and around them walks a sun-broiled assortment of judges—fat men with belts that keep slipping under their bellies, lean men with large Adam's apples, and one midget.

The steers are gradually divided—the best of them designated blue ribbon and brought up along the third-base line, the others relegated to the red-ribbon line out by second base.

The children prod them, stretch them, and pat them. For those in the third-base row, the months of pampering will bring not just honour, but monetary reward as well. The ones that win blue ribbons, and only those, will be auctioned for slaughter at the end of the fair. And auctions are where the money is.

These farm kids must learn early not to get too sentimental about their bovine friends.

"You'd think that," says Hunt, sipping at a Budweiser in the third-base stands. "But Ronnie—well he gets pretty attached. He even gives them all names.

"But I keep reminding him about the bank, and telling him, hey kid, we're in this for the money."

The steers have hacked up the infield and the moon is coming out.

Opening Daze

In the beginning, the Expos played the New York Mets at Shea Stadium in New York. It was April 8, 1969—the best of times and the worst of times, depending on where you were. War raged in Vietnam and Biafra, but the flower children were in bloom in North America. Twenty thousand hippies had just concluded an invasion of Palm Springs, California. But the Expos didn't look like hippies. (Bill Lee was still pitching for the Red Sox.) "What we look like is an ABA basketball team," was the way catcher John Bateman put it, disguising his pride in wearing the Expos' red-white-blue-striped cap on his head like a beanie with a peak instead of a propeller. Bateman, of course, was forgetting that he was too fat to play on an ABA basketball team and that his competition at backstop—5'7" Ronnie Brand—was too short. Both perfect for baseball, though.

A perfect team, in fact, to open against the Mets. The Mets had been an expansion team themselves only seven years earlier, when their record had been 40-120, the most losses in the history of baseball. And although by 1969 Marvellous Marv Throneberry and most of his early Met team-mates had been pardoned from baseball, the Mets had done almost nothing to hint at respectability. In 1968—the final season prior to splitting the leagues into divisions—the Mets had finished ninth out of 10 teams, 24 games behind the league-leading St. Louis Cardinals and only one game up on the cellar-dwelling Houston Astros.

By the end of the 1969 season, of course, they would be known as the Miracle Mets and would defeat the Baltimore Orioles in five games to win the World Series. But who would have guessed? Certainly not the Expos' first manager, The Little General, Gene Mauch—a man widely regarded as a paragon of horsehide savvy. On April 7, 1969—the day before his team opened against the Mets—the Montreal skipper stated flatly that he wouldn't take the New York team in an even trade for the Expos. "Our starting eight," he pronounced, "is better than their starting eight." Who would have guessed if not Mauch?

The opening game seemed to sustain Mauch's vision. Buoyed by sunny skies and a seven-thousand signature telegram from a Montreal radio station, the Expos started tentatively but got bolder and bolder in their inexorable drive to destiny. There may have been momentary doubts when the veteran Mudcat Grant, described in spring-training dispatches as "the 33-year-old magician," dropped his worn right arm into his top hat and pulled out a rabbit ball, which he immediately fed to Met batters, giving up six hits, a walk, and three runs in 1⅓ innings. But what followed prompted the *New York Daily News* to banner "IT AIN'T FAIR!" across its front page the next morning, and of course it wasn't.

The Expos launched five doubles and three home runs, the homers from the bats of rightfielder Rusty Staub, 30-year-old third baseman Jose "Coco" Laboy and—most unfair of all—relief pitcher Dan McGinn. It was to be the only one of his lifetime. The great Tom Seaver, trapped by destiny in the wrong place at the wrong time, was knocked out early. The not-so-great Carroll Sembera saved the game for the winner, Don Shaw, who had relieved Jerry (Hard Luck) Robertson, who had relieved McGinn, who had relieved Grant. The 160-pound Sembera was carried off the field by his team-mates without incident. Had he known they would go on to drop 57 pounds of baseballs while committing 182 errors over the season he might have declined the lift. Sembera would be dropped soon enough. Two months after the opener he'd be given his unconditional release by the Expos, struggling back to pitch seven final innings of big-league baseball the following year before disappearing forever. He was too thin.

On April 8, 1969, though, he was just right, giving up one hit, one walk, and retiring one batter to save the game for the magnificent Shaw, who gave up three hits, four walks, and four runs in 3⅔ innings.

The final score was 11–10. Although he celebrated the victory with his wife at Toots Shore's and would later call the game his greatest thrill of the season, The Little General treated the win as routine at the time. "Our guys knew," sniffed the hubristic Expos pilot, "that they could hit Seaver or anybody else the Mets wanted to pitch."

The next day the Expos, wisely realizing that they weren't going to win consistently if they continued to give up ten runs a game, held the Mets to nine. Unfortunately they could only come up with five of their own. It began to dawn on some of them that this might not be as easy as it looked:

Opening Day Box Score

Phew!

MONTREAL (11)

	AB	R	H	RBI
Wills, ss	6	2	3	1
Sutherland, 2b...........	6	1	0	0
Staub, rf	3	2	2	2
Jones, lf..............	4	1	2	2
Bosch, cf	1	0	0	0
Bailey, 1b	4	1	2	2
Bateman, c	5	1	1	0
Laboy, 3b	5	1	1	3
Hahn, cf	3	0	0	0
Shaw, p	1	1	0	0
Grant, p	1	0	0	0
McGinn, p	1	1	1	1
J. Robertson, p	0	0	0	0
Cline, cf..............	1	0	0	0
Sembera, p	0	0	0	0
Totals	41	11	12	11

NEW YORK (10)

	AB	R	H	RBI
Agee, cf	4	1	2	3
Gaspar, rf	5	1	2	1
Boswell, 2b	5	0	2	1
C. Jones, lf.............	5	1	3	1
Chares, 3b	4	1	1	0
Kranepool, 1b	3	1	1	0
Weis, ss	1	0	0	0
Grote, c...............	3	3	2	1
Harrelson, ss	1	1	0	0
Swoboda, lf	1	0	0	0
R. Taylor, p	0	0	0	0
Dyer, ph	1	1	1	3
Seaver, p	2	0	0	0
Collins, pr	1	0	0	0
Koonce, p	0	0	0	0
A. Jackson, p	0	0	0	0
Otis, lf................	2	0	1	0
Totals	38	10	15	10

```
Montreal . . . . . . . . . . . . . . . . . . . 201 102 140—11
New York . . . . . . . . . . . . . . . . . . .030 300 004—10
```
E—Boswell 3. DP—Montreal 2. LOB—Montreal 11, New York 10. 2B—Bailey, Agee, Wills, 2, Jones 2, C. Jones. HR—McGinn 1, Staub 1, Laboy 1, Dyer 1. SB—Wills, Gaspar, C. Jones.

	IP	H	R	ER	BB	SO
Grant	1-1/3	6	3	3	1	1
McGinn	2-2/3	3	3	3	2	3
J. Robertson	1	2	0	0	1	0
Shaw (W—1-0)	3-2/3	3	4	4	4	3
Sembera	1/3	1	0	0	1	1
Seaver	5	6	4	2	3	5
Koonce (L—0-1)	2	2	3	3	4	1
A. Jackson	1/3	3	3	3	0	1
R. Taylor	1-2/3	1	1	1	1	2

WP—McGinn. Balk—McGinn.
Time—3:25.
Attendance—44,541.

Opening Day Standings

NATIONAL LEAGUE
Eastern Division

	Won	Lost	Pct.	GBL.
Montreal	1	0	1.000	. . . . .
Chicago	1	0	1.000	. . . . .
Pittsburgh	1	0	1.000	. . . . .
St. Louis	0	1	.000	1
New York	0	1	.000	1
Philadelphia	0	1	.000	1

Western Division

	Won	Lost	Pct.	GBL.
Atlanta	2	0	1.000	. . . . .
Los Angeles	1	0	1.000	1/2
San Diego	1	0	1.000	1/2
Houston	0	1	.000	1-1/2
Cincinnati	0	1	.000	1-1/2
San Francisco	0	2	.000	2

TUESDAY'S GAMES
Pittsburgh 6, St. Louis 2.
Chicago 7, Philadephía 6. (11 innings)
Montreal 11, New York 10.
San Diego 2, Houston 1.
Atlanta 10, San Francisco 2.
(Only games scheduled.)

But then an opener isn't really an opener unless it's at home, and the Expos opened at Jarry Park six days after their Broadway debut. By the time they rolled into Montreal, reality had them trapped in a run-down, and their record was 2–4. Mauch denied the young players were jittery, but conceded "there is some anxiety present" after 25-year-old Bill Stoneman made his first appearance giving up three singles, two walks and hitting a batter in ⅓ of an inning. "You know there's something wrong when your right-handed pitcher hits a left-handed batter in the back with a curve ball," said Mauch.

It was, indeed, not easy to separate the jitters from anxiety, anxiety from excitement. What, for instance, did John Bateman mean when he said, "I wanted to throw up before the opening game, and that's never happened before." Had he been looking at his tri-coloured cap again? Or at his pitching staff, which, despite occasional glimmers of talent, would finish with the highest earned-run average in the league? After many of its members had combined to give up nineteen runs in the team's first two games, Bateman seemed a bit punchy. "I wish one of them would go longer than an inning," he moaned. "I'm sick of pulling out my book to look up their names and see what they throw."

Jitters, anxiety, excitement—everybody had them, including the fans. A week earlier the glacier that is Montreal's winter had magically receded and 150,000 had lined the city's streets to welcome baseball back to Montreal. The team they were greeting had a lot of similarities to the one they had lost nine years earlier—the old Montreal Royals. A Dodger farm club, the Royals—stepping stone for such greats as Jackie Robinson and Duke Snider—had been wrenched from the heart of the city by the ruthless Walter O'Malley soon after the Dodgers abandoned Brooklyn.

To be honest, the glacier hadn't completely receded. There were still five-foot snow banks behind the outfield fence, but they provided a fine vantage point from which to watch the action. Neither elements nor personalities could chill opening day spirits—not even Curt Flood, the visiting Cardinal outfielder. It was one thing that Flood felt players were treated like serfs, and he would soon challenge the game's master-servant relationship, opening the flood-gates to free-agency. Fine. But to say of his host's playing field, on the day of the home opener, "I've played on some bad diamonds but this is the worst," is not to be a credit to mankind. Why not celebrate the fact that at this latitude the frost is just starting to leave the ground, leading to some "lumpiness," as he so graphically put it? Of course, it's legitimate to say, "The outfield is rough and its tough to figure out which way the ball is going to bounce." But saying, "I hope I don't get killed out there tomorrow," is tasteless, especially when going up against opponents who would face that risk whatever the condition of the field.

No matter. In a country in which it's still possible to suffer from cabin fever in June, this April day blossomed bright and warm. By game time Jarry Park was swaddled in sunshine, the temperature a balmy 65° without a Celsius in sight. The place was packed long before game time with more than 29,000 people, most of them closer to the action than the richest among them would ever be when the team was later moved to a factory with a hole in the roof. Last-minute preparations were frenzied. The start was delayed for 15 minutes. Renovations at Jarry weren't quite complete and 6,000 folding chairs—hard, but historic—were set up on either side of the field. As the years passed perhaps 100,000 people would remember sitting on those chairs.

As the fans waited, many of them thumbed through special supplements of Montreal newspapers, put together so the public could recognize the home-town squad. Not that they helped much. The photography was baseball traditional: portraits shot at high noon when the players' peaked caps shaded most of their faces, making them indistinguishable and all but invisible—men known by their chins alone.

Each photo was sponsored by a local merchandiser and accompanied by capsule comments describing the player's assets, some of them jammed into a single sentence. Infielder Angel Hermoso—sponsored by Le Martinique Motor Inn, 1005 Guy St.—was depicted as "an exciting ballplayer who should become a big favourite in the Canadian city with his antics on the basepaths." Angel was to steal three bases during the 1969 season. Even if you conceded four antics a steal, that's still only a dozen antics.

Centerfielder Don Bosch had played for the Pirates briefly, before playing for the Mets briefly, before coming to the Expos briefly—probably in a 1954 Ford. One of the captions reminded fans that Pittsburgh Manager Larry Shepard had once been quoted as saying that "in the field, Bosch can be favourably com-

17

pared with Willie Mays"—courtesy of Montreal Messenger and Distribution Service Ltd. At the plate, though, you had to give Mays the edge. Bosch would hit .179 for the Expos in 1969, raising his lifetime average to .164 before going back home.

The game finally started, to wild cheering. The Expos made five errors and gave up seven runs in one inning to the National League champion Cardinals and still came back to win 8–7. Stout left-fielder Mack Jones drove in five runs with a home run and a triple. Jones liked to provide that kind of fun. It was true he couldn't field, and an August slump would leave management disgruntled about him, but in the beginning—when nobody was sure you could sell bad baseball in Montreal—he was crucial.

Coco Laboy hit a double and scored the winning run. Coco, a third baseman, would still be in the running for the sportswriters' Rookie-of-the-Year Award as late as August, and actually won the comparable Sporting News Award voted by the players. By the end of the season, though—with no greater talent waiting in the wings than veteran Bob Bailey, who had acknowledged himself to have been the league's worst third baseman in his prime—Mauch was talking about platooning Laboy the following season. But in the beginning, when this city of some dignity was terrified they would all be mediocre, Laboy was terrific. He led the league in batting for the first month and never did completely fall apart.

And Bateman, glorious Bateman! Chasing a pop fly near the stands, he ran to a spot directly in front of owner Charles Bronfman's box seat, camped under the ball as it parachuted eagerly toward him, and dropped it. Opening Day jitters.

Gazette reporter Ted Blackman, who would follow the Expos for several years, described it all this way: "Employing the rousing fireworks and nail-biting fumbling that have typified their every game, the Expos let it all hang out for a mob of 29,184 enraptured customers who came to cheer at Jarry Park. They left wanting more."

It was the best of times.

Real Opening Day Box Score

ST. LOUIS (7)

	AB	R	H	RBI
Brock, lf	5	0	0	0
Flood, cf	5	1	4	0
Pinson, rf	5	1	1	1
Torre, 1b	5	1	2	2
Shannon, 3b	5	1	0	0
McCarver, c	5	1	1	0
Javier, 2b	4	1	2	0
Maxvill, ss	4	1	2	4
Briles, p	2	0	0	0
Waslewski, p	1	0	0	0
Gagliano, ph	0	0	0	0
Hoerner, p	0	0	0	0
Totals	41	7	12	7

MONTREAL (8)

	AB	R	H	RBI
Bosch, cf	5	1	2	0
Wills, ss	5	2	1	1
Staub, rf	4	2	2	0
Jones, lf	4	1	2	5
Bailey, 1b	4	0	1	0
Bateman, c	2	0	0	0
Laboy, 3b	3	2	1	0
Sutherland, 2b	4	0	0	0
Jaster, p	2	0	1	1
McGinn, p	2	0	1	1
Totals	35	8	11	8

St. Louis . . . . 000 700 000—7
Montreal . . . . 321 100 10x—8

E—Bateman, Wills, Bailey 2, Bosch. LOB—St. Louis 8, Montreal 8. 2B—Flood, Bailey, Staub, Torre, Laboy. 3B—Jones. HR—Jones 2, Maxvill 1, Torre 2.

	IP	H	R	ER	BB	SO
Briles	3	9	7	7	3	3
Waslewski, L (0–1)	4	2	1	1	2	5
Hoerner	1	0	0	0	0	1
Jaster	3-2/3	9	7	2	0	1
McGinn, W. (1–0)	5-1/3	3	0	0	1	0

WP—Waslewski. Balk—Jaster.
Time—2:17.
Attendance—29,184.

The History of Canada and the World: April–October 1969

*There's one thing people forget about that team. And that's
how hard we tried.*
—Manny Mota,
   July 1982

For some pathetic citizens, sports is everything. As the philosopher
Stephen Douglas Rogers has pointed out, fan is short for
"fanatic." Twisted as it will seem to the reader, there are those
who become so engrossed in the day-to-day doings of professional
athletes that they lose touch with the important events of their
times. But while this phenomenon is prevalent in large American
cities, it's rare in cosmopolitan Canadian centres such as Montreal
and Chicoutimi. While a sports team as fascinating as the Expos
will serve as an entertaining and healthy diversion for the good
burghers of such communities, almost all of them will keep a
finger on the pulse of those happenings that determine their fate,
the fate of their children—indeed, the fate of mankind. With this
civilized approach to life in mind, here is what was important to
the hundreds of thousands who added the Expos to their spectrum
of interests in the team's first year of being.
Main characters:
   Pierre Elliott Trudeau, elected prime minister-for-life of Canada, June 25, 1968.
   Charles de Gaulle, first president of the fifth Republic of France (1890–1970).
   Ho Chi Minh, orig. Nguyen That Thanh, Vietnamese political leader (1890–1969).
   Country Joe and the Fish, musical group, played at Woodstock.
   Maury Wills, premier shortstop of the 60s, finished his career with 586 stolen bases, languished in minor leagues for several years before starring with Dodgers, chosen early in expansion draft by Expos, who may have reminded him of the minors, back to the Dodgers.
   Rusty Staub, owner of Rusty's Restaurant, New York.

John Lennon, singer and songwriter (1940–1980).

William Hambly Stoneman, one of 26 major-league pitchers to have thrown two complete games in which his opponents did not hit safely.

Richard Raymond "The Monster" Radatz, 6'6", 235 lbs., appeared on the cover of both *Time* and *Life*. Between 1962 and 1965, throwing for some terrible Boston Red Sox teams, saved 100 games, winning 49 games and losing only 32. Over those four years he pitched 538 innings, giving up 396 hits and striking out 608 batters.

Elroy Face, 5'8", 155 lbs., 1969 room-mate of Richard Raymond "The Monster" Radatz, pitched 16 National League seasons, saving 193 games, winning 104 and losing 95. In 1959 he won 18 games, lost one on a ninth-inning single by Jim Gilliam, and saved ten more.

Richard Milhous Nixon, president of the United States of America from 1969 to 1974.

1969

April 7: 150,000 people lined Montreal streets to greet their new baseball team, many of the younger fans flashing the V peace sign as the players paraded past.

April 8: The Expos came, saw, and conquered in New York, winning their opener 11–10 over the Mets.

April 14: Jarry Park was packed as the Expos stormed back to win their home opener 8–7 over the St. Louis Cardinals.

April 17: The emergence of talent continued as Bill Stoneman no-hit the Phillies 7–0. Don Bosch did his Willie Mays imitation in center field, making a great sliding catch to preserve history.

April 21: Four parachutists descended toward the mound at Jarry in between-game festivities during a double-header. Three of them missed the park, one injuring himself by hitting a parked car. Pitcher Carl Morton had set the tone, an errant tone for them, in the first game, walking five batters and hitting another in four innings of work.

April 26: Morton served up a hanging curve ball to Pirate pitcher Steve Blass, who smacked it for a three-run triple. Expo manager Gene Mauch removed both Morton and catcher John Bateman from the game.

April 28: Charles de Gaulle resigned as president of France after his new constitutional proposals were turned down in a referendum. De Gaulle's feelings were identical to most of the Expos' starting pitchers: *"Après-moi, le déluge."*

April 30: The Montreal Amateur Baseball Fan Club held a luncheon to honour Don Hahn for having been the outstanding Expo at spring training. General Manager Jim Fanning filled in for Hahn, whom he had sent to the minors four days earlier.

May 8: Mauch dazzled with his footwork at Jarry, kicking a rosin bag to deep short and punting a baseball into the dugout after being ejected for protesting a balk call on his pitcher. Balks, he said later, are "insignificant technicalities" that shouldn't alter the course of a game.

May 14: The Expos committed five errors as the Astros clobbered them 10–3. "We owe Abner Doubleday an apology," said Mauch apologetically.

May 15: U.S. President Richard Nixon proposed a gradual, twelve-month withdrawal from Vietnam.

May 17: Tito Francona of the Braves hit a two-run homer to beat the Expos in the twelfth—a legacy for his son.

May 20: Elroy Face celebrated the launching of Apollo 10 to the moon by serving up three home runs in relief. All fell short of the ionosphere. But just.

The Expos had expressed interest in trading slugging first baseman Donn Clendenon to the Mets for a package that would include sophomore pitcher Nolan Ryan, but it was leaking out they were no longer interested because Ryan was said to be having arm trouble.

May 22: Montreal Mayor Jean Drapeau flew off to Europe to lobby for the 1976 Olympics.

May 24: In his first start Jerry (Hard Luck) Robertson allowed only four hits in six innings, striking out nine. The Expos lost to Cincinnati, 4–3.

Gazette sportswriter Ted Blackman acknowledged American newspaper reports that seven days earlier Mack Jones had called him to the back of the team bus, where in "a momentary loss of cool" Maury Wills had demanded that Blackman no longer use his name in stories, then slapped him in the mouth.

May 26: Apollo 10 splashed down safely with Stafford, Cernan, and Young aboard. The first frogman in the water was Louis Boisvert, who was born in Montreal.

May 27: The Chinese government of Mao Tse-tung threatened to wipe out the Soviet Union "resolutely, cleanly, thoroughly, and completely."

May 28: The Expos lost their eleventh straight to the Dodgers. A description of the game's key play: "[First baseman] Bob Bailey started to charge the bunt but stopped when [pitcher] Larry Jaster fielded it. [Second baseman] Gary Sutherland stood behind first base instead of on the bag. Bailey ducked to give Jaster a clear path and the pitcher threw it in the dirt for a two-base error. Sutherland wasn't even there to make the try." (You had to credit Bailey for ducking.)

      Blackman, who had said he had forgiven Wills for slapping him, had nonetheless started describing the back-up shortstop, Bobby Wine, as "a symphony on spikes."

      John Lennon and Yoko Ono held a public love-in in a Montreal hotel bed.

May 29: Starter Jim "Mudcat" Grant shook off the agony of the Expos twelfth straight defeat and announced he would open a disco in Montreal called Mudcat's. Grant explained that if he was going to dance every night it might as well be at his own club. His record was 1–6. Pitching from the Jarry Park mound, he said, was making him sore.

May 30: The Expos dropped their thirteenth straight, losing 3–2 to the Padres. They had held the lead three times in the previous 117 innings. Average offence during the 13 games: 2.5 runs per game. Average defence: 6.5 runs per game.

May 31: The Expos lost their fourteenth straight, again 3–2 to their expansion rivals, the Padres, as Johnny Sipin hit his first, and second-last, major-league homer for the opponents.

June 2: Premier Bertrand proposed holding a referendum to determine Quebeckers' wishes on the status of the province in confederation.

June 4: Maury Wills, the Expos' eleventh pick in the expansion draft, announced his retirement after "a nice visit" with General Manager Fanning, who said he had no doubt that Wills was sincere.

      Mudcat Grant announced his disco would not be opened since he had just found out he had been traded to St. Louis. "That cools that scene," he explained. The Expos lost their seventeenth straight, 8–3 to the Giants.

June 5: "Wegener was doing fine until he faced Murderers' Row," observed Expo manager Mauch. The team lost its eighteenth straight when starter Mike Wegener weakened in the fourth, giving up four straight hits to Giants' catcher Jack Hiatt (.196), shortstop Hal Lanier (.228), second baseman Don Mason (.228), and pitcher Mike McCormick (.156).

June 6: Maury Wills announced he had reconsidered his retirement on advice he had received from thirty friends.

Two pitchers were released: relievers Carroll Sembera and Steve Shea. Shea's ERA was the best on the club, Sembera's was second.

The Expos, having lost nineteen straight, arrived in Vancouver to play an exhibition game against their top farm team, the Mounties. Coach Bob Oldis spoke passionately in an attempt to inspire the parent club. "Go get 'em boys," he said. "This is a sudden-death game, the winner to complete the remainder of the National League schedule." The Mounties won, 5–3, but Oldis reneged.

June 7: They lost again: twenty straight. A month of non-stop losing. Manny Mota and Coco Laboy asked a Spanish brother for a blessing. Mauch commended their attitude. "I'm pleased they asked for a blessing and not the last rites."

June 8: The Expos nipped the Dodgers 4–3 in Los Angeles to end their losing streak, with Elroy Face sewing up the victory in relief. Called upon in the bottom of the ninth, with the Expos leading 4–1, he gave up one run on an infield out, allowed a bloop single, and sent home another run with a balk. Slow Rusty Staub, who had homered, scampered deep to right to catch a ball a foot from the fence, ending the game. At the beginning of the streak the Expos were 12–17. They had slipped to 13–37.

June 9: Wills and Manny Mota, the Expos' first pick in the expansion draft, were traded to the Dodgers for Ron Fairly and change. Wills, who had been manipulating to get out of Montreal, responded to Fanning's informing him of the deal by saying, "Well, I guess that's it" and walking out of Fanning's office, slamming the door in his face.

Fairly, from a long tradition of Dodger winning, was at least cheery. "It'll be fun trying to win with the Expos," he guessed.

Georges Pompidou was elected president of France in a landslide.

June 16: Donn Clendenon was traded to the Mets for pitcher

Steve Renko and others. Renko would have a long journeyman's career with six teams, pitching well enough to survive. No mention was made of Ryan, whose arm was now fine.

June 17: Newcomer Kevin Collins, obtained in the Clendenon trade, impressed the pre-game crowd by smashing six pitches into the upper deck at St. Louis' Busch Stadium. Unbeknownst to anyone he had exactly matched the half-dozen home runs that would be his total major-league output.

June 19: Mudcat Grant, traded to St. Louis two weeks earlier after compiling a 1–6 record with the Expos, pitched 5⅓ innings of scoreless relief against his old club to pick up a win.

June 25: Mauch was jeered as the Expos drop both ends of a double-header to the Cardinals, 8–3 and 8–1, before a capacity crowd of 30,219, with Grant picking up another win. Mauch conducted the jeers with his hands, as though he were leading an orchestra.

Leanne Mauch, the manager's daughter, sat in the Jarry stands with Lowell Palmer, a young Phillies pitcher who had shut out the Expos the previous day with a three-hitter. Reporters called it treason. Palmer was to have a five-year career, winning 5, losing 18, and compiling a lifetime ERA of 5.28. His problem was wildness.

July 1: Newly acquired Ron Fairly slammed his right fist into his left hand and broke a bone in the fist. Fairly was philosophical, saying he once knew a pitcher who broke his arm in four places trying to throw a curve.

Prince Charles was installed as Prince of Wales.

July 2: Dan McGinn, a little lefthander with a terrific sinker, came in in relief and retired ten members of the league-leading Chicago Cubs in order, striking out six of them. The Expos lost, 4–2.

July 3: Cub pitcher Dick Selma was forced to towel off his greasy scalp on the mound after Rusty Staub noticed the ball approaching the plate in a strange way.

Leo Durocher, the newly married Cub manager, was not in the dugout as the Expos squared off against the Cubs. The Cubs publicity office announced he was not honeymooning but was sick, and had regurgitated seven times the previous night. One Chicago newspaper called it a record for a National League manager on Canadian soil.

July 5: A heated battle of words erupted between several players, including Rusty Staub, and pitching coach Calvin (Coolidge Julius Caesar Tuskahoma) McLish. McLish refused to allow the lights to be doused on the bus back to the hotel in Philadelphia so the players could drink their beer in the dark, and he called the players "spoiled."

"When I played we carried our bags a mile from the railway station to the hotel. We never had buses on the runway and a porter to carry our bags. Nowadays they want everything."

July 6: Gary Waslewski, obtained from St. Louis for Mudcat Grant, pitched a one-hitter and gave up only one walk, hitting a two-run double in his own cause and facing the minimum twenty-seven batters, to win his first major league game in more than a year.

July 15: El Salvador guerillas invaded Honduras following a series of violent soccer games between the two countries.

July 17: Willie Stargell became the first player to hit a home run into the swimming pool behind Jarry's right-field scoreboard, 450 feet from home plate.

Prime Minister Trudeau was pelted with grain in Saskatoon, as demonstrators brandished placards exhorting him to "Hustle Grain, Not Women!"

Substitute first baseman Ty Cline went 4-for-4, scoring two runs as the Expos beat the Pirates 5–4.

July 20: Apollo 11 landed on the Sea of Tranquility. "That's one small step for man, one giant leap forward for mankind"—Neil Armstrong.

Police said a complaint will be laid against Senator Edward M. Kennedy for leaving the scene of an accident.

The Expos swept a pair from the Mets on home runs by Jones, Bailey, Wine, and Laboy.

July 23: The National League won its seventh straight All-Star Game behind the home-run power of Willie McCovey and Johnny Bench. Rusty Staub of the Expos made it to the on-deck circle, but not to the plate.

July 26: The Expos became the first team in the league to turn one hundred double plays. Mauch was not surprised. "It makes it a lot easier," he said, "when you give up that many bases on balls."

July 29: The highly strung Adolfo Phillips, recently acquired from the Cubs, had been batting lead-off but was asking to be removed from that position. "Everywhere the pitchers are not so good but I don't hit them," he explained.

Mauch called starter Jerry Robertson "a great man with a lot of courage." The Expos had been supporting Robertson with an average of half a run a game. Despite a decent ERA of 3.95 he would finish the season at 5–16.

August 5: Claude Raymond was presented with a gold medal by an organization called Palestre Nationale for being the best French Canadian in baseball. Raymond was to fashion a 5.25 ERA with the Atlanta Braves before being released and joining the Expos. He beat out Ron Piche, the only other candidate, who was pitching at Tacoma.

August 7: Prime Minister Trudeau took "a stunning redhead" with him on the Grouse Mountain Skyride in North Vancouver. He told reporters her name was "Miss Patterson," but she was later identified as Margaret Sinclair, 21.

August 9: Police were looking for suspects in the murder of pregnant movie actress Sharon Tate and four others.

August 10: The Expos had lost 13 of their last 15, leaving them with a 35–79 record, 36 games behind the league-leading Chicago Cubs. The New York Mets were in second place, 7½ games behind.

August 14: Room mates Dick Radatz and Elroy Face, two of the premier relief pitchers in the history of baseball, went out in tandem at Jarry Park. In a relief stint against the Cincinnati Reds Radatz walked three, threw a wild pitch, and was replaced by Face, who served up a bases-loaded home run to Johnny Bench.

August 15: Elroy Face was given his unconditional release by the Expos. It was his second of the year, having been previously released by the Detroit Tigers, and it marked the end of his career.

August 18: Dick Radatz was given his unconditional release by the Expos—also his second of the year (the Tigers again) and the end of the line. His arm, he said, was as good as it ever was, even when he was on the cover of *Time*. "It's all mental."

The Woodstock Music and Arts Fair oozed to a muddy conclusion on farmland near Bethel, New York, having attracted 500,000 rock fans for a weekend concert.

The Expos lost 9–3 to the Dodgers. Relief pitcher Larry Jaster walked Jeff Torborg (.185) to get to pitcher Claude Osteen, whom he then walked on four pitches. Up strode tiny lead-off man Maury Wills (.222 with the Expos, .297 with the Dodgers), who then smacked the only grand-slam home run of his thirteen-year career.

August 21: The Padres rallied for a run in the tenth to beat the Expos 1–0, for Montreal's eleventh loss in extra innings. They had never scored, let alone won, in extra innings.

August 22: Expos pitchers issued 19 walks—four of them forcing in runs—in losing a double-header 7–5 and 10–2 to the Giants. Bob Bailey hit his hundredth career home run and the public address announcer appealed for the historic ball. Eight of Montreal's finest children showed up, all holding baseballs.

The Expos were 39–87, 38 games behind the Cubs.

August 23: Quebec Justice Minister Remi Paul announced an all-out war against terrorist bombings in Quebec, saying the populace would ensure "these terrorists don't even crawl out of their caves, which reek with the stench of vermin."

The Expos' millionth customer passed joyously through the turnstiles.

August 24: Former Prime Minister Lester B. Pearson, a rabid baseball fan, watched his first live Expos game and said he found the team "staggeringly exciting." The Expos lost to the Giants, 6–4.

August 26: First baseman Bailey, who had once played third for the Pirates, amused reporters with a self-deprecating anecdote about himself and Pirate coach Harry "The Hat" Walker.

Walker, it seemed, had once told Bailey outright that he was the worst third baseman in the league.

"No I'm not," Bailey had fumed.

"Name a worse one," challenged Walker.

(Long thoughtful pause) "I guess you're right," conceded Bailey. Laughter all around.

Bailey didn't mind being the butt of a joke but he quit telling the story in 1970, when the Expos moved him from first back to third. He played there regularly for the next five years—although not quite as well as he had at Pittsburgh, when he was in his prime.

September 1: Padres pitcher Ray Sadecki, hitting .118, was walked three times by Expos ace Bill Stoneman, once with the bases loaded. Sadecki brought his bases on balls total to six in the last two games he had faced the Expos. "It's just one of those things," he said modestly.

September 3: Ho Chi Minh, Vietnamese nationalist leader who led insurrections against the Japanese, French, and Americans, died in Hanoi. A spokesman at the Western White House in San Clemente, California, said President Richard Nixon would have no comment.

Bullet Bob Reynolds, a pitcher called up from Vancouver, arrived with his hair died orange. "Imagine that," said Mauch. "Things like that tell me a man isn't concentrating on baseball. I need people who think baseball every waking minute."

September 4: "Victory is exhilarating," Mauch told reporters. "It's the only thing that keeps you going over a 162-game schedule." The Expos had dropped 18 of their last 21.

September 10: The team has been stricken with spasms of fine pitching. Steve Renko won 6–1; Howie Reed lost 1–0 on a five-hitter; Jerry "Hard Luck" Robertson won 3–2; Mike Wegener lost 2–1, giving up only two hits in 7⅓ innings; Bill Stoneman won 3–0 on a five-hitter—his fifth shutout. In another game Wegener gave up only five hits and two runs over 11 innings, striking out 15.

But then the Mets took over first place from the stumbling Cubs with a double-header win over the Expos.

September 14: The Expos whomped the foundering Cubs 8–2 to cap a four-game winning streak—the longest in club history.

September 18: Singer Tiny Tim, 40-ish, announced he would marry 17-year-old Vicki Budinger, whom he had met at John Wanamaker's department store in Philadelphia.

The Expos had fallen 44 games behind the league-leading Mets.

September 19: 17,084 fans went wild as the Expos swept the Phillies 10–6 and 3–1 in a double-header, storming back from a 6–0 deficit in the first game. Rusty Staub belted homer 28 and Ron Fairly his eleventh in an injury-shortened season. And broadcaster Russ Taylor, his fish net a Jarry Park institution, poked it out of the broadcast booth and finally caught a foul ball.

September 20: Sonny Wade's touchdown pass with 31 seconds left in the game led the Montreal Alouettes to their first CFL victory in more than a year.

Veteran Woodie Fryman, pitching for the Phillies, gave up 12 hits in 9 innings but struggled to a 6–4 win over the Expos on John Callison's three-run homer, which Jose Herrera caught over the outfield fence, then dropped.

September 23: The Expos had won eight of their last twelve games and were being mentioned in dispatches as "the fast-closing division doormats." Rusty Staub was hitting .298 with 28 home runs and everywhere people asked themselves, "Will he round off his numbers?"

Manager Dick Williams was fired by the Boston Red Sox. At his home in Peabody, Massachusetts, Williams attributed his dismissal to lack of communication with his players.

September 25: Shea Stadium in New York was stripped of everything not nailed down by exultant fans as the Miracle Mets clinched the pennant.

The Expos lost 6–2 when Jim Fairey lost a ball in shallow center, leading to a six-run inning. Fairey said he had noticed the sun come out, but didn't think it would bother him.

September 26: The St. Louis Cardinals sat out their regular players and beat the Expos 12–1, with the Expos committing three errors and second baseman Kevin Collins losing a pop-up in the sun.

September 28: An elegant club-house party was held to celebrate the closing of the Expos' first season, a bevvy of four-star chefs laying a table groaning with turkey, chicken, and ribs. The event was marred by the disappearance of one of Mrs. Charles Bronfman's favourite silver forks.

Bob Gibson whitewashed the Expos 2–0 in the final game of the year at Jarry Park, with 23,754 fans sitting through a cold drizzle, many of them under blankets. No balls were lost in the sun and in an emotional 30-minute finale the players' caps were given away in a raffle. "This is a year," manager Mauch told his soaked audience, "that I'll never forget."

Terrorists bombed the Rosemount home of Mayor Jean Drapeau. No one was injured.

October 1: Pirate rookie Al Oliver hit a run-scoring single in the ninth in Pittsburgh as the Pirates beat the Expos in their second-last game of the season. The Expos committed six errors (Bateman, Jestadt, Fairey, Jones, and Sutherland with two) to better their record of five.

October 2: The Expos lost 8–2 to the Pirates, but their six-game losing streak was terminated by the ending of the season. Staub hit .302—tenth best in the league, with 29 home runs. As a team the Expos played 52–110, tied for eleventh and last with their expansion-mates, the San Diego Padres.

The United States detonated a one-megaton thermo-nuclear device 4,000' underground on the Aleutian island of Amchitka without setting off the earthquake some scientists had feared.

October 3: Paul-Emile Cardinal Léger, looking wan, was mobbed by 250 admirers at Montreal International Airport as he returned for a three-month break from his missionary work in Africa.

The daughter of NDP Leader T.C. Douglas, wife of actor Donald Sutherland, was arrested on charges she had purchased hand grenades for the Black Panthers.

US Marine Lance Corporal Normand Corbin, 21, became the fourth Montreal youth to die serving in Vietnam.

October 4: Anna-Machi Malani, a 20-year-old model, was chosen Greece's "Miss Mini-Skirt of 1969" at the annual wine festival in Daphni.

Parts of Saskatchewan were hit by a snow storm, accompanied by 55 mph winds, that left a five-inch blanket over Prince Albert.

The Outcome

		B	Age	G	AB	R	H	2b	3b	HR	RBI	W	SO	SB	BA	OBA
Bob Bailey	1B85, OF12, 3B1	R	26	111	358	46	95	16	6	9	53	40	76	3	.265	.419
Gary Sutherland	2B139, SS15, OF1	R	24	141	544	63	130	26	1	3	35	37	31	5	.239	.307
Bobby Wine	SS118, 1B1, 3B1	R	30	121	370	23	74	8	1	3	25	28	49	0	.200	.251
Coco Laboy	3B156	R	29	157	562	53	145	29	1	18	83	40	96	3	.258	.409
Rusty Staub	OF156	L	25	158	549	89	166	26	5	29	79	110	61	3	.302	.526
Adolfo Phillips	OF53	R	27	58	199	25	43	4	4	4	7	19	62	6	.216	.337
Mack Jones	OF129	L	30	135	455	73	123	23	5	22	79	67	110	6	.270	.488
Ron Brand	C84, OF2	R	29	103	287	19	74	12	0	0	20	30	19	2	.258	.300
Ty Cline	OF41, 1B17	L	30	101	209	26	50	5	3	2	12	32	22	4	.239	.321
John Bateman	C66	R	26	74	235	16	49	4	0	8	19	12	44	0	.209	.328
Ron Fairly	1B52, OF21	L	30	70	253	35	73	13	4	12	39	28	22	1	.289	.514
Kevin Collins	2B20, 3B16	L	22	52	96	5	23	5	1	2	12	8	16	0	.240	.375
Don Bosch	OF32	B	26	49	112	13	20	5	0	1	4	8	20	1	.179	.250
Maury Wills	SS46, 2B1	B	36	47	189	23	42	3	0	0	8	20	21	15	.222	.238
Joe Herrara	OF31, 2B2, 3B1	R	27	47	126	7	36	5	0	2	12	3	14	1	.286	.373
Floyd Wicker	OF11	L	25	41	39	2	4	0	0	0	2	2	20	0	.103	.103
John Boccabella	C32	R	28	40	86	4	9	2	0	1	6	6	30	1	.105	.163
Donn Clendenon	1B24, OF11	R	33	38	129	14	31	6	1	4	14	6	32	0	.240	.395
Manny Mota	OF22	R	31	31	89	6	28	1	1	0	0	6	11	1	.315	.348
Angel Hermoso	2B18, SS6	R	22	28	74	6	12	0	0	0	3	5	10	3	.162	.162
Jim Fairey	OF13	L	24	20	49	6	14	1	0	1	6	1	7	0	.286	.367
Marv Staehle	2B4	L	27	6	17	4	7	2	0	1	1	2	0	0	.412	.706
Don Hahn	OF3	R	20	4	9	0	1	0	0	0	2	0	5	0	.111	.111
Gerry Jestadt	SS1	R	22	6	6	1	0	0	0	0	1	0	0	0	.000	.000
MONTREAL 6th 52-110 .321 48 TOTALS			29	162	5419	582	1300	202	33	125	542	529	962	52	.240	.359

	P Age	W	L	Pct.	Sa	G	St	CG	IP	H	W	StO	ShO	ERA
Bill Stoneman	R 25	11	19	.367	0	42	36	8	236	233	123	185	5	4.39
Dan McGinn	L 25	7	10	.412	6	74	1	0	132	123	65	112	0	3.95
Howie Reed	R 32	6	7	.462	1	31	15	2	106	119	50	59	1	4.84
Steve Renko	R 24	6	7	.462	0	18	15	4	103	94	50	68	0	4.02
Mike Wegener	R 22	5	14	.263	0	32	26	4	166	150	96	124	1	4.39
Jerry Robertson	R 25	5	16	.238	1	38	27	3	180	186	81	133	0	3.95
Roy Face	R 41	4	2	.667	5	44	0	0	59	62	15	34	0	3.97
Gary Waslewski	R 27	3	7	.300	1	30	14	3	109	102	63	63	1	3.30
Don Shaw	L 25	2	5	.286	1	35	1	0	66	61	37	45	0	5.18
Claude Raymond	R 32	1	2	.333	1	15	0	0	22	21	8	11	0	4.09
Mudcat Grant	R 33	1	6	.143	0	11	10	1	51	64	14	20	0	4.76
Larry Jaster	L 25	1	6	.143	0	24	11	1	77	95	28	39	0	5.49
Carroll Sembera	R 27	0	2	.000	2	23	0	0	33	28	24	15	0	3.55
Carl Morton	R 25	0	3	.000	0	8	5	0	29	29	18	16	0	4.66
Dick Radatz	R 32	0	4	.000	3	22	0	0	35	32	18	32	0	5.66
Leo Marentette	R 28	0	0	.000	0	3	0	0	5	9	1	4	0	7.20
Bob Reynolds	R 22	0	0	.000	0	1	1	0	1	3	3	2	0	27.00
Steve Shea	R 26	0	0	.000	0	10	0	0	16	18	8	11	0	2.81
	28	52	110	.321	21	162	162	26	1426	1429	702	973	8	4.33

The Chosen

Many years passed. Players with names like Pete Mackanin, Don DeMola, and Bombo Rivera came and went without incident. Mack Jones moved to the Owen and Corning Fiberglass Co., in Atlanta, Georgia, where he became an attendant on the packing line. Bill Stoneman became the only American Expo ever to settle permanently in Canada when he took up a job as an advertising executive with Royal Trust in Toronto.

John Bateman left the Expos in 1972 and later went on to play with Ed Feigner, "The King and His Court," a four-man comedy softball team. The Expos continued their own comedy routine right through 1976, when they bottomed out at 55–107, their worst year since the opener.

In 1979 they put on their first credible performance, winning ninety-five games and finishing only two games behind the Pittsburgh Pirates.

They were close again in 1980—only a game behind the Phillies—and in the shortened 1981 season they beat out the St. Louis Cardinals to win the National League East, despite the fact that the Cardinals had a better won-lost record over the two halves of the split season.

By 1982 the Expos had become fashionable, even in America. The baseball magazines began rolling off the presses in early February, two months before baseball's 4,422-game, 10,000-hour festival was due to begin.

The Sporting News, marketed as "baseball's Bible," polled its twelve National League correspondents and found the Expos "the overwhelming choice" of ten of them. *Sports Illustrated* picked Montreal for first, Philadelphia for second. Its rival, *Inside Sport*, had Montreal first and St. Louis second, as did *Baseball Digest*. "The Expos' starting line-up may be the strongest in baseball," enthused the *Digest*.

Tommy Kay's Big Book of Baseball and *Ken Collier's Baseball Book* both picked the Expos to win the East and keep on going. "Look for Montreal to make it all the way to this season's fall classic," said Tommy. "Our neighbours to the north of the border will be in the post-season classic," added Ken.

Seasoned baseball writer Zander Hollander zeroed in on growth amidst decay: "The overall prospects for a second straight [Montreal] pennant are solid simply because top contenders Philadelphia and St. Louis don't look improved and the Expos should be better."

The Tribune Co. Syndicate Inc., with a monicker that certainly made them sound like bookies, put out odds that listed the Expos as 3–1 favourites to win the East, with Philadelphia at 4–1 and St. Louis at 6–1.

Any lingering doubts of the less faithful were exorcised when the two most beautiful baseball writers of the 80s added their blessings. Thomas Boswell of *The Washington Post*, author of the classic *How Life Imitates the World Series*, predicted a dynasty:

> The Montreal Expos will win the National League East this season. They will win it again in 1983. Some things are simply ordained. Just as the Yankees and the Royals each made the play-offs five times from 76 through 81, so the Expos—who are by far the most misfortune-proof team in baseball, have already begun such a reign. Nothing stands between Montreal and greatness.

Bill James, the statisticians' guru and author of *Bill James' Baseball Abstract*, was equally enchanted. "Let's face it, folks," he told the folks who read *Esquire*. "The Expos are without a doubt the best team in baseball today."

Of the biggies, only one dissented. *Sport Magazine* picked St. Louis to beat out Montreal with Philadelphia finishing third, and nominated Jim Fanning as the manager most likely to be fired. "When it starts to get hot," intoned *Sport*, "he'll be reminded he's a front-office type working in the dugout."

So what did the people at *Sport* know? If they wanted to sound authoritative they might have thought twice about picking the Texas Rangers to win the American League West.

In March West Palm Beach's bars and beaches are dotted with as many Expo caps as sun hats, and the chatter is as much in French as in English, and hardly at all in southern drawl. Under the caps are people who are shipped south in freezer bags each year, dipped in a warm saline solution, and transported to West Palm's

Municipal Stadium, there to lie out like mad dogs in the noon-day sun, absorbing cold beers, the worst hot dogs anywhere, and *nos amours*, Les Expos.

The main topics at the bars and in the stands in the spring of 1982 were these:

Question 1: Who should play second?
(a) Steady-fielding Rodney Scott, who ran the bases well and thought he could hit right-handed pitching, but couldn't seem to?
(b) Rookie Wallace Johnson, who ran the bases well, seemed to be able to hit, but fielded like a man eating mashed potatoes with his hands?
(c) Hall-of-Fame candidate Tim Raines, who ran the bases extremely well, hit left-handers and right-handers with equal abandon, and looked like he might be athletic enough to play anywhere back of the pitcher's mound?
Answer: Wallace Johnson. He hit .339 at spring training and stole five bases without getting caught. Rodney Scott was in the doghouse for not hitting the way Harry "The Hat" Walker told him to. Tim Raines' agent was nervous about him playing second base. So everyone had become more and more confident about Wallace's capabilities in the field. Except for those who were paying attention.

Question 2: Who should we trade for?
In the graphic words of Duke Snider, the Expos needed a "big left-hander with hair on his butt" to drive in clutch runs. Snider himself had been a big left-handed clutch hitter, but he was 56 now and the hair on his butt was grey. Should the Expos go after:
(a) Dave Parker?
(b) Al Oliver?
(c) Sasquatch?
Answer: Al Oliver. In late March a West Palm radio station confided that Larry Parrish and Al Oliver would trade uniforms. Expos President John McHale denied the rumour, saying that he had merely agreed with a reporter from the station that he would be crazy not to be interested in somebody like Oliver who hit .300 and drove in runs, and the crummy reporter had gone off and "created the rest of the story." The next day McHale announced he had acquired Oliver for Parrish and right-handed first baseman Dave Hostetler, the latter a throw-in bonus the Rangers later ad-

mitted they hadn't expected to get. Oliver was more pleasant than either Parker or Sasquatch and hit better than either of them.

Question 3: Jim Fanning?

Fanning and his coaches had taken over as manager from Dick Williams on September 8, 1981. With the forty-man September roster available Fanning had deftly inserted into the line-up farmhands he had supervised while he was director of player development. He had also been rah-rah, in the manner of Little League. Some players had been embarrassed about this, but others preferred talk—even pep-talk—to being grunted at in the Williams tradition. When Fanning and his merry men took over, the Expos had been 1½ games behind the Cardinals in the race for the second-half championship. Under the new regime the team promptly lost three in a row, then rallied to beat everybody around except the Cardinals themselves, who luckily enough started losing to other people. At the end it was the Expos by half a game—4½ innings in front with time run out. They beat the Phillies three games out of five to win the division finale, and they lost to the Dodgers three games to two to lose the National League pennant by one Rick Monday home run. Their overall record under Fanning and Co. 21 wins, 16 losses. Was this guy for real?

Answer: Who could be sure? As he himself put it, "I have no idea what kind of manager I am. I'm sure things will shape up during the season as to whether I'll be conservative or whether I'll be a gambler. I haven't managed enough to know just what my style is."

Question 4: Over the winter the Expos had fallen a couple of vibrations short of shaking the baseball world by trading a minor-league junkballer named Steve Ratzer to the Mets for Frank Taveras, once a respectable shortstop. Taveras had led the majors in stolen bases in 1977 with 70 and averaged over .270 with the bat between 1977 and 1980. Incumbent Chris Speier, known more for his intelligence and diligence than his motor skills, had been doing a slow but thoughtful fade at short since he'd hit .271 for the Giants in 1975. But faded or not, his performance in 1981 had never lacked self-respect. Taveras, on the other hand, had put in such a lackadaisical year that Nelson Doubleday, chairman of the Mets' board, was reported to have offered a pair of Gucci loafers to any of his executives who could get as much as a rosin bag in trade for Frank. Were Frank's hands still quick enough to grab the Expos' rescue rope?

Answer: No. Chris didn't look any more acrobatic than he ever had at spring training, but at least he looked smooth. Frank only looked smooth when he was standing beside Wallace Johnson.

Question 5: Of the eight years Larry Parrish had put in at third base for the Expos, one had been fine (he'd hit .307 with 30 HRs in 1979), two had been ordinary, and the rest had been mediocre. Could Billy DeMars, the Expos' new batting coach, help Larry find the long-lost magic words? And if he couldn't, why did Billy keep walking around saying things like "Wham! Wham! Ptew!"?

Answer: No man, no matter what frustrations he had heaped upon his public, deserved to be sent to right field in Arlington. Wham! Wham! Ptew!

Question 6: Charlie Lea and David Palmer were both superb young pitchers who'd had arm problems. Lea was 25, Palmer 24. Before arthritis set in in 1981, Lea had pitched a no-hitter and gone 28⅔ innings without allowing a run. Palmer had been 18–8 over 1979 and 1980 and one of the top pitchers in the league before undergoing elbow surgery in November 1980. In 1981 he'd floundered in the minors, throwing more balls than strikes, none without pain. The odds on both of these young talents regaining their form was probably about 50–1 against.

Answer: The question was unanswerable, at least at spring training. So you didn't ask. You just crossed your fingers.

The club that left spring training hadn't jelled. Jim Fanning didn't like all the talk about new people playing new positions everywhere you looked, but there they were:

Tim Wallach replacing Larry Parrish at third. Wallace Johnson in for Rodney Scott at second. Al Oliver at first, sending Warren Cromartie to right field. Tim Raines in left, with half a season under his belt. Chris Speier at short again, but with Frank Taveras in the wings and Bryan Little making threatening gestures from Wichita.

Only two positions were immutable. Andre Dawson patrolled the vast skies of center field and Gary Carter was squatted firmly behind the plate.

For months the line on the Expos had been that they were strong and standing pat. *Gazette* columnist Michael Farber had described Expos' President John McHale as being "as daring as dentist's music," but the beat had changed. Suddenly the faithful found themselves at Studio 54, full of the boogie and dizzy.

To look at the Cardinals' and Phillies' box scores toward the end of spring training was to detect flaws here and there but to sense harmony in the enemy camp. To watch the Expos jockeying toward the starting gate was like watching a Team Canada hockey squad off to play the Russians: this was a lot of individual talent, hastily flung together.

Comparing infields with St. Louis and Philadelphia made watchers especially queasy. Tight infields have been treated with veneration since Tinker-to-Evers-to-Chance and the other guy. Tight infields aren't everything—pitchers who make a lot of mistakes have a special affection for outfielders who are quick and wise—but it's intimidating for batters to be surrounded by the sure and the nimble, caught in a corral of barbed wire, as it were. Good infields absorb balls the way blotters absorb ink. And St. Louis and Philadelphia entered the 1982 season with infields that were better than good. A comparison:

INFIELD
First Base

Montreal: Al Oliver, a finely polished antique and a truly gifted hitter. Played first base with grace many years ago before being stricken with a bone spur and tendonitis in his shoulder. Had become a designated hitter with Texas, giving up fielding for life, it had seemed.

St. Louis: Keith Hernandez, a fine clutch hitter in the Oliver mould, coming off seasons in which he batted .344, .321, and .306. The most graceful first baseman in the league.

Philadelphia: Pete Rose, winner of the NL batting championship in 1968, 1969, and 1973, with a lifetime batting average of .310. Going into the 1982 season on the verge of overtaking Hank Aaron for second place on baseball's all-time hit list, climbing the mountain road toward Ty Cobb. A tired arm and not much range, but adequate around the bag.

Second Base

Montreal: It was hard to say, and would get harder.

St. Louis: Tommy Herr, coming off an astounding first full year in which he proved himself a fine second-spot hitter (.268, 41 RBIs, speed), led the league in fielding range by handling 5.73 chances a game, and in fewest errors and most double plays.

Philadelphia: Manny Trillo, for his three years with the Phillies the best second baseman in the league. Hit .287 in 1981 with an audacious little dash of power, and finished only a split hair behind Herr in fielding range.

Shortstop

Montreal: Chris Speier—"Mr. Routine." A savvy fielder known for playing hitters well, never making a mental error, being fast on relays, smooth around second, but without the gifts to dazzle. A streak hitter and a survivor.

St. Louis: Ozzie Smith, either the best or second-best shortstop in the NL, give or take the incredible but seemingly unfulfilled talent of Garry Templeton. Without as strong an arm as Templeton, but more consistent; a great diver, with a quicker release and more hustle. A banjo hitter with speed.

Philadelphia: Ivan DeJesus, rated well behind Templeton and Smith defensively but ahead of Speier. Dragged a respectable lifetime average of .275 down to .257 in 1981 by hitting a yucky .194, somehow getting on base often enough to steal 21 times.

Third Base

Montreal: Tim Wallach, a slugger in the minor leagues who hit only .236 in 1981, his first major-league season. A right-handed hitter, he somehow hit .281 against right-handed pitchers and .136 against lefties. Smoother than Parrish in the field without his gun of an arm. Soft hands.

St. Louis: Ken Oberkfell, a left-hander with an even .300 batting average over the previous three seasons, feasting on the league's predominance of right-handed pitching. Not far behind Mike Schmidt as the best-fielding third baseman in the league.

Philadelphia: Mike Schmidt himself, coming off two straight MVP seasons, who with the help of batting coach Billy DeMars (then with the Phillies) transformed himself from a strikeout-riddled slugger into the best-overall hitter in the game. Hit .286 with 48 HRs and 121 RBIs in 1980. Climbed to .316 with 31 homers and 91 RBIs in shortened 1981.

Double plays: Montreal 88, St. Louis 108, Philadelphia 90.

Overall Infield Rating (out of 10): St. Louis 9, Philadelphia 9, Montreal 6.

Not our forte, really. But what's an infield without a catcher? What's a team without a catcher, for that matter? Which inevitably takes one back to Casey Stengel, who was asked why the 1962 Mets had taken a catcher as their number one pick in the expansion draft. "You have to have a catcher," explained Stengel. "Because if you don't, you're going to have a lot of passed balls."

CATCHERS

Montreal: Gary Carter, great arm, great bat, great handler of pitchers. The best going into 82—potentially the best ever.

St. Louis: Darrell Porter, coming off alcohol and rotator-cuff problems. A decent hitter with 558 lifetime RBIs spread over a decade. MVP in American League in 1979 while with the A's. Arm now suspect.

Philadelphia: Bo Diaz, over from Cleveland, known as "The Cannon," for his arm. Replaced Bob Boone and Keith Moreland because they couldn't throw out base-runners, but who could with most Philly pitchers' tardy wind-ups? Hit .313 in 1981—a shocker, given his previous high of .236.

Catchers' Rating: Expos 9, Cardinals 7, Phillies 7.

That's more like it. On to the outfield.

OUTFIELD
Left Field

Montreal: Tim Raines, fast but often confused, with a mediocre arm. But a fine, quick switch-hitter who'd be even better if he'd bunt for the odd base hit. Hit .304 in his rookie year, with 71 stolen bases in only 88 games, a prime candidate to break Lou Brock's record of 118.

St. Louis: Dane Iorg, a consummate doubles hitter with a craving for right-handed pitching and a .327 batting average in 1981. Murder against the Expos (.438 in 1981). Thus the traditional Quebec nursery rhyme:

Iorgy, Iorgy
Puddin' and pie,
Kissed the ball
And made us cry.

Not much of a fielder, with less of an arm. Whitey Herzog said he intended to replace him with defensive specialist Tito Landrum in the late innings.

Philadelphia: Gary Matthews, error-prone in the outfield but a terrific hitter, especially in the clutch. Hit .301 with 21 doubles, nine HRs and 67 RBIs in 1981, stealing 15 bases in 17 tries.

Center Field

Montreal: The incomparable Andre Dawson. Fast, powerful, graceful, fierce, and determined. Saddled with incredible expectations. In a game in which it has been considered awesome to accomplish 30 HRs and 30 stolen bases in the same year, the forecasters were demanding 40–40 from Himself.

St. Louis: Lonnie Smith, known for running fleetly, but often straight for invisible banana peels left scattered around the outfield. A .327 batting average over his first two years in the majors, and a budding burglar on the basepaths.

Philadelphia: Garry Maddox, of whom Ralph Kiner once said, "The earth is two-thirds covered by water, and the other one third is covered by Gary Maddox." Had an off year in 1981, hitting .263 after hovering over .290 for most of a decade. At 32, seemed to have lost a step.

Right Field

Montreal: Warren Cromartie, your average leftfielder with your average-leftfielder's arm, playing in right where you need more than that. A maker of delicious and awful plays, sometimes in the same inning. A left-handed .300 hitter with some power who had always hit best when he was whistling them on a line to the opposite-field gap. A history of messed-up bunts and grounding into double plays, but a potential .325 hitter.

St. Louis: George Hendrick, probably the best rightfielder around, with the deterioration of Dave Parker. Reliable in the field and usually around .290 at the plate, with around 20 HRs and 90 RBIs and an almost-extinct phenomenon—a rightfielder's arm.

Philadelphia: With Bake McBride gone to Cleveland it was hard to say who'd fill the gap. The possibilities included George Vukovich, who had trouble with the curve ball but kept the Phillies in there against the Expos in the 1981 divisional playoffs; Dick Davis, the veteran who'd hit .333 in 96 at-bats the year before; and Bob Dernier, the American Association all-star who'd twice stolen more than 70 bases in the minors. Stay tuned.

Overall Outfield Rating: Expos 9, Cardinals 8, Phillies 7. Dawson, Dawson, Dawson.

PITCHERS
Starting Pitchers

Montreal: Rogers (12–8, 3.41), Sanderson (9–7, 2.96), Gullickson (7–9, 2.81), Burris (9–7, 3.04), Lea (5–4, 4.64), and maybe Palmer. The finest staff in the majors, hampered only by the absence of a more reliable lefthander than Bill Lee (5–6, 2.93, but like rolling dice). Rogers and Burris churned out masterpieces throughout late 1981, and the fine young arms of their cohorts were coveted around the league.

St. Louis: Bob Forsch (10–5, 3.19) and Joaquin Andujar (8–4, 4.10) looked like quality, but the rest were iffy. John Martin (8–4, 3.41) had been useful in 1981 but hardly overwhelming. Steve Mura (5–14, 4.27) had given up 156 hits in 139 innings pitched with the Padres. John Fulgam, a fine young pitcher in 1979, had been unable to rebound from arm surgery. Bob Gibson had retired in 1975.

Philadelphia: Steve Carlton (13–4, 2.42), owner of the most uncanny slider in baseball, had long since qualified as the best at his trade from port or starboard. Mike Krukow had performed with hopeless valour at Wrigley Field and looked like a strong third starter. Which raised the question of whether anyone looked like a strong second starter. Dick Ruthven (12–7, 5.14) had fallen apart completely during the second half of 1981. Maybe he would come back. Or maybe it would be Marty Bystrom (4–3, 3.33), the 1980 whiz kid who'd had some arm and attitude problems. Or Larry Christenson (4–7, 3.53), talented but erratic, who'd rejoined the Phillies after becoming a free agent.

Starting Pitchers' Rating: Expos 9, Phillies 7, Cardinals 6.

Relief Pitchers

Montreal: Jeff Reardon (3-0, 8 saves, 2.19), with a 94 mph fast ball and a new curve, as the right-handed stopper. Woodie Fryman (5-3, 7 saves, 1.88), with a fine, hard slider and a 42-year-old arm, as the left-handed stopper. Wild Bob James as a fast but unknown quantity. Bill Lee (5-6, 2.93) as the junk man.

St. Louis: Bruce Sutter (3-5, 25 saves, 2.63), with a split-fingered fast ball that dipped at the plate and made him the best reliever in baseball. Doug Bair (4-2, 1 save, 5.07), another right-hander, had once been good at Cincinnati. And Lefty Jim Kaat (6-6, 4 saves, 3.40), 43, with 278 lifetime wins, looking for 280.

Philadelphia: Lefthanders Tug McGraw (2-4, 10 saves, 2.66), Sparky Lyle (9-6, 2 saves, 4.44), and Sid Monge (3-4, 4 saves, 4.34); righthanders Ron Reed (5-3, 8 saves, 3.10), Ed Farmer (3-3, 10 saves, 4.58), and Warren Brusstar 0-1, 0 saves, 4.50). All had been outstanding at various points in their careers—the veterans Reed and McGraw as recently as 1981. But McGraw had undergone elbow surgery over the winter. A grab bag.

Relief Pitchers' Rating: Cardinals 8, Expos 7, Phillies 6.

Before the final tabulation, consider this as an All-Star line-up drawn from only three teams:
Catcher: Gary Carter, Expos
First baseman: Keith Hernandez, Cards
Second baseman: Manny Trillo, Phillies
Shortstop: Ozzie Smith, Cards
Third baseman: Mike Schmidt, Phillies
Leftfielder: Tim Raines, Expos
Centrefielder: Andre Dawson, Expos
Rightfielder: George Hendrick, Cards
Right-handed starter: Steve Rogers, Expos
Left-handed starter: Steve Carlton, Phillies
Right-handed reliever: Bruce Sutter, Cards
Left-handed reliever: Tug McGraw, Phillies

Apologies to Rose, Oliver, Herr, Reardon, and Matthews—the core of an awfully decent bench.

And now, assuming the three teams would shake down with about equal bench strength, the envelope please:

Montreal Expos 40 (wild applause), St. Louis Cardinals 38, Philadelphia Phillies 36. Nobody else counted. The Pirates were old and didn't have any pitching. The Mets couldn't field, nor were they likely to hit or pitch. The Cubs had a lot of character but were dead in the vines.

Hallelujah! Bring on the Dodgers! Bring on the Yankees! And if Fanning turned out to be a better manager than Herzog, it would be icing on the cake. And if he didn't?

> *This team has so much talent*
> *we don't need a manager.*
> —Rodney Darrell Scott
> April 8, 1982

Titanic Meets The Icebergs

Spring came a few weeks late in 1982. The blizzards between Montreal and Pittsburgh had left dozens of cars and vans stranded and trailers jack-knifed on the highways on the route to Opening Day, which was cancelled, cancelled, and cancelled again. That was Jerry Manuel, upside down in the ditch. Over there, Larry Parrish, his lights still blinking feebly. Even at 20 mph in a snowstorm, life imitates baseball for the demented.

So Montreal had finally opened in Philly, at two degrees over the freezing mark, with the Expos favoured by everybody and the Phillies dugout a home for the aged. There were a lot of friendships between the two clubs, despite the fierce play-off battles the teams had split over the last two seasons. Not that Jeff Reardon would talk to opponents or Steve Carlton would talk to anybody. But Pete Rose and Chris Speier had spent half an hour kicking things around at the indoor batting cage before the first game. Expo coach Vern Rapp walked the corridor between dressing rooms with Rose, arms over each other's shoulders, jawing at each other, waiting for the snow to stop and batting practice to begin. Tommy Hutton, an Expo sub until late into the 1981 season when he moved to the broadcast booth, was staying at the home of his brother-in-law Dick Ruthven, the Philly pitcher.

There was a notice posted on every club's bulletin board warning that the anti-fraternization rule remained in effect, a fifty-dollar fine if you were caught being buddy-buddy in public with an opponent. But these folks looked like they'd gladly pay fifty bucks to talk to one another.

So you could see how some of the Expos might feel a little sorry for the Phillies. The Phils had been right in the thick of it for several years, but Bake McBride was gone, and once you got by Gary Matthews and Mike Schmidt in the line-up . . . they were hitting George Vukovich fifth. Vukovich had 84 major-league at-bats behind him, with 12 RBIs. The idea with the Phillies, Gary Carter had explained, was simply to pitch around Schmidt and go at the other guys. Friendships or not, business was business.

The Expos had won the opener 2–0 on a three-hitter by Steve

Rogers and coasted home in the second game, 11–3. The Philadelphia press was treating the Expos with a respect verging on awe, gasping that just the way it had been in the fall of 1981, so was it in the spring of 1982—the Expos invincible.

And then there was this story headlined in one of the Sunday papers: "Schmidt on Expos: 'They can't hit with us . . . play defence with us.' "

It started like this:

> Their name is the Montreal Expos, and they have been built up, all of a sudden, as baseball's next super team.
>
> "They've got a $2 million man (Gary Carter). They've got the game's most underappreciated superstar (Andre Dawson). They've got maybe the best under-25-year-old righthander in the game (Bill Gullickson).
>
> "They've got the whole magazine-cover formula: an ace for the rotation (Steve Rogers), a flame-thrower in the bullpen (Jeff Reardon), the swiftest base-stealer in the game (Tim Raines), and, finally, the left-handed bat they have always needed (Al Oliver).
>
> "But Michael Jack Schmidt, who plays for another team in the National League East, looks that Montreal roster up and down and shakes his head. He isn't ready to concede.
>
> " 'Montreal hasn't proven anything to me,' Schmidt said one day toward the end of spring training. He was quite serious.
>
> "Now you might recall that the Expos did indeed beat the Phillies last October in the first and (hopefully) last NL East mini-playoffs. But to Mike Schmidt, that series proved zero.
>
> "To me, that was sort of a freak win," said Schmidt.

And it went on like that.

Perhaps the key phrase was that Schmidt had allegedly said these things at spring training. Here, further to the north, reality was cold, no?

"No, that story was exactly right," he said, thawing out his blue-white muscles in the dressing room.

"Your bullpen has to rely on one guy, Reardon, your so-called stopper," he went on. "And what does he do but throw fastballs? If Woodie Fryman comes up with any kind of a muscle pull at his age or if anything happens to Reardon, where are you?

"Defensively you've got us in two places. Gary Carter is the best catcher in baseball and Dawson and Maddox are 1-2, like this," he said, holding his finger and thumb close together. "But who would you pick at the other six positions? Who's better than Trillo at second? Is Speier better than DeJesus at short? Wallach is new at third, isn't he? How good is Raines in left field? I thought Oliver was a designated hitter.

"Don't get me wrong—Montreal has a great ball club, and we're going to have to beat you to win this division. And I've never doubted the effectiveness of Montreal's starting pitching. I've got all the respect in the world for the Expos. They think they know how to win, and maybe that's right. But they still have to prove it to baseball. So far they've only done it over a shortened season, and at that they barely squeaked in. Can they field? Can they put more than two hits together at a time to score runs? We'll see."

Poor Schmidt. But you had to admire his pluck in this, the year of the Expos.

The Expos lost the third game of the series, but it was a 1-0 squeaker and the run off Burris was unearned. Wallach made one of those silly little rookie errors, pulling Oliver off the bag.

Then it was back to Montreal for the home opener, with Jerry White pinch-hitting a two-run homer to beat the Pirates, 5-4. Oliver and Speier had trouble with a couple of grounders, so two of the Pirate runs were unearned.

There was some consternation when Oliver made a strange throw to home plate in the style of a shotputter, but he was jocular about it. "I figured just to get the ball in the area and Gary would do the rest," he laughed, and indeed, Carter moved with alacrity to make the tag.

The next day big Al charged the plate to cover a bunt, whirled toward Scott covering first, and threw a high fly ball over his head to Cromartie in right. It was a sobering moment. Conjecture began to stir that Oliver had tried to throw the ball through the hole in the dome, to prove that he'd recovered from the tendonitis he'd suffered from in Texas.

What could you expect? It was cold. The press box was a sea of toques and gloves. Olympic Stadium has a lot of concrete, and none of it seems dry until June. After eight games the Expos were 5-3 and every player in the line-up had made an error save Cromartie. He had started off looking like stardom was finally at hand, hitting .323 with a pair of homers. When he wasn't slicing the ball to the opposite-field gap he was pulling it toward or over the right-field fence.

Duke Snider told his radio listeners that the Cro was hitting the ball as purely as he had at any point in his career. The Duke had never come on as a rabid Cromartie supporter, so the praise was large indeed. Cromartie's *Crobar* chocolate was selling well for cancer research, memories lingered of Cromartie waving the Canadian flag on foreign soil, and he was even fielding well—handling balls cleanly in right field, ranging far over into center to back up Dawson, and, on at least a couple of occasions, hustling in behind second and first to take balls the inexperienced right side of the infield wasn't moving back on.

It seemed in order to compliment the Cro, but the Cro wasn't taking compliments. "Everybody says how I haven't made any mistakes out there. It seems like everybody's just waiting for me to make one. Well I ain't made one and I'm not going to." Flying high or not, the Cro was squawking.

Rowland Office, the substitute rightfielder, was released to make room for John Milner, who had been out with a pulled rib muscle. Office (black) was probably more talented as an outfielder than Mike Phillips (white) was as an infielder, but the infield was uncertain and there were five outfielders—Dawson, Raines, Cromartie, Francona, and White—who were going to play ahead of Office. So he was dropped. Maybe, guessed Cromartie in company, it was "because of his tan."

Racial aspersions had been cast on Expo management's decision-making since 1969, when some American black-power activists decided the Expos had too many white faces. They circulated again when rightfielder Ken Singleton, who had married a white Quebec girl, was traded off to the Baltimore Orioles for nothing. That one gained credibility because nobody could think of another reason for such a stupid trade. It had become traditional, every time a black infielder like Dave Cash or Rodney Scott was having trouble holding his job, to suggest that two brothers would make a better keystone combination than would Chris Speier and a brother forced to play second fiddle at second base.

But this time the Expos had just traded two white players (Hostetler and Parrish) for Cromartie's black idol (Oliver), and optioned Brad Mills (white) to Denver, bringing up Dan Norman (black). Cromartie waited a couple of days, then denied he'd said what he'd said.

The pitching was superb. After 12 games the Expos staff had a collective earned-run average of 2.32, but the team was only 7-5. When the league's weekly statistics came out Expo starters Rogers, Sanderson, and Burris ranked one, two, three in ERA. But Burris was 0-3 and, as it turned out, going under fast.

The hitting was somewhere in that hazy area between just-about-adequate and mediocre. As Thomas Boswell has pointed out, big innings are important in baseball. In most games, the winning team scores more runs in one inning than the other team does in the whole game. Between their seventh and twelfth games the Expos left the bases loaded without scoring three times.

But if there was uneasiness about squandering all that pitching while St. Louis was forging to a lead there were no signs of panic. There's nothing more unfashionable than early panic in a 162-game baseball schedule. You can take more contradictory road signs for life from baseball lore than you can from the Bible. If a manager wins a game in April, it's customary for him to remind you that "a win in April is just as important as a win in September." If he loses, he's likely to remind you that "it's early" or "for the contenders, the season starts September 1." The team in front at the All-Star break is also supposed to win its division, unless your team isn't in front, in which case the September 1 rule applies.

"He gives 110 per cent" is the way baseball describes a player who goes beyond his limitations to win games. "He's learned to play within himself" is the way baseball describes a player who's stopped destroying himself by trying to give 110 per cent, having learned that you play better when you just give 100 per cent.

Anyway, nobody was panicking, which is just as well since it's a difficult game to play if you're nervous. The Expos were 8-5 when they took to the road for a tour of the West Coast, their traditional foundering ground. And they didn't look too bad, losing a series 2-1 to the Giants but beating the Dodgers, for years their nemesis, by the same margin. In fact they might have won all three against the Dodgers; they lost the second one 2-1 and had runners on first and second in the ninth inning. Fanning put Scott in to pinch run, but sent him to first to replace Speier instead of to second in place of Cromartie. Cromartie was thrown out at the plate when Wallach lined a single to left.

But the Expos blew the Dodgers out 13-1 in the final, giving them their first series win in Los Angeles in five years, and in its wake they strutted into San Diego, clubbing Dick Williams and the Padres to bring their record to 12-8, two games back of the Cards.

And at that point, the Mike Schmidt hex took hold.

A win in the second game against the Padres, the last of the road trip, would have brought them home with a winning Western record at long last. They would also have swept Dick Williams in their first series against him since he had been dumped as their manager in the middle of the 1981 pennant race. Williams was certainly up for it. "Any time you play a team that canned you," he mused, "it gets the adrenalin flowing. I'd really like to beat the shit out of them."

Which the Padres proceeded to do. When the dust cleared it was 7-3 for the Padres. Burris, master of location and change-of-pace since the middle of 1981, had lost whatever he had. After giving up first-inning homers to Garry Templeton and Sixto Lezcano, he threw a ball into center field on a fielder's choice, letting one run score, and watched Gary Carter do the same on a steal. Instead of leaving the fans savouring a successful road trip, the game left them brooding over Fanning running Scott for Speier instead of Cromartie four games earlier.

Gentleman Jim finally took to the airwaves to defend himself, saying he was sure he'd done the right thing. "Cromartie is a good baserunner. If I'd known Tim Wallach was going to hit a line-drive bullet to left field I might have done it differently."

But line-drive bullets are the reason managers insert pinch runners. On routine singles, nearly anybody will score from second.

But if Fanning was sowing seeds of doubt about his managing, his players were fertilizing the field. Duke assured the fans that all that was needed was some home cooking. Who would have expected a bout of food poisoning in your own home town?

Year after year it is the subtle, yet totally accessible fundamentals of the game that keep us attached to baseball as we see common sense, alertness, and perseverance rewarded, while the slipshod is relentlessly punished.
—Thomas Boswell, 1982

Beginning with the finale in San Diego, the Expos punished themselves relentlessly over the next fourteen games. Thirteen of them were at home, where they had racked up a 145–72 record during the preceding three years.

The Dodgers followed them to Montreal for a four-game series. Dusty Baker, Steve Garvey, Pedro Guerrero, and Ron Cey were all trapped in slumps. No problem, gracious hosts.

Rick Monday lost no time reminding the locals how he had ended it for them in the autumn, driving a triple in game 1, inning 1, in almost the identical spot he had homered to to win the pennant for the Dodgers in his last at-bat at Olympic Stadium.

Dawson might have caught the ball if it had been hit in the ninth. In the first, it probably didn't seem worth the chance of leaving his teeth in the wall. Tim Wallach had let a Garvey liner get by his backhand before Monday did his number, and by the time the Dodgers were out of the inning it was 3–0.

The Expos had come out of 1981 with the image of a team that didn't come back. Bill James' statistics showed that they had been the best team in the league at holding a lead, and the worst at coming from behind. The Phillies had come back thirty-four times in 1981, compared to fifteen for the Expos. The Phillies came back from four-run deficits seven times in 1981. The Expos never did. Maybe Mike Schmidt was onto something about knowing how to win.

This time Gary Carter hit two solo home runs, but it wasn't enough. Final score: Dodgers 3, Expos 2.

In the second game, the Dodgers again struck early with five runs in five innings off Steve Rogers, who was whacked in the elbow with a line drive in the first. They won it 6–2. The Expos were shaky. Carter threw a ball off Taveras' glove on a steal and Dawson didn't back up the play. Steve Sax stole a base on a pitchout. Raines barely held on to a routine fly ball in left. When he'd led off the game he'd hit a difficult little popper in fair territory and stood watching as catcher Mike Scioscia dove to make an unlikely catch. And Cromartie let a ball hop over his head, although it appeared to bounce off a seam.

But the drama was in the clubhouse.

A reporter asked Fanning whether he was considering playing Raines at second base, since Wallace Johnson had been sent down on the coast trip. Fanning replied, "We haven't got a timetable for it, but it's fair to say that's part of the plan."

Since spring training Fanning had been saying the thought of shifting Raines to second was never very far from his mind, but it was now obvious for the first time that he intended to do so. Johnson had been hitting .184 and couldn't field. Taveras was at .057 and Scott at .208.

In the changing room adjacent to the manager's office, three men stood in various states of undress: Terry Francona, who had expected to see a lot of outfield action after Fanning had predicted he'd get into 110 games in 1982, but who had been to bat only 7 times in 23 games; Tim Raines, who had on several occasions said he'd prefer to stay in left field because playing second was riskier for the legs (Francona was later to prove that left field could be just as risky); and Rodney Scott, the fierce and moody incumbent, currently sulking over Fanning's obvious determination to relegate him to back-up status after three full years as a starter.

Raines seemed ready for the news. He smiled, turned the palms of his hands to heaven, and nodded. "Well then I guess I have to go to second base. I'm not the one who says where I have to play."

Francona appeared surprised. For one brief instant he tried to suppress a smile, then gave up and ordered in dimples. "I guess I hoped that would happen—it's what I've been waiting for. I've been getting a little antsy. I've played two innings in a month."

Scott was wearing an African comb in the back of his hair, adorned with a black-power fist pointing to the ceiling. For a moment he looked like he was sitting in a court room and the judge had just passed the death sentence. He recovered quickly and spat dry spit at the floor.

"I just hope he wins, for his sake—that's all. I just hope he wins."

On Friday night Jim Fanning had said he didn't have a timetable. On Saturday morning Rodney Scott was gone. On Saturday afternoon Terry Francona was in left field and Tim Raines at second.

John McHale told Scott he was a disruptive influence and, moreover, he had evidence that Scott smoked marijuana every night. That was a low blow. Marijuana is weaker, less expensive, far less trendy, and not as widely used among big-league athletes as is cocaine. It was like telling a guy you knew he got drunk on beer when the smart set was into martinis.

"Anyway," said Rodney, "there ain't a way on this earth I'm going to smoke marijuana every night. I don't care who I'm with or where I am. Not every night."

Bill Lee, an eccentric and prescient man, had expected something like this. Descending on the players' elevator the day before, he'd been asked whether he thought he'd be playing. "No, not me," he had replied. "I'm in the doghouse, just like Rodney Scott. We're both on sabbatical."

In fact, Lee did pitch in the 6–2 loss to the Dodgers, giving up three hits and a run in three innings to bring his ERA down to 4.38. Season totals: 19 hits and a walk in 12⅓ innings pitched, with seven strikeouts. Not very good.

When he learned Scott had been dumped, Lee went to Fanning's office, where he left a branch of fruit blossoms and a note saying "Come and get me." He then went to a Hochelaga Street tavern where he drank three bottles of beer and played pool with his friend Terry Mosher, "Aislin" the cartoonist. "Maybe," he told Mosher, "I'm just Don Quixote."

The windmill struck back with a vengeance. Lee returned to the stadium in the seventh inning, ready to do his Grover Cleveland Alexander act after seeing the Expos were in need of relief pitching on the TV at the brasserie.

The most he was able to do, however, was turn his manager into his former manager, telling Fanning he was more-or-less a dictator and throwing his ripped-up Expos jersey at him. McHale fired him the next day, adding a $5,000 fine to the injury.

"The most serious breach of a player's contract is to make himself unavailable during a game," said McHale.

"They treated [Scott] like a dog," said Lee. "They kick him, then wonder why he snarls . . . all they think about is filling the stadium and making money. They don't understand the game is played by players."

"Bill Lee and me are friends," said Woodie Fryman. "But we're both question marks at this stage in our careers. You don't do these things when you're a question mark."

"We're a better team now," said McHale.

Not that it showed.

In the third game against the Dodgers the Expos ran up a 9–3 lead and hung on to win 10–8, with Dusty Baker going 5-for-5 with two home runs and five RBIs. Pitcher Bill Gullickson and Terry

Francona, the new man in left, accounted for the day's quota of errors.

Warren Cromartie was inserted into the second spot in the batting order, behind Raines. Batting second meant taking strikes, moving the runner over, bunting, and the like. Could Cromartie handle the pressure? "When you've got a guy like Raines with a 90 per cent steal ratio in front of you," replied Fanning impatiently, "you could be Humpty Dumpty and hit second. All I want Cromartie to do is pull the ball through the hole. With a runner on base the whole right side of the infield is open."

Unfortunately Warren had fallen into something of a slump (.256), and all the king's horses and all the king's men couldn't put his bat together again.

And there were other factors that made one wonder. Cromartie had always hit best when he was going to left center most of the time, and Fanning was asking him to pull to right. He was also a terrible bunter and had messed up badly on two simple sacrifices the previous week. Both Fanning and batting coach Billy DeMars were well aware of his deficiency. DeMars contended any major leaguer could learn to bunt if he practised, while Fanning thought it was probably too late to teach an old crow new tricks. It really didn't matter who was right, because Cromartie wasn't about to practise.

When a pro golfer messes up a round he marches himself to the nearest practice tee and works on his stroke until he gets it right or his hands are bleeding. In baseball, it is traditional to start off batting practice by laying down two bunts. The day after one particularly clumsy sacrifice attempt Cromartie did just that. The first bunt landed in the air near third base, two feet foul. The second popped over the batting-practice pitcher's protective screen. "Hit away," he muttered self-consciously. Bunting practice was over.

The fans were starting to turn on him, for his batting average, his bunting, other things. In the opening game of the Dodgers' series he'd taught Tim Raines all he knew about not running out a ball. With two men on and two out in the ninth, losing 3–2, he popped up to the infield, turned around, and walked back to the bench. Bill Russell caught it, but he needn't have bothered.

It seemed a strange time to be asking Cro to take over as the second hitter, and it didn't work. Over the next ten days he went 4-for-29, lowering his average to .212. He was finally replaced by

Francona, who bunted well, poked the ball to all fields, and hit .327 in the second slot before shattering his knee in St. Louis.

Why had Fanning ever thought Cromartie was the man for the job? "Because he'd hit so well for us in 1981 when he batted in the lead-off spot." (While replacing the injured Raines the previous September Cro had hit .467 in 12 games, with an on-base percentage of .571.) But surely there was a big difference between batting number one—when your job was to get on base—and number two—when it was to move the lead runner over whenever he got on.

"Yes, but in many cases the number one batter gets out. Then the number two batter is just like a number one batter."

Which seemed to mean that when the first six batters get out, the number seven batter is just like the number one batter as well. Cromartie was finally moved to the number seven slot.

The Dodgers took the wrap-up game, 5–4. The Expos went 1-for-10 with runners in scoring position and dropped below .500 for the first time in the season. Burris took the loss again, giving up seven hits and four walks in six innings.

San Francisco came to town, and it was like the circus coming in, except most of the performers were local. "It was Ringling Bros. out there," said Al Oliver, but the Expos came from behind to win a game for the first time in the season.

They'd been leading 2–1 when the Giant's Johnnie LeMaster laid down a bunt with Milt May and Jim Wohlford on first and second. Pitcher Charlie Lea tried for the force at third but fired the ball past Wallach. Francona picked it up in left field and fired it the other way past Wallach. Lea, who'd been stomping around the mound fretting about his throw, didn't back up on the play. The Giants had a 3–2 lead.

They'd scored their first run earlier when, for the first time in memory, Andre Dawson soured on a baseball. Jack Clark doubled to left center. Dawson dropped the ball on the bounce, allowing Clark to coast to second. He then stood glaring at it for a couple of seconds, and Clark went on to third, coming home when Chris Speier dropped a pop fly for another first time in memory.

On the other side of the ledger, the Expos stole five bases (with only two runners picked off) and put together a three-run rally in the eighth to win the game, with key hits from Oliver, Wallach, Dan Norman (the new right-handed pinch hitter), and Raines. "It was a farce," said Carter in the dressing room. "But we'll take it."

The next night the Giants won 5–4, scoring two runs when Raines hesitated on a throw to first and Wohlford beat out a two-run single that should have been an out. While Raines took a rap in the press for "nonchalanting" the ball, his problem was quite the opposite. So cautious was he being about his throw he didn't put enough on the ball. Not having played at second during any of the exhibition games in spring training, he was feeling his way around.

In the final of the three-game series Rogers gave up only three hits in seven innings, but lost 3–2. The Expos committed five errors, three of them in the third inning when the Giants scored their three runs without benefit of a hit.

Wallach fielded a Wohlford liner cleanly and threw it over Oliver's head. He then wrestled with a LeMaster grounder, losing. One walk and two outs later third baseman Tom O'Malley bounced a soft hopper to Oliver, who blocked it with his body, then lost it. The throw from first to home was late, and another runner scored.

"We're just going through some growing pains," said Rogers after the game. "We've got some new guys in some new positions. But I hope we're going to be adults now, because we've sure had some adolescence problems over the last week or two."

There was booing now, and the scene was being set for more booing later. These fans weren't your three-times-a-year-to-the-ballpark-if-the-weather's-nice variety. The stadium was still cold and uncomfortable. The home-opener crowd had gone and the summer bunch wasn't here yet. These were hard-core fans. And they were not happy.

The Expos won their next two—the opening games of a four-game series against Williams and his Padres. In both cases the margin was one run, and in both cases they came from behind in the late innings.

In the first game Cromartie broke an 0-for-19 hitless streak with an RBI single in the eleventh to win it 6–5 after the Padres had blown it in the ninth by getting mixed up on a squeeze bunt. In the second, Dawson's two-run single topped off a three-run rally in the eighth after Padre third baseman Luis Salazar made a two-base throwing error.

The Padres then came back for 6–2 and 8–2 victories on the

weekend, and Williams left town laughing. In the Saturday game the Expos weren't able to hit Chris Welsh, who threw a four-hitter after entering the game with a 6.94 ERA, and in the second game they had been leading 2–1 in the ninth before the stoppers, Reardon and Fryman, fell apart.

The Braves came to town, and Steve Rogers rose up to beat them 4–0, on a two-hitter. But even what looked like a night to celebrate turned into a night to ask questions. Plate umpire Jerry Dale took Rogers' glove away in the fourth inning after Braves' manager Joe Torre had asked him to check it. They found a foreign substance on it. Under rule 8.02(b) they were required to eject him from the game, but didn't.

Torre claimed it was pine tar, used to make bat handles sticky and, in this case, to make Rogers' fingers just tacky enough to give his breaking balls that little bit extra. Rogers claimed the substance was a combination of Neatsfoot oil (used to soften leather) and dirt. So you could see how the oil, which usually soaks into the glove, might hang around the surface and mix with the dirt and look dark and gooey, just like pine tar. Although you'd wonder where it got the pine-tar smell.

Many sportswriters play a little ball themselves, usually quite badly. Being enthusiasts, many of them soak a lot more Neatsfoot oil into their gloves than any real athlete would ever be bothered with. Being clumsy, many of them grovel around in the infield dirt with their gloves, trying to squish baseballs to a standstill. None of them could remember ever being able to build up a residue of dirt and Neatsfoot oil in the pocket of his glove.

"I don't care whether any of you believe me or not," snapped Rogers. So nobody did. But neither did anyone actually push him too far. Nobody asked to see the glove, for instance. Because it *was* his night. In a string of awful nights, he had pitched a two-hitter, giving up one with the old glove and one with the new one. And if his fingers might have been a little sticky, the balls were coming in clean. Times had been tough for the Expos, but so far Rogers had been even tougher.

The Braves won the next one, 6–4. Brian Kappler of the *Gazette* had figured out that, if the Expos kept making errors at the rate they had been, they'd break the club record of 184 set by the first Expos team ever. So the Expos bore down, holding the evening's total to one.

But Speier was left stranded at third with nobody out. And when Francona laid down a perfect bunt for a base hit in the third, with Oliver on first and Dawson on second and nobody out, Dawson tried to score and was thrown out easily. In the fifth he was picked off first.

The Expos were down 3-2, but still in the game when a tired Bill Gullickson walked Rafael Ramirez and hit Claudell Washington with a pitch in the seventh. Fanning left him in. Dale Murphy hit a one-hop single to left. Francona dropped it and threw wide of third; and catcher Tim Blackwell didn't back up the throw. Two runs scored, and the Expos were out of it again.

Gary Carter, one of the few batters who'd been hitting well, came down with conjunctivitis. And in the final game of the Braves series and the home stand, the Braves won 9-1.

Jim Fanning said he would shoulder the blame for the Expos' ineptitude. Asked why he should, he said, "Because I'd be the easiest to take the blame." There is probably no greater sin for a manager than to forget that old baseball adage: *Martyrs finish third.*

Gentleman Jim

Somewhere in the wonderful area of Hartley, Iowa—from his family, his friends, his teachers—the right mix of intelligence, character and personality was put together to give the baseball world Jim Fanning.
—John McHale
Jim Fanning Testimonial Dinner
Hartley, Iowa
July 17, 1971

Jim Fanning's home town was Moneta, Iowa, eight miles down the road from Hartley in the black-earth country of northwestern Iowa. But Moneta, population one hundred when Fanning was a boy, is nearly gone now. Besides, the people of Hartley feel a legitimate claim to him, too. He played his American Legion ball there, and when they held the testimonial for him, three summers after he'd been named general manager of the Montreal Expos, the *Daily Reporter* from nearby Spencer, Iowa, pulled out all the stops:

> It's been a long time simmering on the fire. But now it's on the table ready for a big serving because today is "Jim Fanning Day" in Hartley.
> Born of the germ of an idea which was popped into the head of Verlyn Jipson, long-time and close friend of the honored guest, "Jim Fanning Day" took shape in a slow kaleidoscope of changing patterns and grew to a psychedelic dizziness of events.
> The day is filled with activity, from a children's parade at noon to a testimonial dinner in the evening.

When the kaleidoscope had stopped whirling, there was a bronze plaque embedded in a brick archway leading to Jim Fanning Park, in honour of a man who had played there and gone on to hit .170 in 64 major-league games.

Hartley isn't the only community that has staked a claim in Fanning. Spencer itself, thirteen miles from Hartley, has already been given one of his old uniform tops and wants more, to be put on display in the foyer of radio station KIDC. Spencer solidified its credentials by holding a Jim Fanning Roast in December 1981.

Fanning has declared himself "a very private person," which mainly means he doesn't want to talk about why he never married, any more than Steve Garvey wants to talk about why he ever did. Or about other personal things. Nevertheless, his stern gaze softens for the briefest of a flicker when he talks about these tributes from people who have held onto him long after he went away.

The archway in Hartley? "Obviously it makes you feel good," he says, looking down at his feet. The roast in Spencer? "A real big event," he says, already recovered and matter-of-fact again. "Some people I hadn't seen since high school."

He's not smiling on this fine summer day in Philadelphia. Not even that half-way, barracuda smile of his that's indistinguishable from a grimace. It's not the emotional side of himself or the folks he grew up with in Iowa that Fanning wants to talk about.

It's the fibre, the toughness, the resilience of the stock he comes from that's on his mind because he's having trouble finding it in and around his dugout.

"All of us kids in these little towns were eager to work, and we had all kinds of jobs," he remembers. "I didn't play Legion ball sometimes because I was working. I worked on town jobs—there was an apiary—and farm jobs—I bailed hay and milked cows.

"All the kids I knew were industrious. One kid in my class owns a great big automated farm now—he presses buttons from the house to feed the animals. That boy, with his older brother in the service and his younger brother helping him, worked the farm for his mother. He'd plough all night and come to school in the day time. I always had great admiration for that guy—he's a millionaire farmer, but he did it the hard way.

"The kid who lived next to me on my little block went into the service and retired about five years ago as full colonel. He's in the real-estate business in Colorado now and doing quite well.

"The kid who lived next to him went into the navy and is now a top business executive in St. Louis."

He pauses, clenches his jaw, shakes his head, marvelling at the impact that one tiny town with a will had made on the world.

"So many young guys have left that area and went off and became very successful. The whole town was an industrious little place where everybody worked."

Jim Fanning was an only child. His father was a labourer. When he worked during the depression it was for a dollar a day.

Only child or not, the young Fanning learned fibre. Sandlot games were rough and tough, often breaking up in the morning in a fight, but always resuming in the afternoon. There was a game in town—wagered on by the men who sat in Moneta's only tavern—to see if anyone, big or small, could throw a baseball hard enough or devious enough that little Jim Fanning couldn't catch it. Whatever they threw, he never backed away.

By the time he was a teenager there was nothing he couldn't catch, and at twenty-two he signed a professional contract with the Chicago Cubs.

For the next four years he played in towns with names like Springfield, Des Moines, Rock Hill, Nashville, Cedar Rapids, and Beaumont, moving around so much he picked up the label "The Wandering Man." Finally getting his major-league break with the Cubs in 1954, he hit .184 with one RBI. Overall he hit .170 in bits of four seasons with the Cubs and .258 in 11 minor-league seasons with 14 different clubs from Class C to Triple A.

While doing all this Fanning was smart enough (a) not to complain; and (b) to get a master's degree in physical education from the University of Illinois, writing a thesis called "A Cinematographic and Mechanical Analysis and Comparative Study of the Catcher's Throw."

By the time he was thirty his label had been firmly attached: "good field, no hit." All that sweat, all that work, all those dusty minor-league roads and double-headers, and that was it. The label was fair, he says, his eyes hardening, bracing to acknowledge professional failure and get on with it.

Bob Uecker has wound a broadcasting career out of ridiculing his own performance as a major-league catcher. Uecker caught 297 games and hit .200. Fanning is unamused at his. "I had my best years in Double A and did not have good years at Triple A. I was able to play in the majors because I had mastered the defensive aspects of the game."

His record is placed right up front in the Expos Media Guide. Right up front. If he were embarrassed about hitting .170 in 141 at-bats, with no home runs and five RBIs, it wouldn't be there. Carnegie Hall is Carnegie Hall, whether you're soloist or third fiddle. Especially if you fought to get there.

The public image of Jim Fanning is one of a refined gentleman, a decent man with enthusiasm for the game and affection for his players. But there is a bitterness here that doesn't show in the bland, post-game interviews in which patience and understanding are the theme.

When he came up, he says, "survival of the fittest" was the theme. There were lots more teams, lots more competitors every year, and when you finally got to Double A you thought "maybe there's an outside chance, some way, somehow, that you could get through the Double A's and the two Triple A's and finally make it, just maybe." But you never talked about it. "We only felt we had to do as good as we could and let the chips fall where they may."

And if you didn't get much of a chance when you got there, you accepted it. That's the way the system worked. "My opportunities in the major leagues weren't all that many, but still, I had enough at-bats to do something, and didn't."

When Fanning was a player, baseball and the people who ran baseball challenged you. You faced the challenge, and, if you failed, you packed your bags with dignity and went away. Quietly.

The trouble with players now, he says, is that very few of them will accept a challenge. "There are some undisciplined players who should be handled toughly," he says. "But most of them can't handle the tough part. It's an affront to them to be challenged in this great era of everyone being handled so fair, so equally. Years ago you took the challenge, you said to yourself, boy, I've got to do this thing.

"The players have changed drastically. How prepared are they to accept the great disappointments and discouragements of professional baseball? Most all of them haven't done a day's work in their lives. Most of them . . . I shouldn't use the word spoiled, but all of a sudden they're in a man's game."

The message is that Fanning is trapped in a time warp that won't let him manage the way he'd like to. He would like to deal warmly with some, sternly with others, mixing and matching as the occasions arise. He is forced to deal warmly with all.

Images: Of Easter Sunday in Philadelphia, in a dressing room flooded with Warren Cromartie's latest disco rock tape, the manager moving from player to player, clasping their hands with both of his. "Happy Easter, Rodney. Happy Easter, Al. Happy Easter, Warren." Of Tim Raines, walking naked toward the showers, having a bad first half, the manager calling out to him, "Tim. Tim!" Raines turning, Fanning clenching his fist and winking to commend him on a good game, feeling the gesture is not enough, calling "Tim" again, walking over, putting his arm around his shoulder, whispering a message of congratulations. Of Warren Cromartie marching back to the dugout through a chorus of boos in August, having struck out with men on base once again, and Fanning clapping for him, encouraging him, even though you could get a Cromartie quote any day of the week dumping on Fanning as a manager.

These are seemingly the gestures of a kindly man, a man daring enough to come on as a scout leader amidst the macho world of tobacco spit and profanity. But this is also a man who'll tell you his players don't have any pride and he doesn't care what they think of him. And that they're a bunch of spoiled babies, anyway.

And you realize that what you're listening to is a man who feels cheated—not by the system, which spat him out as a player but took him back as a workaholic administrator, but by Dr. Spock's grandchildren, the players.

Taking over from the vitriolic Williams, whose approach to motivation was to pull the players' wings off for the press, Fanning refused to say a negative word about any of them. By the second week in the season reporters' eyes were starting to glaze over.

"Errors are a part of baseball," became a refrain. Many errors —which is what the Expos were making—were part of bad baseball. And mental errors—which the Expos were also making— were part of terrible baseball. But in Jim Fanning's office, the players rarely made a mistake. They were just part of baseball.

The tone was "we're all human." But the effect, ironically enough, was to dehumanize the game.

Fanning appeared to think of it as a daily exhibition of his patience, after he'd decided that handling modern-day ballplayers required patience because so few other avenues were open to a manager.

"Not too many years ago, in the 50s, if you couldn't handle it— from a physical or emotional or psychological standpoint—you just got lost. Nobody messed with you. You were gone. We can't do that today. We have more major-league clubs than ever, we have fewer good players coming into baseball, and I would guess that most baseball management people are more patient, more tolerant. We recognize our investments."

When players became "undisciplined" and were deemed to be

marginal investments (Rodney Scott, Bill Lee) the Expos could play it the old way—dump 'em. But if Tim Raines didn't show up for a game without telling anybody until five minutes before it was going to start, it was grit your teeth and go back to patience.

On the other side, some of the players were patient with Fanning and some were less so. It infuriated him that they had that option; he hadn't had it in the 50s. And it was even more infuriating that some of them would exercise the option against him when he was biting his tongue and showing martyr-like patience while they kept screwing up.

Bill Lee and Cromartie struck early, soon after Fanning took over in 1981.

"Another goddamned General Patton," railed Cromartie. "We're a game and a half out, everybody's future is on the line, and we've got a guy coming down from the booth."

Lee bordered on incoherent, but you got the point. "We've changed horses in mid-torrent," he raged, "and we haven't even got on the horse, and now we're tumbling over and over down the river of despair."

Fanning survived all this by winning the National League East, despite a curious ending that lost the pennant to the Dodgers. With the score tied going into the final inning of that final game he brought in Steve Rogers to pitch, despite the fact that he had his ace lefthander, Woodie Fryman, and his ace righthander, Jeff Reardon, in the bullpen. Rogers, who had pitched brilliantly down the stretch as a starter, had nothing in relief and proved it by giving up a vicious fly ball to Ron Cey that took Raines to the warning track. Nevertheless Fanning left Rogers in to pitch to the left-handed Rick Monday, who flied out to God deep over the right-field fence. To this day Fanning says Reardon's shoulder was injured, Reardon says it was fully recovered, and Fryman says he'd loved to have pitched to Monday.

But it had been a successful season and the fans were forgiving, especially since Fanning had intrigued people by inserting some players and making some moves that, if not hints of genius, were at least a relief from Williams' boring repetitiveness.

But spring training left the second-base question unanswered and Fanning's favourite, Wallace Johnson, soon proved inadequate. There were some questionable tactical decisions about batters, baserunners, and the like; the team had no consistency and little flair for adventurous baseball; and by the All-Star Game Fanning was getting booed.

Scott bitched, sulked, and was fired. Lee raged about fascism and was fired.

"Fanning gives that appearance of almost being too nice a guy to be a manager," said Lee. "I never saw that in him. I saw a vengeance and a venom in the first team meeting he held. He didn't like the way Williams had run the club, and he told us we would be a great ball club if we had discipline. Hell, that's the reason we had been such a good ball club, because we were undisciplined. We swung the bat, we struck out a lot, we ran the bases with reckless abandon, and we intimidated teams. We didn't need an organization man with no managerial skills."

Cromartie grumbled, even though Fanning played him every day long after decency or judgement required him to.

Andre Dawson, who prides himself on getting along with people, said he liked Fanning a lot but wondered if he was the right person to be manager.

"You can't really point the finger at Jim, because he's still learning and he didn't even ask to be here. There have been occasions when there's been a lot of second-guessing—you even hear guys saying Jim will have to ask the coaches what to do now.

"Things like that tend to get into the air and before long everybody's talking about it. And it's not good, because then you start going out and blaming him, and playing for yourself and not for the team.

"I tend to believe I can play for anyone and I think what my problem is is that I realize just what kind of a predicament he's in and I go out and try to over-play, try to do too much. If he makes a move, like batting me second, you want to go out and try to show it's the right move, even if you don't think it is. You want to make the guy look good.

"Like I say, he's still learning, but it's tough to go out and be a consistent winner if you've got a manager who's just learning the game. He just doesn't have the personality of a manager. But I like him a lot."

Steve Rogers hated Dick Williams and was thrilled to see him fired. He felt Williams had tried to destroy him with malicious comments and that, with Fanning, there was much less interpersonal hostility on the team.

Would it be fair to say, then, that replacing Williams with Fanning has made the Montreal Expos clubhouse a better place for a baseball player to go to work?

"That's not too far wrong. On the other hand, as much as negative personality is bad, it's not so terrible as it can make or break a season as long as the actual managing of the game—the physical decision-making—is sound. And Williams was good at that."

As far as handling people is concerned, Rogers preferred Fanning, with reservations.

"Fanning may make reporters' eyes glaze over, but for five years they haven't had to write a story. They'd stop in Williams' office without ever coming to see the players, and after everyone had been sufficiently ripped for twenty minutes they'd go away.

"There has to be a happy medium between a guy like that and what Jim seems to do at this stage of his development—never acknowledging a mistake, pretending it didn't happen.

"You need somebody to say 'you screwed up and I want to talk to you about it, remind you about it.' Everyone has enough pride not to want to mess up, but it often takes that little bit of an additional boost to constantly improve yourself, whether it's man-to-man, in front of the other guys, or even in the press. Sometimes that works, too."

This was one of the team's statesmen, its representative on the players' association, acknowledging that, if you're not abusive about it, it doesn't hurt to kick ass now and again. Talking about a manager who thought the same thing but lamented that in the modern game a manager couldn't get away with it.

When Jim Fanning took over in 1981 he gave an interview to Allen Abel of the *Globe and Mail*, saying emotional connection with the players wasn't that important to him, but he wanted "dialogue" with them: he wanted them to feel free to walk into his office and talk about what was going right and what was going wrong.

Has that dialogue worked?

There is a long pause in a Philadelphia hotel room.

"Well, I think there is a hesitancy of a player . . . I suppose on this club there's a division of players. The players who have come through our system in the last three or four years, particularly guys I've had a lot to do with, they're anxious to learn everything there is to know about baseball. They have a rapport and a freedom with me that others don't have, others who have been here longer and probably think that's beyond them. And that's fine."

Indeed, Tim Wallach and Terry Francona would probably have made out all right in the industrious little town of Moneta in the 50s. But it's hard to say how Rodney Scott and Warren Cromartie, John Milner or Bill Lee would have fit in.

And Whitey Herzog, the Cardinals' manager, battling Gentleman Jim for the pennant—how would he have fit in? At one point in the season the Expos beat the Cardinals three out of four at Olympic Stadium. After the Cards lost the second one—knocking them two games behind the Phillies—Herzog stretched naked behind his desk (if the word "stretched" can be used for such bulk) bemoaning his fate with black-tongued humour.

His hair, gold on top and dark at the roots, was still wet from the shower. He looked at his hitters' records against the Expos' next-day pitcher, rattling off histories that included a 1-for-19, 0-for-12, and 1-for-16 in the heart of his line-up, and he cackled: "Hee, hee, hee. Fuck! I sure hope it rains." Still chortling, he was off for a rubdown.

"He's probably the best manager in baseball," remarked Cardinal starter Dave LaPoint. "And he spends most of his time hunting and fishing."

How would Whitey have fit in in Moneta? We'll never know. Moneta is all but gone now, down to fewer than fifty people, and Jim Fanning doesn't drive through it any more.

"It's a honey town now. The apiary has taken over. The town hall is filled with extracting equipment. The store, the garage, the building that was the tavern—they've all been taken over."

No more men sitting around quaffing their beers and betting over who could throw a ball through little Jim Fanning.

Just the buzzing of bees, going about their work. Bees with fibre. Busy, busy, busy.

Good Boys and Bad Boys

Andre Dawson

This is the endless Hawk
soaring in the field,
hovering
like a shadow to the lines.

At the plate he scowls
and pounces,
rips
miles around his shoulders

—misses—

glares out,
eyes burning,
hands as quick as talons
whipping sinew to the ball;
his swing too sweeping
but his hands too quick
and his eyes too hot
to be denied.

And again
into the field,
where he floats
glides
and always arrives just then,
catching it at the knees,
holding the ball now,
staring fiercely at the bases,
angry once again.

Andre Dawson probably wouldn't have fit perfectly into Fanning's little community of Moneta, but not because he didn't share its work ethic. No one has worked harder at making himself a complete ballplayer than Dawson. But in the beginning everyone saw a flaw. Wise old white men with faces disguised in leather watched the young Andre Dawson play baseball and somewhere in the backs of their minds said no, he wouldn't do.

The Kansas City Royals, not knowing that he would some day steal bases when he wanted to and cover more ground than all the others in all their fields, thought he was too slow. That surprised him—he thought he had run fast for them. Perhaps they were afraid of the knee brace he wore from football.

The Dodgers didn't think he could hit. Danny Menendez, the Expos' chief of scouting, remembers a Los Angeles scout saying that a bunch of them had gone down to see him play in a college game, but he hadn't got a hit. The consensus was that he had speed but his bat was too light.

It was in college that they all discovered that he couldn't throw. His coach at Florida A&M moved him to shortstop so a scout could get a look at his lateral movement, and he hurt something in his arm. It took years to heal.

But he healed it, working with weights and making long throws, heating it, rubbing it, stretching it. In the beginning he couldn't lift it without pain. When he was finished he could stop runners in their tracks just by looking at them.

He healed it with some luck and a lot of patience. "I just felt if it was strong at one point in my career why couldn't it be again? And I worked in that direction."

When he got to the minors they wondered if he could field. "He had a funny sort of short-stride running gait," recalls John McHale. "He was kind of a rag doll defensively. He'd catch everything, but he was awkward and he didn't have a good throwing arm."

"We had no clue he would become the player he is," says Menendez. "The odds against it were astronomical."

Acting on scout Billy Adair's advice, the Expos selected Dawson in the eleventh round of the June 1975 free-agent draft, after 250 players had been taken. Of the 251, he was the best.

In August of 1977 *Sports Illustrated* did a feature piece on the Expos' young "blackbird outfield" Warren Cromartie, Andre Dawson, and Ellis Valentine. For a start, the article pointed out, they were a bargain. Valentine was making $35,000 that year, and

Cromartie and Dawson $25,000 each. Valentine was lauded for having the best arm in baseball, which he did, and was also described as "the complete player" of the three. Dawson was "the silent partner." "Andre has to be more aggressive and take charge in the field," said manager Dick Williams.

So Andre did. Cromartie has survived as an off-and-on fielder and an on-and-off hitter. Valentine has tried to drown his talent in a vat of self-indulgence, though it still struggles to the surface for the odd gasp of air. But Dawson ranks with Mike Schmidt and Gary Carter as the glory of their times.

"I think [Dawson's] the best player in the league," says former Expos coach Ozzie Virgil. "I played with Willie Mays, and Dawson is pretty damned close to him."

"There's no sense comparing him to anyone else," says Pittsburgh manager Chuck Tanner, "because he's the best."

Andre Dawson caught 327 fly balls during the 1981 season. Omar Moreno of Pittsburgh was closest with 302. Philadelphia's Garry Maddox, playing in nine fewer games than Dawson, had 251. The same Maddox of whom Ralph Kilner said, "Two thirds of the world is covered by water. The rest is covered by Garry Maddox." Dawson would get his feet wet.

About three or four times a year Dawson-watchers will wonder whether he might not have gotten to a ball that dropped in. Not that anybody else would have—it's just that, being Dawson, maybe he could have. Being purists, they pride themselves on being open minded.

He isn't perfect. On May 6, 1982, Rick Monday hit a triple to the right-center-field fence that Dawson might have had a shot at if he had run full tilt at the wall and timed a perfect jump. On May 10 he dropped a one-hop double to left center off the bat of Jack Clark and stood and glowered at it for a couple of seconds, allowing Clark to go to third. And there was a shallow liner in an August series that nobody seems able to pinpoint. But there was agreement at the time that he might have made the catch if he'd gotten a perfect jump. There were others. But not many.

At bat Dawson is a windmill in a hurricane. There are spots for a pitcher to shoot for because of the enormity of his swing, but his hands are so fast he can often adjust in time. His compulsion to crush everything within two feet of the plate and drive it into the left-field stands may be wrong headed . . . is undoubtedly wrong headed. He should wait out more bases on balls. But his swing is a glorious thing to watch and who would unscrew the first bolt to try to up-grade a .300 hitter with power? Perhaps the man himself. "I'm at my peak in the field," he says, "but I know I haven't reached my peak offensively."

Dawson calls himself a serious person and he looks serious. His forehead is sculpted in a frown, he has embers for eyes, and he's built like a light-heavyweight without hips. He looks strong and intense enough to do exactly what he wants to: "be aware of my surroundings, contain myself, and maintain control of my situation." He's about as funny as the Old Testament until he laughs. It's so unexpected and always so genuine a Dawson laugh is worth waiting for, even working for.

He grew up without a father close at hand, but he didn't need one. His grandmother's specialty was discipline. His mother's specialty was affection and hard work—she supported eight children, of whom Andre was the eldest, by baking cakes in a cafeteria. His uncle Ted's specialty was philosophy and baseball—he was a third baseman with the Pirates' organization. He spent a lot of time telling his nephew that you can achieve anything you want in life if you set yourself in that direction and go after it.

His grandmother spent very little time informing him that he could forget about signing a baseball contract and rushing off to the minors. He was going to university first. There were race riots while Dawson was growing up in Miami, but he didn't take part: they were held past his curfew. Moreover, he "wasn't a problem child."

"Which is particularly why I think I'm in the situation I am today. My mother has visited Montreal. She's quite proud of me because, being raised without a father, I could have chosen to go either way."

Dawson understands those who went the other way but has limited patience with them. Dick Williams had a reputation as a disciplinarian when he signed on to manage Montreal; but he turned out to be more of a barker than a biter, letting Ron LeFlore, Ellis Valentine, and Rodney Scott run free. Dawson needled them about it, but they knew he wasn't being funny.

"Some ballplayers come to the park whenever they like," he told a reporter. "The rules have been obliterated."

What he wanted to see was the kind of structure he'd grown up with in Miami: enough discipline to keep people productive, but enough flexibility to let them express their own personalities. He doesn't have much time for the spoiled-black-athlete syndrome, typified by LeFlore, Valentine, and Scott. But he resents the attitude that everybody should be middle-American boy scouts.

It is conventional wisdom, based on testimony from Menendez, that one of the reasons Dawson was overlooked by scouts was that the whole team at Florida A&M, a small black college, was so lackadaisical. They didn't run on and off the field, and there was little of the rah-rah that people associate with enthusiastic baseball.

This makes Dawson mad. "What a lot of people fail to realize is just how much talent there was on that ball club, and what we did with it. We played between thirty-five and forty games a year, and the most we ever lost was about five. We beat the University of Miami in a double-header when they were number one in the nation. They were a big school. We weren't. The scouts didn't see rah-rah, so they didn't like us. But I'll tell you one thing—that's one of the best teams I've ever played with or been around."

For Dawson, the 1982 Expos didn't rank, although he liked the 1981 version, with Rowland Office, Rodney Scott, John Milner, and Bill Lee. "We had everything you needed to win. We had experienced guys who could come off the bench and win a game for you. That's all gone, though."

1982 brought too many uncertainties for him, too many changes that didn't make sense. He was critical of Rodney Scott when Scott indulged himself at the expense of the team. But he calls Scott's release in May "one of our biggest mistakes."

"We miss Rodney more than any other player who's left the team this year. We've run through so many second basemen. How many second basemen steal seventy bases? How many second basemen score eighty runs? He was the type of player who would intimidate you, force you into mistakes. He liked to make things happen.

"They got rid of him because they felt he had an attitude problem. I don't think he was a problem player. He went out and played hard every game.

"If he was pitch-hit for, he'd say something to the manager, and that would be showing the manager up. Chris Speier says something to the manager and nothing is thought of it. But to them Rodney had an attitude problem, and they thought he could be replaced.

"You can't take all the character out of a team. You cannot have all similar personalities on a ball club. You've got to have some guys rah-rah around, like Cromartie. You've got to have some guys down to earth. You've got to have some daredevils, and even a few who don't seem to care about anything. I don't think you can have one personality for twenty-five ballplayers."

He says he doesn't much like some management decisions made over the year or the "military camp" atmosphere when the team has been at home in Montreal; but, with a contract that stands to pay him six million dollars over five years if he performs in the manner to which he has been accustomed he's not about to let any distractions get in the way of his performance.

"I think when I retire I'll be looked at as having been a complete ballplayer. I hope my average will be above the .300 level. I want to average between 35 and 40 stolen bases a year, between 25 and 30 homers, and between 85 and 100 RBIs.

"In the outfield I've sort of taken the approach that I'm a gambler now. I'll force you to hit the ball over my head. I'll take away the gap against a pull hitter and force him to hit the ball the other way."

And if he had to assess himself, what stands out the most?

"I am not a problem ballplayer. That probably stands out more than anything else."

True enough. Because when they hit that ball to center—no problem. We have Endless Andre Dawson, like a shadow to the lines.

Deep down in my heart I know somebody is thinking about me helping them to play winning baseball. But who that is or where they are I really don't know.
—Rodney Scott
   May 14, 1982

Rodney Scott could never say he wasn't a problem ballplayer. The best he could do was, "I never meant anybody any harm."

Yet it's hard to think of anything that did the Montreal Expos more harm in 1982 than the firing of Rodney Scott, for which he must take some blame.

In fact, much of the stupidity of the Expos' 1982 season could be summed up in the words Rodney Scott. Much of the stupidity was Rodney's personal property; but when you put that aside, there was a truck-load left over. It was everywhere.

Scott was the other 60s black kid. Dawson had an absentee father, love, and guidance. Scott had an absentee father and love until one rainy day, when an old man, standing behind the screen back of home plate at a little-league game in Indianapolis, fell down, the victim of a stroke.

His name was Charlie Woodruff. He was a steelworker until he retired, when he made pocket money cleaning up at a barber shop, assisted by his grandson Rodney Scott.

"He was my greatest booster when I was growing up. He came to all my games. He really didn't tell me a whole lot, but he'd shake his head and tell me how good I'd played, and make me feel special. Always, later, when I'd be playing ball I'd think how if he were around he'd be watching me. I still feel him watching me."

When Charlie Woodruff died, his grandson became his own booster. He would be great, he was going to be great. And soon, he felt, he was great.

Not in terms of numbers, maybe. In baseball you are what you add up to. After seven years Scott added up to .237, with three home runs and 203 stolen bases. But he was larger than his numbers. As they said in the Expos' souvenir program before the company line changed, "In the opinion of many observers, Rodney Scott is the most consistently underrated player in the majors today."

He was combative. He intimidated teams with his audacity, especially on the bases. When Scott batted second, baserunning was a joint adventure with the great Tim Raines, as it had been with Ron LeFlore the previous year. Without Scott, Raines looked alone, unsure, a soggy firecracker trying to remember what fireworks were all about.

Between them Scott and LeFlore stole 160 bases in 1980, a major-league record for a tandem performance. Scott and Raines combined for 101 in the shortened 1981 season. And then it was over—just like that.

The rationale was that Scott had become a .200 hitter, and that the Expos had to get more offence out of the second-base position. Except that Scott, who probably wasn't as gifted a second baseman as he was cracked up to be, was a much better offensive player than he was given credit for.

Because he drew a lot of walks and stole a lot of bases, only six National League second basemen ranked ahead of him in Total Average in 1981, and that was in an off year, when Scott had a .205 batting average. And he wasn't a selfish hitter. He took hundreds of potentially hittable pitches to allow LeFlore and Raines to steal, and he took them as obstructively as he could.

Lou Brock, the all-time base-stealing champion, studied Scott and Raines. "Scott was one of the keys to Tim Raines last year," said Brock during Raines' 1982 difficulties. "He had learned to do what Ted Sizemore and Curt Flood did for me, which for a batter involves a complete deprogramming. All his life a batter has been trained to move forward, into the ball. But the best thing you can do for somebody trying to steal is to stay back so the bat head bothers the catcher. No catcher likes to come up near the head of the bat. Scott knew how to do that, and not many batters do."

And when he got on base, with LeFlore, Raines, or Dawson, you had the Quebec Track Team. Steals of second. Steals of third, many by Scott while the catcher was tossing the ball back to the pitcher. Double steals. Fretting pitchers. Runs scored. Fastballs to hit.

"Not only was he quite a bit better than an average fielder," acknowledged Hugh Hallward, ten per-cent owner of the Expos and a member of the team's decision-making troika. "From second to home he was the best baserunner on the club. His intuitive baseball skills were marvelous."

"I miss Rodney incredibly," said Raines toward the end of his second season. "It was amazing the things he'd do for me at the plate. He'd do anything he could to distract the catcher. He'd always give me a chance. There were only two times all last year that he swung the bat when I was going. This year it's probably happened twenty times. We didn't really have a second-place hitter this year."

Which, after Terry Francona was injured, was true. The Expos finally got so frustrated they used Andre Dawson to hit second, telling him to forget about all the little things a second-place hitter is supposed to do—take pitches, hit to the opposite field, etc.—

and just swing away. It wasn't very clever baseball, and Dawson only hit .275 from the second spot, but there wasn't much choice.

The others they tried there—Cromartie, Youngblood, Gates, White, Taveras, Johnson, Little, Raines, and Phillips—averaged .190 and scored a run on average of once every nine at-bats, a sad record considering the formidable war clubs that followed them to the plate.

And the people who replaced Scott at second base fielded worse than those who replaced him in the second hitting spot. Raines couldn't turn the double play, and was hesitant and unsure on his throws; Gates was inconsistent; Taveras showed no sign he had once known how to play the game; and Johnson was a designated hitter in the wrong league.

It is difficult to guess how many runs the merry-go-round at second cost the Expos before Doug Flynn arrived 102 games into the season. Judging from statistics on errors, double plays, put-outs and assists, and on day-to-day observations, these six members of the Gang of Eight probably gave the opposition forty or fifty total bases that Scott or Flynn wouldn't have.

That would have been bad enough in itself, but they were bracketed by Speier at short and Oliver at first, generous people themselves.

There is a theory that Bill Lee, who survived on ground-ball outs, didn't throw his fit so much because he loved Rodney as he did because Scott's release meant doom to him as a pitcher.

Lee still had enough guile left to fool some of the people some of the time by making the ball shudder, wince, sidle, hesitate, stall, crumple, and shrivel before the batter's very eyes; so that when it mingled with the bat it wanted to scurry into the friendly arms of an infielder rather than vault, jump, explode, or otherwise celebrate its freedom. But where were the friendly arms?

Not that Rodney Scott ranked with Manny Trillo, Tom Herr, and Juan Bonilla as a second baseman. But he was pretty decent.

So how could anybody release a guy like that and swallow his $300,000 contract in the process?

Simple. John McHale is a disciplinarian with Middle-American values. Rodney Scott was a spoiled brat, a bad apple, a sulker, fierce, disruptive, and a poor role model for the young players—many of them black—whom the Expos hoped to work into their line-up over the next few years.

He was also a doper, although how heavily he partook of what ingredients remains an open question.

His skills might have been deteriorating, although he still looked good on the basepaths and hit a reasonable .256 in spring training. But he had gone from a .224 hitter with 63 stolen bases in 1981 to .205 and 30 stolen bases in two-thirds of a season in 1982.

Was dope robbing him of his skills? "I can't really say that it was," he would say many months later. "And I'd be the first to know."

But the Expos were worried sick about Tim Raines, who had a drug problem of his own. It was time to weed the garden, as Whitey Herzog had done at St. Louis. Office, Lee, Milner—anybody who smelled suspicious. And most especially, Scott.

McHale said it was because Scott was a .200 hitter, pure and simple, and he didn't like .200 hitters. What he meant was that management will go a long way to try to save a talented ballplayer such as Raines but not any further than it has to with someone closer to the fringe, like Scott.

McHale elaborated at a news conference at the All-Star break. "He was released because he wasn't participating any more. He wouldn't practise. He wouldn't attend team meetings. He'd be lying down on a table in the clubhouse while the game was going on. . . . We sent him for batting lessons to Harry "The Hat" Walker. It didn't work out. He wouldn't have anything to do with [batting coach] Billy DeMars. He wouldn't accept the role of utility man we had allotted him."

It was all true. Fierce little Rodney Scott was sulking. He'd been sulking since the Expos had fired manager Dick Williams the previous September. Williams had been his protector and had pampered him after giving him Dave Cash's job at second in a surprise move at the beginning of the 1979 season.

Scott, LeFlore, and Ellis Valentine had been allowed to set their own rules under Williams. It had rankled some of the other players, including Dawson, and it had certainly rankled the front office.

But Williams, like Scott, was fiercely independent, and nothing could be done. Until Williams was gone.

For Scott, losing Williams was like losing Charlie Woodruff one more time. He was left with being his own booster again.

"When you have a guy of gifted ability, he stands out anywhere," he said jauntily after his release. "I make it look so easy they think I'm not trying. I rate myself among the best. On the field I couldn't pick none of them ahead of me.

"I don't think none of them can run the bases like I run the bases. I've got a good eye, get a lot of walks, take a lot of pitches. If I was a selfish kind of guy I could probably hit higher, but I like to see everybody do good."

Sometimes he'd be jaunty like this. And sometimes he'd be gloomy. Either way, nothing went right. Williams couldn't convince management at San Diego to sign Scott to the long-term contract he wanted. The Yankees signed him to a minor-league contract, then gasped when he refused to come up to the big team unless they offered him a better, long-term deal.

They brought him up anyway. He'd been hitting over .370 at Columbus and finally agreed to play for them. The Yankees only had to pay him the major-league minimum because he was still on his Expos contract.

In his first game he batted second, getting two hits and stealing a base. Could he be the one to finally get George Steinbrenner's ballyhooed track team out of the starting blocks?

The answer turned out to be no. He went hitless for a few games, they dropped him down to eighth and then ninth in the batting order, and he complained.

"I was just concerned about what they had planned for me. The way they were using me, that didn't give me much incentive to play."

He got on the wrong side of some people. It became known that manager Clyde King didn't want him on his team.

"Somebody's always going to dislike you or not like your ways," said Scott after the Yankees released him. "That's the trouble with life in general."

"It was his habits," said Hugh Hallward. "What a waste Rodney Scott is. What a hell of a waste."

"Everybody's going to like a guy who just does what they tell him to do," said Rodney Scott.

"Impossible," said Charles Bronfman. "He was impossible."

"I'm going to survive my life a lot better without people saying a lot of untrue things about me," said Rodney Scott.

"These guys are making tremendous money," said John McHale. "We have a right to expect them to be ready to play, to be in shape."

"You know all these guys they're sending to rehabilitation

79

centers," said Rodney Scott. "They're going to be sorry, because somebody will always be reminding them about it. If you're a man, you should be able to help yourself without someone else interfering. I don't want anybody manipulating me."

He was 29, and unemployed.

The Winning Streak

It seemed flawed. When you talked about it as a winning streak of the first rank, you had to admit it lacked length. You could argue that it had breadth and depth, but to what point? You could marvel at its consistency, pointing out how uninterrupted it was by loss, but even second-rate winning streaks are uninterrupted. You could rave on about its fine play, soaring spirits, luck, and the rest. But there hardly seemed time, even for that.

For a start it seemed wrong to begin calling it a winning streak for the first five or six games. Until then the truly professional announcer will hold himself to, "So the Expos sweep the three-game series . . ." or "That's five in a row for the Expos, who may have something going here. . . ."

And sure enough, after the next game they did. The Expos, suddenly, were riding the crest of a six-game winning streak. And seven! And eight! And suddenly—it was over. Two games short of the club record of ten, set in 1979 and tied in 1980. Five games short of the showy thirteen-game streak the Braves opened the season with. And thirteen games shy of the major-league record of twenty-one, achieved twice by the Cubs, in 1880 and 1935, before they got hooked on losing.

Eight does seem a bit short. But at the time, it was just right. Nobody really wanted too long a winning streak. Hadn't there been enough pressure stumbling through the first six weeks of the season while the Cards sauntered along in front?

No, what the fans wanted was for the Expos to slip into a winning stride. Not the stupidity and bungling of the 4–10 home stand that had preceded the streak. Not the unreality of winning nine straight games. But a comfortable, realistic compromise: maybe win eight, lose one; win six, lose one; win seven, lose one. . . .

In hindsight, of course, the winning streak was too short. And the players, in cutting it short because they sensed that's what the fans wanted, probably made a mistake. If they had chosen to keep it going there's not much doubt now that they could have won fifty or sixty in a row and coasted the rest of the way. But it's easy to second-guess.

Because people didn't want a winning streak at the time many have forgotten that there was one. To some the season seems like one long blur of not being up to the mark. But for eight short days it was different.

The Expos had left Olympic Stadium like the scene of an accident. "Expos Finish Home Stand on New Low," read the sports-page headline in the Montreal *Gazette*, after the Braves had whipped them 9–1 to leave them with a 4–11 record in their past 15 games.

Charlie Lea signalled the revival on the first day out in Cincinnati, pitching a two-hitter and driving in a run with a single as the Expos whitewashed the Reds 2–0. The win reeked of fortitude. The Expos were forced to scratch for their runs off the overpowering Mario Soto, who whiffed eleven of them.

But they did. Raines doubled on the first pitch of the game and came home on a bunt and a sacrifice fly. Cromartie doubled in the second and came home on Lea's bad-hop single. Then the Expos held tough: Lea pitched out of a bases-loaded difficulty in the sixth, Fryman relieved and got his second save of the year in the ninth, and all of a sudden it was one in a row.

The next night Warren Cromartie, hitting .216, rapped a home run and a single, driving in two runs as Scott Sanderson pitched a six-hitter through 7⅓ innings and beat the Reds 4–2, lowering his earned-run average to 1.68. Jeff Reardon gave up a hit and two walks without retiring anybody in the eighth, in what was to be the only mediocre pitching performance of the streak; but Fryman came on to record his second save in two nights.

On Sunday the Expos completed the sweep, evening their record at 19–19. Steve Rogers stranded seven Reds in the first four innings and went on to win a 4–2 decision. Reardon pitched 1⅔ innings of perfect relief. Rogers gave up 10 hits, but finished the game with an ERA of 1.70. The Expo batters were like butter in the box as Bruce Berenyi sliced through twelve of them in a row to open the game; but Oliver, Cromartie, and Raines came through with timely hits in the fifth to score three runs.

The Expos then nipped over to the Astrodome in Houston, where Bill Gullickson followed up on Rogers by stranding six runners in the first three innings and going on to win a seven-hit shutout. Fryman picked up his third save of the embryonic streak, giving up one harmless single in the final inning. The Expos were held to three hits in seven innings by Bob Knepper and had to be lucky to score.

But they did, twice. Former Expo Tony Scott, who enjoys showing his stuff against his former team-mates, came close to making a breathtaking, diving catch off a sinking liner from the bat of Terry Francona. But he couldn't hold it. Francona scored when Denny Walling threw wide of Knepper at first on a high Andre Dawson hopper, and Al Oliver lined a single to score Dawson after he'd stolen second. Four in a row.

Four looked like the limit when the Expos sent David Palmer to the mound the next night. Palmer hadn't pitched in the majors since October 1, 1980, and he'd been struggling to recover from elbow surgery.

Palmer's control, once a source of pride to him, was shaky as he walked six men in six innings. But he gave up only two hits and one run. Bryn Smith came in and recorded his first major-league save with three innings of runless relief, and the Expos won 6-1. Winning had become infectious—just like Gary Carter. Carter had been out of the line-up with *pink eye* or conjunctivitis for short. But after extra batting practice before the game, he blasted a two-run homer off the scoreboard above the left-field fence. Andre Dawson hit two solo home runs and a two-run double. Five in a row.

And then Charlie Lea, the guy who started it all, came back to win a pitchers' duel against Don Sutton, who'd come into the game with a 7-1 record. Sutton gave up only five hits in nine innings, then had to sit back and watch the Expos score four off relievers Frank LaCorte and George Cappuzzello in the tenth.

Lea gave up one hit and no walks over nine innings, with Reardon giving up one hit in the tenth but shutting the Astros down for a 4-0 two-hitter.

Which meant that three of the five wins had been pitched by cripples. Neither Lea (2 wins) nor Palmer (1) had figured to make the team in spring training. One of them would have been a bonus. Two comprised a Godsend.

In the sixth game LaCorte walked three in the tenth before Tim Raines drove home a run with a sacrifice fly and Tim Wallach followed up with a three-run homer. Six straight.

The Expos came home, which in 1982 should have ended the streak. But Scott Sanderson pitched a six-hit complete game and got good support in the field as the Expos beat the Reds again, 4–2. Ron Oester hit a two-run homer to account for the Cincinnati runs, but the Expos had already scored three in the first off three Berenyi walks, three wild pitches, a double by Dawson, and a single by Wallach.

John Milner filled in for Al Oliver at first. He started a neat 3–6–3 double play and scooped a bad throw out of the dirt. Warren Cromartie raced far into the right-field corner to rob Oester of a double. That made it seven.

Gary Carter clubbed a tremendous, high home run over the center-field fence with two runners aboard on Saturday, May 29, to break a 1–1 tie and gave the Expos a 4–1 victory over the Reds.

The homer was his third in four games and the win was the Expos' eighth straight. Steve Rogers went the distance, scattering eight hits and striking out six batters and lowering his league-leading ERA to 1.67.

The Expos, who had been floundering at 16–19 a little over a week earlier, were strutting at 24–19, "with the momentum," as they say.

The Saturday game had been covered by NBC television and both the French and English CBC.

"Today," said Gary Carter, looking at the world through rose-coloured eyes, "a lot of eyes were on us and people across the United States and Canada are realizing that the Expos are for real."

During the eight games the previously porous defence made only four errors, and gave up no unearned runs. The pitchers gave up eight runs in eight games, and because one lasted ten innings there combined ERA for the streak came out to 0.99.

But Charlie Lea wasn't quite finished. Gullickson and Reardon fell victim to home runs on the Sunday, and the Reds snapped the streak with a 7–1 win.

But the next day, against the Astros, the Expos played as close as their fans will ever see to a perfect game, led by Lea again.

Lea pitched a four-hit shutout, giving up no walks and stretching his scoreless-inning streak to twenty-six. Two of the hits were meaningless singles in the ninth.

The Expo batters, meanwhile, racked up five runs off Don Sutton in the first inning and piled up five more by the sixth, coasting to a 10–0 conquest. They collected fifteen hits, and nobody in the starting line-up went without one.

Raines stole two bases. Jerry White climbed the wall in left center, nearly knocking open the access gate to the field, to rob Phil Garner of at least a double. Cromartie made a fine running catch off Jose Cruz to take a double away from him.

Tim Wallach made a teensy throwing error to first that didn't lead to anything for the only Expo miscue of the game, and made up for it by going 3-for-4 at the plate with a massive home run deep into the left-field bleachers and four RBIs.

That the Expos were still 3½ games behind the Cardinals seemed incidental. How was St. Louis, with its Steve Muras and Bob Forsches, going to match Montreal pitching down the stretch? Especially now that the fielding was starting to come around?

But what about the hitting? In 1981 the Expos had seemed to have a decent offensive line-up, but had batted a collective .246—tenth best in a twelve-team league. There was obviously plenty of potential: they'd been second in home runs and fifth in RBIs. But .246 wasn't going to be enough against high-average teams like St. Louis and Pittsburgh.

Bring on number two, Mr. Billy DeMars, stolen from the Philadelphia Phillies over the winter along with a batting tee so worn from use that Billy could raise and lower it in his sleep to simulate high pitches and low pitches.

Once—admittedly while fully awake—DeMars was simulating the batting stance of one of his Philadelphia protégés in an elevator at Veterans Stadium. Oblivious to all around him, he continued to pose as the doors slid open, presenting to a lone, defenceless lady the statue-like spectre of a wild-looking, watery-eyed man with his fists in the air, seeming ready to swing an axe she couldn't get a glimpse of. Nor did she want to. He thinks she took the stairs.

DeMars hit .237 in 80 major-league games between 1948 and 1951, dividing his time between Philadelphia and St. Louis. He never hit a home run, but he was a shortstop, so he wasn't expected to. In 211 trips to the plate he hit 45 singles, 5 doubles, 1 triple, and drove in 14 runs.

It is an unimposing record for a batting coach, but there is a simple explanation.

"My thumb," says DeMars.

He used to wrap his thumb over his forefinger on his bottom

hand on the bat. How was he to know? Nobody told you anything in those days. Babe Ruth had a lucky grip.

"When you put your thumb over your forefinger, it acts as a brake on your swing," he says, and sure enough, if you try it, it does. "If I had taken that thumb off—well, you don't know, do you, I might have been a superstar." He laughs.

Despite DeMars' batting average, which Rodney Scott used to sneer at when management would talk about him changing his hitting style, DeMars had credentials.

Two examples are enough. After eleven years as a successful minor-league manager, DeMars spent thirteen years as a coach with the Phillies. During those years two of the players most involved in making the team a contender were shortstop Larry Bowa and third baseman Mike Schmidt.

"Bowa was the worst batter I've ever seen," says the man who became his batting coach. "It was like there were seven infielders when he came up. Everybody crowded around."

Bowa hit .211 in 1973 and, despite his early agility at shortstop, looked ready to spend the rest of his career in the showers. At 155 pounds he was too small to hit the walls and wasted a lot of at-bats lofting the ball into shallow places. DeMars taught him to sting the ball through the infield; and since then Bowa has had some helpful years at the plate, hitting over .280 twice, over .290 once, and over .300 once.

Bowa has had a few problems since moving over to the Cubs this year. DeMars chuckles. "He says he'll pay me the first $20,000 of my salary if I come over there."

Schmidt is his masterpiece. Schmidt always had power; but his long, looping swing was vulnerable to pitchers competent enough to find the hole in it. By 1976, Schmidt had led the league in homers for three straight years with 36, 38, and 38; but he'd also led the league in strikeouts in each of those years, with 138, 180, and 149. His career batting average by the end of 1976 was .252.

DeMars worked with him, trying to get him to do the two things that come hardest to a power hitter: swing down on the ball, or at least think down while you're swinging even instead of uppercutting it; and keep your shoulders in and stroke forward, instead of trying to jerk everything down the line.

Because power hitters are going for the downs they tend to try to lift the pitch out of the park. It can be done—Dave Kingman hits a lot of home runs. But because his swing goes in a loop, there is only one small spot where his swing will do anything with a given pitch. If his timing is at all off—by microseconds—not much is going to happen. A batter with a level or slightly downward swing has much more leeway for a timing error, and is likely to hit the ball hard somewhere.

And for the second part: a batter who throws his shoulder into a pitch, jerking his hands around behind it, thinks he's getting out there more quickly to pull a pitch. In fact, if he keeps his shoulder in and hands back, and then comes through in a short quick stroke, he not only has a much smaller chance of getting fooled on a pitch, he is actually quicker getting his bat head to the ball.

Before 1977, Schmidt struck out six times for every five hits he got. From 1977 to the end of 1981, he struck out four times for every five hits he got. The difference is the 250-odd times he's put the ball in play over those five years instead of striking out.

When DeMars approached Tim Wallach in spring training and suggested that they shorten his swing, Wallach rolled his eyes and figured he was done for. Batting is as much confidence as anything, and when you start dismembering a man's swing you're tinkering with just about everything that ever got him anywhere. A batter simply can't go to the plate thinking about trying to do more of one thing and less of another. There's already far too much to worry about just trying to figure what the pitcher's putting up there and whether your reflexes might be up to getting the bat in the right vicinity.

Ted Williams says there is no more difficult task in sports than hitting a round ball moving at more than 90 mph, often in devious directions, with a round bat. Of course he never tried to hit a square ball with a square bat. But even Yogi Berra said you can't think and hit at the same time.

So Wallach wasn't encouraged. Nevertheless, everywhere you went you saw the angelic blue eyes of Wallach, 6′3″, staring at the gimlet eyes of DeMars, 5′10″, as the latter went through the same motions with the same words, over and over and over. It was Chinese water torture.

From a distance you'd see DeMars, his left fist clenched, thumb toward his stomach, suddenly shoot that fist straight forward as though he were trying to pull an arrow out of his navel without making too much of a mess.

And there were secret words that he'd say as he pulled the arrow out. Sometimes it was "ptew." Sometimes it was "boom."

"It's hard to find just the right word for the quick and abrupt use of power you need to throw the bat head into the ball," he says. "I keep searching for the perfect word."

One of his perfect words is "we"—as in "sometimes when we hit the ball . . ." or "one mistake we often make . . ." When you hit the ball for Billy he's standing right in there with you.

Much of his work is done underground, in an interior alleyway behind the Expos dressing room, where someone has managed to squeeze a batting cage between the delivery trucks and fork lifts.

"If you love me, let me go . . ." wails a radio from a potato-chip truck, fighting to be heard over the grunts of a fork lift.

"Super," shouts Billy DeMars, fighting to be heard over the radio, as Chris Speier whacks one from the stolen hitting tee.

"Thwack!" "Great!"

"Clock!" "Super!"

"Crack!" "Not good."

"Smack!" "OK, super!"

"Thlock!!" "Now isn't that easy power? Huh?"

The fumes from the assorted vehicles spew forward and the rumbles from their engines shake the alley by its throat. But the hitters carry on, preparing the show for the audience above.

"At first I didn't like it, because when I went to the plate there were all these things whirling through my head," says Wallach. "Now when I go up there, I don't even think."

Eat your heart out, Yogi.

Wallach was named the National League's Player-of-the-Month for May. He hit .367 during the month, smacking six homes runs, six doubles, and driving in 23 runs. When the news came through, reporters tried to reach him for comment in Pittsburgh, where the Expos were playing; but he was out hitting balls off a tee.

Al Oliver won the award for June, with eight homers and 26 RBIs.

What was supposed to happen when the Expos acquired Oliver, who had hit over .300 for six straight years, and DeMars, who had taught people to hit over .300, did happen. The Expos, with the exception of Warren Cromartie, began to hit. The more Cromartie slumped, the more he seemed to press; and the more he pressed, the more he tried to pull the ball; and the more he tried to pull the ball, the more his average sunk. His strength had always been the ability to drive the ball toward the opposite-field gap. Either he had forgotten how to do it or decided that he was a power hitter after winning a few games with home runs. Whatever it was, he slumped to the .220s, struggled over .250, and lost his grip again. The irony was that the old Cromartie style was just what DeMars was preaching. But there was little apparent communication between the two men. Cromartie was not one of those who spent extra time in the batting cage.

But the rest of the Expos were hitting. Even Speier, who bottomed out at .183 in the middle of the winning streak, finally began to emerge from his eight-year slump. By the All-Star break he was hitting .263 and climbing.

Carter was at .313—48 points over his lifetime average—and had hit 19 home runs with 55 RBIs. A notorious streak hitter, he had become much more consistent.

Oliver, who'd hit 4 home runs in 1981, had 14 by the half-way mark in 1982. He was also hitting .321 with 60 RBIs.

Wallach was respectable at .265 with 11 homers and 48 RBIs— quite an accomplishment given his .233 debut in 1981. Tim Raines was having his problems at the plate as everywhere else, but was hanging in at .288.

Overall the team was batting .266, third in the league to the Pirates (.281) and the Cardinals (.268), and well above their 1981 embarrassment of .246. They were third in the league in home runs, just behind Atlanta and San Francisco, and second to the Pirates in RBIs.

Despite normal mutterings about not enough clutch hitting, the Expos were hitting better than any team other than the Pirates by the All-Star break.

And the Pirates didn't have much pitching, even with the resurgence of John Candelaria, Don Robinson, and Kent Tekulve. The Expos did. They led the league in club ERA at 3.40.

Yet Montreal was in fourth place at the break, with a 43–42 record, four games behind the Phillies and Cardinals and 1½ back of Pittsburgh. Pittsburgh, who most people had picked for fifth. Pittsburgh, who'd been 10 games behind in last place the day the Expos won the eighth game of their May streak.

The Expos hadn't fallen apart after the streak; in fact, they'd played pretty good ball for a while. They did lose four out of five immediately after the streak ended. And there were hints of what the problem might be. The stunningly terrible fielding displayed on the home stand just prior to the streak was hiding out, underground. (Chris Speier was not dropping pop flies, for instance, and probably never would again.) It was changing from flagrantly bad to quietly mediocre.

You only had to examine two paragraphs. The first was from the Montreal *Gazette*, an Ian MacDonald story describing the Expos' 5-4 loss to Pittsburgh in 10 innings on June 3. The italics are added:

> Smith walked Jason Thompson to lead off the tenth inning and after a perfect sacrifice by Mike Easler, Tony Pena ripped a hard grounder *just out of shortstop Chris Speier's reach* to cash Thompson with the winning run.

The second was from a Brodie Snyder story in the Montreal *Express* the next day, describing a 2-1 loss to the Atlanta Braves:

> Gullickson had retired 13 of 14 men when Dale Murphy started the Braves winning rally *with a groundball single past shortstop Chris Speier* with one out in the seventh.
>
> Murphy scored when Chris Chambliss, swinging late on a Gullickson fast ball, managed to slice a fly ball down the left field foul line:
>
> Jerry White caught up with the ball after a long run, *but it ticked off his glove for a double.*

The Expos had for the most part stopped making the errors they had in April and early May that would have set a club record over a full season. But the problem hadn't been solved, and moving Raines to second base wasn't likely to be the answer.

But perhaps it didn't seem that important to John McHale or Jim Fanning at the time. The fact is that, after the brief 4-out-of-5 bout with losing, the team started winning again.

Over the next 16 games the Expos won 12 and lost only four. They came back to beat the Braves 6-3 on June 6, having been down 3-0.

They took two out of three from the Cardinals in the series everybody had been waiting for. Cromartie hit a ninth-inning home run to win the first game, 3-2. Woodie Fryman, who went into the series with a 1.49 ERA, looked lousy in a brief relief stint, but Fanning got him out in time. Reardon mopped up and the whole thing was treated as a momentary aberration.

But the next night Fryman failed again, losing a 5-4 decision when he gave up two runs in the tenth.

The Cards looked flashy and exciting, with Willie McGee, Tommy Herr, David Green, and Ozzie Smith dancing the bases, and Whitey Herzog gambling from the dugout. In the first game, he had catcher Glenn Brummer lay down a bunt with the bases loaded that came within an eyelash of working, and the Cards scored the winning run in the second game on a suicide squeeze by Ken Oberkfell that brought home McGee.

All doubts were dispelled, though, when the Expos won the rubber match 5-1, with Gullickson cruising behind a Carter two-run homer in the fourth. But Fryman warmed up again in case he was needed. In the club's first 52 games he had either warmed up or appeared on the mound 72 times, a considerable burden for a 42-year-old man. With Lee gone, he was the only left-hander in the bullpen.

The Expos pulled to within two games of the Cardinals by dumping the Cubs three straight, scoring twenty-one runs in the process. Then it was a three-game return engagement in St. Louis. In the first game, Chris Speier, a smart shortstop with hustle, pulled off the old hidden-ball trick to tag out Ozzie Smith leading off second. Then Ozzie Smith, a gifted shortstop with hustle, took over.

He extinguished an Expo rally in the sixth when he snared an impossible Dawson liner and turned it into a double play. He made an even more beautiful and disheartening play to start the next inning, flinging himself into the hole to snatch a hit from Oliver.

And in the ninth, with only one out and the bases loaded, Smith completed a double-play pivot as Tim Wallach slammed into him, and the game was over.

The next night the Expos were leading 2-1 with two out in the ninth and Keith Hernandez on third, when pinch-hitter Lonnie Smith smacked a ball to Tim Raines at second. Raines picked it up cleanly, then threw wide of first to pull Terry Francona off the bag. The Cards won, 3-2. In both games the difference had been defence.

The Expos scored five runs in the second inning of the final and breezed to an 8-3 win, but not before Francona went to the wall for a ball off the bat of Julio Gonzales, twisting his knee into a pulp and damaging enough ligaments and cartilage to put himself out at least for the rest of the season. It was a major loss. Francona had been proving himself as the perfect number two hitter, was a steady if unspectacular fielder, had a good head for baseball and a sense of fun in the clubhouse. But it wasn't like losing Dawson or Carter, and the show went on.

The Expos lost a terrible 12-8 game to the Cubs, and then reeled off five straight victories, beginning with a 4-0 win the next day, when Carter and Bill Buckner exchanged unpleasantries and punches. Carter had deliberately broken Buckner's bat after the first baseman had lined into a double play. Which came a week after Buckner had smashed Carter's mask with his bat when Carter was going after a Buckner pop-out. All of which came to not much after Fanning, in his reasonable way, convinced the umpires that the fans' best interests would not be served by kicking the two out of the game.

The following day Jerry White hit a two-run pinch double in the top of the eighth to key a four-run rally as the Expos overcame a 2-1 deficit and won 5-2.

Wallach and Oliver clubbed homers in the finale as the Montrealers won a laugher, 11-5.

Then on to the Big Apple. Carter hit two home runs in the first game to back the five-hit pitching of Charlie Lea and Ray Burris for a 5-1 win.

The Expos were shaky in the second game as both Oliver and Wallach fumbled with the ball, and they were out-hit 11-5; but Randy Jones walked four batters to start the game and Cromartie singled to give them three of the four runs they needed to win 4-3.

Cromartie smacked two home runs the next day, and Steve Rogers ran his record to 9-3 with his fifth shutout as the Expos triumphed 5-0 and moved into first place in the National League East, .005 percentage points ahead of the Cardinals. After the game, Rogers patiently dispensed homilies to reporters, trying not to overstate either his or the team's performance to date. "First place in June," he mused, "doesn't mean as much as first place at the end of the season."

Oh, that it did! This is when they should have called another strike: June 24, 1982. In the morning. With the Expos in first place at 38–27, having gone 22–8 over their last 30 games, with 20 games to go before the All-Star break. Any fool knows that if you're in first place by the All-Star break you're going to win. If you're in second, third, or fourth place you know "it's still early—this thing won't be decided until September."

Over the next 20 games the Expos mired themselves in the second category. There is no sense chronicling these three weeks of misery on a game-by-game basis. But if you're ever wondering when it all began to unravel, consider the game of June 24 against the Mets in New York, the fourth of a four-game series. The Mets won it, 3–1. The Mets got all their runs in the sixth inning on a combination of two decent hits, one close play on a bunt, two line shots off the gloves of Mike Gates and Brad Mills that were scored as hits, and a collision between Gates and Cromartie.

When asked about the "hits" that lost the game for him, Bill Gullickson's tongue succumbed to sarcasm. "Oh, were they hits? . . . The official scoring this year has really been awful. I mean a hit's a hit and an error's an error. Those guys [the scorers] can't kiss everybody all the time."

As frustrated as he was, Gullickson stopped short of denouncing his fielders. Outright. By name. On billboards all across Canada, in French and English. But he did seem to be hinting at something.

Over the next twenty games the Expos made nineteen official errors, and countless other balls skittered through the infield when they shouldn't have. Gates had been called up from Wichita to play second when Francona was injured and Raines went back to left field. He started a few nice double plays, which was a relief, since Raines had become involved in only eleven in thirty-six games, about half the league average. But Gates doesn't cover a lot of ground, and balls kept going into his glove and popping back out again.

Wallach was proving to be a decent third baseman with smooth moves and an adequate arm, but as a rookie at the position he was making rookie errors, both with his glove and arm.

Speier had always been regarded as steady at short without much flash. But anybody who bothered to look at the 1981 fielding statistics knew that he ranked only seventh in the league in fielding average at .964. And far more significantly he was eighth in range, turning an average of 4.92 balls a game into outs. Smith got to 5.98, which meant he was saving his pitchers the equivalent of about a base hit a game on balls hit to the shortstop that Speier wasn't. Not that every major-league shortstop is going to play like Ozzie Smith. But of regular National League shortstops in 1981 Speier out-performed only four: Larry Bowa, then of Philadelphia; Craig Reynolds of Houston, since displaced by Dickie Thon; Johnnie LeMaster of San Francisco; and Frank Taveras, the worst in the league, who had since become Speier's back-up.

As for Al Oliver at first, he hadn't played the field for a few years and had atrophied. It was recognized early in the year that he could not make the throw home after plays at first, and the opposition began running on him. He had little range, and "just under Al Oliver's glove into right field" became a common expression. In fairness to Oliver it should be said that he gave every appearance of enjoying his work and wanting to be part of successful plays. But in fairness to history it should be noted that his affliction was there.

And while the Expos had three-quarters of a good outfield in Andre Dawson, Raines' judgement was inconsistent in left and Cromartie was off-and-on in right. Dawson was out with an injured knee for seven of the final twenty games of the first half. It's probably not noteworthy that the Expos lost five of those games, but it is noteworthy to remember what it was like without him in center. It was terrifying.

After the Expos lost that last game to the Mets in New York they came back to Olympic Stadium, where the Pirates bashed them before 51,360 witnesses in a double-header, 4–3 and 9–7. Each team had 7 hits in the first game and 14 hits in the second game, but that's the only thing that was close about either game. In this case fielding wasn't the problem; it was pitching. Scott Sanderson gave up two home runs to Tony Pena and one to the opposing pitcher, Don Robinson, in the first game, and good friends Ray Burris and Woodie Fryman got hammered together in the second.

The Pirates got 19 hits on Saturday to smother the Expos 14–5. The score was tied 4–4 in the seventh when Speier made a one-out error. Four hits later it was 6–4, despite Cromartie making a good throw to cut down a runner at the plate. Fryman and Bryn Smith gave up eight hits and eight runs while retiring three batters between them. But only three of the runs were earned; Fryman and Brad Mills both made throwing errors on force plays.

On the Sunday David Palmer set the Pirates down on three hits and Dan Norman and Tim Wallach hit homers as the Expos won 5–2.

But then the Mets came in and won two out of three—both victories coming by one run. The Mets won the first one 5–4 when Burris gave up Ron Gardenhire's first major-league home run. The Expos took the second 4–1 behind Gullickson with Carter and Wallach hitting homers, but the Mets won the deciding game. Scott Sanderson pitched a seven-hit complete game and didn't give up an earned run; but Wallach threw wildly to first on a Mookie Wilson grounder that tied the game 1–1, and Bob Bailor followed with a single to drive in Wilson, the winning run.

The Expos then flew to Pittsburgh, where they were beaten 6–3 and 7–2 in a double-header. The Pirates blew out Charlie Lea in the second inning, sending ten men to the plate and scoring five runs. The Expos still had a chance in the eighth with the bases loaded and nobody out, but Kent Tekulve struck out Wallach and Oliver, and got Carter on a well-hit fly to shut them down.

Dick Davis hit a three-run homer for the Pirates in the nightcap, and the Bucs had no problem solving Dan Schatzeder for eight hits and six runs in six innings.

Jason Thompson hit a two-run homer the next day and the Expos fell 4–2. They were now 1–7 against the Pirates.

All those innings of frustration seemed to evaporate in the first game of a double-header the next day as the Expos went wild, looting, pillaging, burning, and devastating their hosts 16–6. Cromartie hit his tenth home run and Rogers won his tenth game.

No problem for the Bucs. They came back to take the second game 10–4.

And then back to Olympic Stadium where the Expos built up a 6–0 lead over the Padres, were leading 6–1 as Scott Sanderson cruised into the seventh, and then gave up six runs on a combination of hard singles, past-the-glove singles, an off-the-glove single, and a crucial single that Cromartie could have caught but pulled up on.

The next night the Padres won 5–1 as Ray Burris lost his eleventh and the offence managed only four hits. Suddenly they were in fourth place.

And then the Dodgers came in and the Expos out-hit them 8–4, but lost 3–1. Manager Jim Fanning said he wasn't discouraged. "We're just not getting the breaks that the other teams are."

The Expos won the second game 7–3. Cromartie had a double

and two singles. Three more days until the All-Star break. One last chance to look respectable, to finish the first half on a four-game roll. The Giants were coming to town. Marginal talent. They had taken two out of three at Olympic Stadium earlier in the year in the "circus series"—nobody could forget that one. It made you shudder to think about it. There were a lot of visiting reporters and dignitaries already in town for the All-Star Game. They'd all been wondering from afar about what was wrong with the Expos. Time to strut, big team. Show them what you've got.

Rogers started the first of a three-game series. The All-Star starter in a warm-up bout. Nothing too difficult. Just enough of a challenge to help keep his edge.

After five innings everything was going according to the script. The Expos had a 1-0 lead on a Carter RBI single. But in the sixth Rogers gave up a lead-off home run to Joe Morgan, a single to Chili Davis, and a home run to Jack Clark on a hanging slider. Oliver hit a solo home run in the bottom of the inning and that was the end of the scoring. Giants 3, Expos 2. There were 31,339 spectators.

The following night 36,076 showed up to watch the Expos do everything right. The Giants made two errors—by Joe Morgan and Champ Summers. The Expos made none. Andre Dawson had three hits and four runs batted in, and the Expos won easily, 8-4.

Which set the stage for the finale. Was this a classy team going through hard times or just another bunch of well-paid, over-rated jocks? The crowd was the biggest of the series, 36,090.

After four innings it was Giants 4, Expos 1. The visitors were carrying hand-held SAM-7 missile launchers with them to the plate, and by the time the treachery was discovered Reggie Smith, Milt May, Champ Summers, and Joe Morgan had all been credited with solo home runs off Scott Sanderson—the first three coming back-to-back-to-back in the second inning, with Morgan going it alone in the third.

Gary Carter hit one for the Expos in the second, and four singles and a sacrifice fly produced two more in the fifth, leaving the Giants with a 4-3 lead.

The Giants scored two more in the sixth when Fanning decided against walking third baseman Tom O'Malley with runners on second and third to get to the pitcher. O'Malley slapped a single to right to score both runners.

And scored again in the seventh when the Giants pulled off their second double steal of the game—Johnny LeMaster scoring from third as Carter tried to throw Chili Davis out at second.

It was time for some heroics. As the Expos entered the bottom of the eighth, it was 7–3, Giants.

The Expos scored three runs on five singles in the eighth and might have got more had Chris Speier not been slow in moving off second on a ground ball to the left side that turned into a double play.

They scored another in the ninth to tie the game, but again might have had more had they not made another baserunning mistake. With Oliver on second, Cromartie on first, two out and the score tied, a ball seemed to squirt away from May, the catcher, and Speier signalled for the runners to move.

Oliver knew better and didn't. Cromartie didn't and did, ending up in a run-down and tagged out.

Cromartie thought Oliver should have run. May thought it would have been stupid for him to run. "It's a cardinal rule of baseball never to make the third out at third base. I think I would have had Oliver if he'd tried to run."

May smote a long home run off Jeff Reardon in the tenth, and the Expos were out of comebacks.

The Expos were 43–42. They had lost 15 of their last 20 games. The hitting had been decent, if not always as timely as perfection would demand. The pitching had at first been superb and later off-and-on: During the last 20 games Fryman's ERA had been 6.98 and Reardon's 3.00—not quite what had been hoped for from the bullpen stoppers. Over the same period the entire bullpen had given up 45 runs in 87⅓ innings. That terrible total was only mitigated by the fact that eight of those runs were unearned.

Which brings one back to fielding. The enormity of the disaster that was the Expos infield in the first half of 1982 can, at least to some extent, be documented.

That Wallach at third and Speier at short had made eleven and ten errors respectively was inconsequential. Both totals were about average for the league.

That the various players who had taken a shot at second—Johnson, Scott, Phillips, Taveras, Raines, and Gates—had totalled thirteen errors was unsettling but not surprising. Remember, though, Rodney Scott had totalled eight for the entire short 1981 season. Only one other team had a worse record and that was the Chicago Cubs, where Bump Wills wore a steel-toed glove.

That Al Oliver had fourteen errors at first was breathtaking. The much-ridiculed Met Dave Kingman was second with eight, and nobody else had more than six. Steve Garvey had two and had gone through the whole 1981 season making only one.

But with the exception of Oliver's total none of these figures were disasterous, primarily because errors don't mean very much as indicators of a team's defensive abilities. The guys who go after and get to more balls usually commit more errors, because they're dealing with tougher chances. An infielder who fields 30 balls during a week and drops three others is obviously more valuable than an infielder who only gets to 20 balls and doesn't drop any of them.

The measurement of an infielder's ability to get to balls is known as his Range Index or Range Factor. The Range Index is obtained by totalling the number of chances (put-outs plus assists) a player is credited with over a given period of time and dividing it by the number of games he played during that period.

There can occasionally be problems measuring particular players if they don't always play complete games. A player's Range Index won't look as good, for instance, if he's credited with playing a hundred games but was taken out for a defensive replacement in the seventh inning of ninety of them. Obviously if he had completed every game he would have racked up more chances. But that doesn't happen very often with infielders and adjustments can be made when it does.

Here are the range indices recorded around the Montreal infield over the first half of 1982, compared to:
1. The best in the league at that position.
2. The worst in the league at that position.
3. The league average at that position.
4. The Expos 1981 performance at that position.

Third Base	Chances/Game
Player	
Wallach, Expos	3.00 (third)
Salazar, Padres (best)	3.27
Horner, Braves (worst)	2.23
League Average	2.77
1981 Expos: Parrish	2.61 (ninth)

98

This meant that Wallach was getting to a lot more balls than Parrish had been. If their figures were extrapolated over a 162-game season, Wallach would be involved in 63 more put-outs than Parrish would have been (3.00 — 2.61 × 162).

Wallach was also better than the league average over the first half of 1982, and if his performance kept up over 162 games he would either make or assist in the making of 37 outs more than would our mythical, average third baseman. So far, so good.

Shortstop Player	Chances/Game
Speier, Expos	4.31 (tenth)
O. Smith, Padres (best)	5.78
Reynolds, Houston (worst)	3.87
League Average	4.72
1981 Expos: Speier	4.92 (eighth)

Speier wasn't getting to as many balls as he had the previous year. Over 162 games, the difference would be 99 outs. And comparing him to the non-existent average shortstop over the first half of 1982, he would fall 66 outs short of being ordinary.

Putting it another way, Speier and Ozzie Smith were about equal at the plate over the first half. When you considered hits, power, walks, and steals they each accounted for about 15 total bases a week, based on 30 at-bats in an average week. But based on a 6½-game week, Smith was saving his pitchers about 10 total bases a week that Speier wasn't (5.78 — 4.31 × 6.5 = 9.56 chances). Anybody who thinks defensive differences are of only marginal consideration in evaluating players had better think again. If Smith's defensive superiority over Speier were transferred to offense for the purposes of comparing them you'd be comparing a .260 hitter with a .400-plus hitter.

Second Base Player	Chances/Game
First half 1982 Expos (Scott, Johnson, Taveras, Raines, Gates)	4.67 (eleventh)
Sax, Dodgers (best)	5.73
Backman, Mets (worst)	4.36
League Average	4.92
1981 Expos: Scott	5.09

1981 Expos: Scott + Manuel	5.11 (ninth)
Bernazard, Chisox (1st half/82)	6.09

You'll notice there are a few extra entries here, the most noteworthy being Tony Bernazard, who was traded away at the tender age of 24 to the Chicago White Sox for Richard Wortham, a talented left-handed pitcher who developed a psychological aversion to home plate and was released from the Expos' minor-league system in 1982.

Over 162 games the Expos conglomerate at second fielded at a clip that would have seen them record 41 fewer outs than the composite average National League second baseman—not too bad, considering the number of players involved. But 68 outs fewer than Rodney Scott would have accounted for, based on his 1981 performance. That does seem silly.

As for Bernazard, why cry over spilt milk, eh? Why worry about 230 extra outs over a year? It's only the defensive equivalent of the difference between the worst-hitting team in the National League and the best-hitting team.

The Philadelphia Phillies compiled 1424 total bases in 1981, the best in the league. The Chicago Cubs managed 1205, the worst in the league. The difference was 219 bases, the difference between a team that hit .273 and a team that hit .236. That's also the approximate difference between playing Bernazard at second and playing the pre-Flynn collection. Bernazard had more balls hit to him because the American League used the designated hitter. But not that many more.

First Basemen	Chances/Game
Player	
Oliver, Expos	8.69 (eleventh)
Garvey, Dodgers (best)	11.00
Smith, Giants (worst)	8.57
League Average	9.89
1981 Expos: Cromartie	8.38
1981: Cromartie + Wallach	8.65

Range Index may not be the best way to measure first basemen in the field. Most of the "chances" a first baseman gets are throws from other infielders, and the number of throws they get over to him is likely to affect his Range Index much more than the number of line drives he catches or unassisted plays he makes on ground balls.

Another way of looking at first basemen is simply by the number of assists they get. Assists require coming up with a ball and throwing it to the pitcher covering first or to another base.

First Basemen	Assists/Game
Player	
Oliver, Expos	0.60 (tenth)
Buckner, Cubs (best)	1.06
Kingman, Mets (worst)	0.47
League Average	0.69
1981 Expos: Cromartie	0.51
1981: Cromartie + Wallach	0.47

Neither method is perfect for first basemen. Bill Buckner is not the best defensive first baseman in the game—Keith Hernandez is. Hernandez finished second in assists per game, at 0.89. Oliver, who has a bad shoulder, was better than two regulars: Dave Kingman and Dan Driessen. In Range Index he was better than one: Reggie Smith. In errors he ranked last. On the other hand the first-base situation probably wasn't any worse than it was the previous year. Cromartie and Wallach made only four errors between them during the whole year, but they didn't get to much.

Double Plays

In 1981 the Expos turned only 88 double plays, second worst in the league to Houston, and far behind San Diego with 117 and St. Louis with 108.

In the first half of 1982 the Expos turned 53 double plays—the worst. Chicago was next most awful at 60. Atlanta had 104.

Fielding Percentage

In 1981 Montreal tied for third in the league in fielding percentage, with a .980 average, behind only St. Louis and Cincinnati at .981. In the first half of 1982 the Expos were ninth at .977.

Conclusion

When NBC's Game of the Week crew came into Olympic Stadium to broadcast an Expos–Giants game on the Saturday before the All-Star Game, Don Drysdale seemed mystified that the Expos could be leading the National League in pitching, be third in hitting, and still be trudging along just above the .500 mark.

"It must be *something*," he said, shaking his head.

It was fielding.

Expos owner Charles Bronfman can be very poetic about baseball, and he sees the duel between pitcher and batter as an archetype.

"You have a very classic confrontation that goes back to caveman days. You have a man with a rock going against a man with a stick, and they're both out there in the middle and nobody can help them."

On some teams there were people helping the guy with the rock.

Portrait of the Artist

On the mound he talks to himself. He curses an inadequate pitch, exhorting himself to a superior effort. If he is particularly displeased, he remains in his follow-through for a moment, his feet firmly planted, and then executes a tiny leap in the air. He lands on both feet, squat and tense like a Sumo wrestler. He throws up his hands in disgust and turns his back on the batter. Hands on hips, he glares at the center-field flag pole. He shakes his head angrily and, to punish himself, refuses to breathe out, his cheeks swelling with his stifled exhalation. The effort becomes increasingly painful. His features are contorted into a slit-eyed grimace. Finally, before he explodes or faints, Steve Rogers of the Montreal Expos exhales and begins contemplating his next pitch.
—Pat Jordan
Sports Illustrated
April 1974

For years they told Steve Rogers he'd never be a good pitcher unless he surrendered his emotions before he took the mound. He disagreed. He wanted them with him, he said. He'd make them work for him.

They sighed. But the more they sighed, the more he sighed, right out there in front of the hordes. And not only did he sigh, he sagged. Nobody can sag like Steve Rogers. Every muscle goes slack.

Most often it's after he's made an inadequate pitch after several innings of nothing but beauties. He shakes his head at his own foolishness to get it started.

His brow knits. His head lolls forward against his chest, then back against his spine. His cap is off—he's mopping his brow. His pelvis tilts forward, his shoulders droop, his eyes roll skyward, and his moustache takes charge of a pout. He's as vexed with himself as he used to be as a young phenom; but he's grown more used to being vexed with himself, so the ritual has changed slightly over the years.

His cheeks still swell with stifled exhalation just the way they did in 1974, and he still stares at flag poles as though they were malevolent shrines to the God of Hitting. But gone are the tiny leaps into the air, landing squat and tense like a Sumo wrestler—who wants to be tense? At least the gestures that have survived into his thirty-third year are the ones most likely to rid his body of the demon of tension.

The mound is a public confessional, at which he is both priest and sinner. He berates and absolves himself in the same moment, acknowledging his ridiculous humanness for having thrown such a stupid pitch, even as he rises above humanity by making it clear there would have been no hit had be been in his right mind.

Finally, he regroups. He exhales, his moustache twitches, and his shoulders rise. He stares at the site of the indignity, then looks at the ball in his glove, turning it with the tips of two fingers and his thumb as though fiddling with a lock to which he has forgotten the combination.

At that moment he has been likened to Hamlet, examining the skull of Yorick. He has contemplated his next pitch. More likely than in 1974, it will be a good one.

Aha! *More likely than in 1974 it will be a good one.* A dangerous statement! One compares this man's present worth as a pitcher with his worth at any point over the last decade at one's peril.

Imagine yourself with Rogers in a taxi, crossing Philadelphia in the direction of the ball park. You open the conversation with what you think is a compliment about the blossoming of Steve Rogers as a pitcher.

You remind him of spring training a few years back, when the Yankees were scouting him and bad-mouthing his talents; you recall that at that point in his career people weren't sure whether:

(a) he had his best years behind him;

(b) he would blossom in his thirties; or

(c) he would "flatten out" and maintain the level of competence the fans had become accustomed to over the years.

It wasn't the kind of remark you would make unless your personal conclusion was obviously (b), but still it raises his hackles. He is fuming. The taxi has become uncomfortable. And all because of (c). The word "flatten." Too many people, he thinks, believe his career was flat, ordinary, mediocre, until a few years ago—primarily because he'd lost about the same number of games as he'd won.

Despite having broken in with a splashy 10-5 record in 1973 and recording winning seasons for five straight years between 1977 and 1981, Rogers' lifetime record going into the 1982 season was 114-113. He had two bad years in terms of losses: 1974, when he led the league in losses and went 15-22; and 1976, when he was 7-17 with a team that was 55-107. His personal earned-run average that year was 3.21. Phillies ace Steve Carlton had an ERA of 3.13 and was 20-7. John Candelaria of the Pirates had a 3.15 ERA and was 16-7.

Rogers doesn't care if you meant "flatten out" to suggest neither an improvement nor a decline, but simply a continuation of good quality.

"The inference to me is certainly a lot more negative. What you were saying to me is that two years ago people didn't know whether I was going to be good, bad, or stay mediocre.

"Somebody will always come up to me after a game and say, 'Well, now that you've finally reached your potential . . .' And I want to say that that's judgemental of my other years. I may not have a lot of wins to show for those years, but the team didn't either. And I've got a lot of great personal statistics which were, at the time, all I really had to go on. And to have people sit in judgement three, five, six years later and suggest that was nothing bothers me.

"People can say I've never won twenty games, and I can't argue with that—I haven't. But to have that colour someone's opinion of what I feel I've done for this ball club throughout the years—that always tends to make me angry at the person judging me."

Last year, to be judgemental, Rogers was the best pitcher on one of the two best pitching staffs in baseball.

Expo pitching would have been good even without him. The young starters—Gullickson, Lea, Sanderson, and Palmer—all have their foibles, and Palmer's gutsy career may even be over because of recurrent elbow damage. But they've all shown strong arms, good stuff, and outstanding control over the past few years; and there isn't a team in the majors that wouldn't have been delighted to insert any one of them in their starting rotations last year.

Jeff Reardon was intimidating out of the bullpen; Woodie

Fryman was, in his advanced years, still smart, strong, and, except for a few weeks, better than his ERA indicated; Bryn Smith was as good as any of them when his palm ball was working; and Ray Burris showed occasional flickers of his 1981 genius in a disappointing year.

Together they were good. With Rogers they were great. Without him the first half of the season would have been a shambles instead of just awful. He went 10–4 while the team was going 43–42, and he lost two games to errors. In 18 starts he was blown out once, giving up eight hits in five innings in a 6–2 loss to the Dodgers. Without him the Expos would have entered the second half hand-in-hand with the Astros and Reds—forgotten.

Between halves he won the All-Star Game. He was a couple of pitches short of brilliant; but he dug in, hung on, and gave up only one run in three innings.

In the second half of the season he was 9–4, finishing at 19–8 with a 2.40 ERA, 14 complete games, 4 shutouts, and 277 innings pitched—third highest in the league. He had one lousy game in the second half. He was knocked out after 5⅓ innings against the Cubs in the finale of the disasterous mid-September series that ended all hope; he gave up ten hits and five runs in the game, which Bryn Smith eventually lost. He also pitched a mediocre game back on July 4 against the Cubs, coming out after 5⅔ innings having given up 4 runs; but the Expos went on to win.

That was it. For the rest he was either good or superb. He lost a game to Houston on August 20 without giving up an earned run over eight innings: Joel Youngblood and Andre Dawson collided and dropped a third out.

In all, he lost three games to errors and won one that he might not have because of an opposition error—Rafael Ramirez booted a routine grounder to break a tie and give the Expos a win on September 6. Rogers' record should have been either 22–5 or 21–6, and he should have won the Cy Young award or finished a much closer second than he did to Steve Carlton.

It was a sunny year and a fine harvest, but Rogers was reluctant to celebrate. To single out this season, for him, would be to diminish all those other years—to acknowledge that something had been missing because he couldn't always pull himself out of the quicksand of shabby fielding support, indifferent hitting, and even his own imperfections that, for all his brilliance, left his won-lost record flat.

He may huff, sag, and pout, but he doesn't cry about any of this. He is simply adamant. Those years were friends when times were tough. He's not about to snub them when he's winning. If you want to drink to this year, drink to those.

Steve Rogers' parents remember him as a bright, good-looking kid with long eyelashes, a winning smile, and a charming way with teachers. He remembers himself as an introspective, pigeon-toed young man whose primary source of self-confidence was the pitcher's rubber. Probably he was both.

Conventional wisdom around the Expos front office is that the trouble with baseball today is that there are too many spoiled ballplayers around, many of whom grew up pampered, either in the ghettos or the suburbs. The theory is that this breed may be talented but lacks the toughness required to be a winner.

Rogers, who has had a decade of quality pitching, doesn't come from tough roots. He was a lucky, middle-class kid whose father, an orthodontist, was a nice enough man to set up a home plate and a rubber in the back yard and pretend he was Roy Campanella while the kid pretended he was the great Steve Rogers. Which was fine until little Steven started to get great and his father's shins started getting pummelled.

Rogers knew where he was going and how to get there. By the time he reported to the Winnipeg Whips, the Expos' Triple A affiliate, he was a graduate in petroleum engineering. He wasn't likely to go near oil unless his arm fell off; but if it did, he wouldn't have to apply for food stamps. A prescient gesture, considering nobody else in the Whips' line-up the night he made his debut made it to the majors.

He got pounded 7–4 by the equally obscure Tidewater Tides before 1,913 people in Norfolk, Virginia, giving up 12 hits and 3 walks in 5 innings. All despite a scouting report that prophesied, "can't miss—just a case of getting control of all his pitches—when he throws enough strikes he'll be in Montreal."

This game marked the beginning of his relationship with the press. One Winnipeg paper fell all over itself explaining that the kid was nervous in his first professional game. Not so, said Rogers, in what may have been the first of several hundred post-game seminars he has conducted over the years. They usually have one central theme: rhythm.

"It wasn't so much nervousness," he tried to explain patiently, "as not having my rhythm." For Rogers, life has been a search for the secret of endless rhythm. Physical and mental harmony. Strength, timing, and confidence. All that and more.

He arrived in Montreal in July 1973, with the Expos in the middle of the only pennant race they'd get close to in the first decade of their being. He was making $15,000—the major-league minimum—and he earned it all in the first couple of weeks by scoring shutout victories over Steve Carlton and Jon Matlack plus a 6–1 win over Fergie Jenkins.

With the entrance Fernando Valenzuela made in 1981 and the scant attention the Expos pay to their own history, Rogers' debut has been all but forgotten. But it was incredible. After his first four games, his ERA was 0.77. His shutout against Carlton was a one-hitter. He beat Tom Seaver and the Mets 3–1. He was a giant killer. He kept the Expos—mostly a likable pack of discards celebrating their fifth year of hanging on in the majors—in the pennant race well into September.

At the end he was 10–5 with a 1.54 ERA and had earned from his team-mates the nickname "Cy," after the immortal Cy Young of the 511 wins. Part of the nicknaming may have been teasing, but part of it was respect.

He was second to Gary Matthews in voting for NL rookie of the year, and named NL rookie pitcher of the year by *The Sporting News*. He was the first burst of top-of-the-line talent to emerge from a farm system that would eventually produce a lot of it, and the fans responded with ovations that exceeded even Jarry Park standards of adulation.

"No man," intoned Gene Mauch in Winston Churchill cadence, "has ever delivered so magnificently for me over so many straight games. He pitched the greatest 2½ months of baseball in my experience. I've never seen him beat himself."

Mauch's statement would be questioned time and again in years to come, when Rogers started losing more than he won—an inevitability for a young man honing his craft amidst mediocre hitting and fielding. There were baseball people convinced that he was beating himself.

This, too, was inevitable, because Rogers was different. He fretted and agonized on the mound. How much psychic energy was he dissipating, seized with the need to be perfect? It was respected baseball tradition that if a pitcher couldn't look mean, he should at least look blank. Looking vulnerable—even if only to your own frustrations—meant being vulnerable. Or worse, precious.

If Rogers had the right stuff to be a champion, it was argued, surely he would overcome the light hitting and the mediocre fielding. Steve Carlton had gone 27-10 in 1972 while the Phillies were going 59-97, so it could be done. Rogers should quit fussing around, stop getting tired in August, and just do it.

He went 50-67 over the next four years as the team's ace pitcher, throwing too many innings because of bonus clauses. In 1977 he threw 302 innings. In 1982 Carlton led the league with 295 innings and was the toast of the baseball world because of his mythical strength. Yet, Rogers was somehow always thought of as fragile.

At the end of 1977 he proved he was, going under the knife to repair ligament damage to his elbow. In the spring of 1978 there was a famous airport scene, initiated by Norm Sherry asking Rogers how his elbow felt after the operation.

Fine, said Rogers, but his shoulder was hurting. Nobody had bothered to explain to him that this was a natural temporary consequence of inactivity due to the elbow operation. Manager Williams, having refreshed himself liberally over the long flight, overheard. "If you can't pitch," he growled at his ace, "we'll get somebody who can."

The animosity between the two festered for five long years, until Williams was fired in September 1981. At one point Rogers asked to be traded, feeling that Williams and Ron LeFlore had combined to poison attitudes toward him during August 1980. The team was struggling to keep pace with the Phillies, who ended up winning the division by one game. Rogers' elbow was hurting him, and he was having trouble finishing games.

Twice he came out of games early, both times leading 7-2. Each time the team failed to hold the lead, and lost. Some, including the noisy LeFlore, blamed him for coming out. Why did Rogers give in so easily? Why had he never won twenty? Why wasn't he made to perform?

Williams started leaving him in when he was both hurting and struggling; meanwhile, Williams made fun of him to players and reporters. Rogers endured. He went 4-2 down the stretch, finishing at 16-11 with a 2.98 ERA. (LeFlore, coming off four years at Detroit where he'd averaged .310, slipped to .257.)

"I felt a coldness," Rogers remembers. "The same warmth as a team wasn't there. I remember talking to my wife and saying 'something's weird.' Guys who had been talking to me still talked, but they weren't saying anything. I didn't know what was going on.

"Then I threw back-to-back shutouts at the end of August, and everybody was my friend. Right toward the end of the season John Tamargo was living with me, and he told me a lot of the guys had been mad at me. He said that they thought I was jaking out—quitting.

"I said I had talked to my wife two or three times about how I didn't think they were really putting out for me when I was pitching. He said, 'You're right—they were all talking behind your back and saying why couldn't you win twenty games.' "

So that was it. Twenty games. The bench mark of greatness for a pitcher, or at least a requirement to qualify. And Rogers has never done it. He watched when Ross Grimsley did it with mirrors for the Expos in 1978 with a 3.05 ERA, while Rogers was winning 13 with an ERA of 2.47.

Of his more noteworthy contemporaries, Jim Palmer has won twenty games eight times, Fergie Jenkins seven, Steve Carlton seven, Tom Seaver and Gaylord Perry five, Luis Tiant four, Phil Niekro, Vida Blue, Tommy John, and Dennis Leonard three, Nolan Ryan and Joe Niekro twice, and Bert Blyleven, J.R. Richard, Ron Guidry, and Rick Reuschel once each.

Yet over the decade that he has been in the majors, Rogers has been as good a pitcher as many on that list. Between 1973 and 1982 only a handful of the six-hundred-odd pitchers who fought their way to the majors posted better numbers than Rogers in hits, walks and runs allowed, innings pitched, games completed, and the like.

Carlton, Seaver, Palmer, Richard, John, and Don Sutton outrank him, and Ryan, Blue, and Phil Niekro probably deserve an edge.

Statistically, Rogers ranks with Blyleven, Guidry, Reuschel, John Candelaria, and El Tiant over the decade, and ahead of Jerry Reuss, Joe Niekro, Dennis Leonard, and many talented others.

And more important—whether he chooses to acknowledge it or not—he is a better pitcher now than he has ever been.

If he's lost three or four miles per hour off his quickest fastball over the years, he still gets the ball up there at 89 mph with a delivery that may not be classic but is particularly intimidating to right-handed batters.

At the beginning he had exceptional finesse for a power pitcher. Now he has exceptional power for a finesse pitcher. So deftly does he combine and arrange his assortment of fastballs, sliders, curves, and change-ups that true aficionados sometimes stay at home if he's being televised—the better to watch him work the batters, through the magic of the center-field camera.

He doesn't like to be called an artist. "It's not art—it's hard work." So, of course, is art. But being thought of as an artist, perhaps, suggests a certain delicacy and a greater interest in a flawless performance than in one that has been spoiled slightly. By a stupid pitch, for instance.

Part of Rogers' maturing—and at least he admits to having matured—has been in his recognition that great artists don't make every stroke with a fine brush. "I think the biggest learning process has been that it doesn't take a perfect pitch if the action on the ball is of a significant quality. It doesn't have to be right on the corner every time. The level of frustration available to grab on to in baseball is high enough as it is. You don't need to create any more for yourself.

"I think I'm probably more mature with regard to frustrations. Some people take that as my not caring as much. It's not that. It's a matter of setting priorities about what matters and what really doesn't matter, and the overall result is all that matters. The magnitude of how much it matters on each individual pitch is less."

He has been talking seriously, pondering all this, trying to articulate the search for endless rhythm. Suddenly he laughs. He has realized the absurdity of imagining that even a thousand years of maturing could ever eradicate a man's essence.

"It's all easier than it sounds," he says. "The truth is I want to make every pitch perfect."

Last year Rogers won the second-highest number of games in the National League, pitched the third-most innings, was fifth in strikeouts, fourth in complete games, and had the best earned-run average and won-lost ratio.

The numbers sketch a portrait of the artist all right—the artist as a strong man. He has always been a fine pitcher, but in 1982 he blossomed.

No matter what he says.

The Sophomore Jinx

Baseball gives you every chance to be great. Then it puts
every pressure on you to prove that you haven't got what it
takes. It never takes away the chance, and it never eases up
on the pressure.
—Joe Garagiola

When they got him, froze him like that, you had to think of Lot's
wife—the one who got turned into a pillar of salt for glancing back
as she fled Sodom. Nitpickers and naysayers, of course, will say
the analogy doesn't hold. First base isn't intrinsically evil the way
Sodom was, they'll say, and fleeing it is just part of baseball. (If
first base were evil, would Willie Stargell have hung out there?)
And Tim Raines, they'll go on, didn't look like a pillar of salt, or
pepper, when they got him. Fair enough. But when you're used to
looking at Tim Raines as a blur, well, there he was, a pillar—
freeze-dried, one hand pointed to second and one hand pointed to
first.

It was May 11, 1982, in the middle of the bad times. The
Dodgers had left town two days earlier after sweeping a four-game
series. A day after Andre Dawson—a man management had
regarded as a responsible employee—went on radio to say Rodney
Scott should be playing second base rather than Frank Taveras.
Instead Scott was dumped along with Bill Lee. Raines was shifted
from left—where he had said he wanted to stay—to second—a
spot his agent had advised him to eschew like flashing spikes coming at million-dollar legs.

In his first three games there he had looked athletic but raw, and
the jury was still out. The Expos had lost five of their last six, the
one win coming in a come-from-behind victory over the tradi-
tionally humble Giants. That one evened their record at 13–13,
and left them stuttering along four games back of the league-
leading Cardinals, a position they'd soon become familiar with.

The first game had been exciting because it had been the first
time in twenty-six games they'd come from behind in the late innings to win—a trick the Cards were pulling off with appalling

regularity. If the Expos could pull it off two nights in a row, perhaps the bad times were over and their march to destiny was on.

But by the time they reached the ninth inning of the second game in the series they were down 5–3. In the bottom of the ninth, Brad Mills, the reserve third baseman, led off with a single, and Tim Blackwell sliced a pinch double to put runners at second and third. Raines, who had doubled-in the winning run the night before, came to the plate. He slashed a single that scored Mills; Mike Phillips, running for Blackwell, held up at third. Only one run down now. Runners at first and third and nobody out, with the heart of the batting order coming up. It was a dollar to a dime they'd score at least one.

A sizable residue of the 16,298 paid had remained to the end on this fine spring evening, and they began chanting and clapping in unison, like very dry dirt farmers at a prayer meeting. The drought was coming to an end—Hallelujah! It was a moment to savour, and the Giants donated the time. Their great, aged second baseman, Joe Morgan, called a conference on the mound. No sense in worrying about the runner at third, he counselled catcher Milt May. He was almost certain to score anyway. What was important was keeping Raines out of scoring position.

While it didn't seem like a steal situation—since even a double play would score the runner from third and tie the game—Raines just might be going anyway, to put two runners in scoring position with nobody out, or even to let the tying run waltz in if May threw the ball into center field trying to get him. Couldn't worry about that.

If Raines took off, Morgan told May, try to gun him down. Even though Raines had stolen 71 bases in 88 games in his rookie season. Even though he had stolen three bases off May the night before—one of them on a pitch-out. Even though Expos first-base coach Steve Boros had statistics alleging that if Raines got his normal jump, the odds against throwing him out were prohibitive with the best of catchers, let alone Milt May.

May is the son of Pinky May, who played third base for the Phillies during the Second World War. Both father and son preferred the slow lane. Pinky stole 13 bases during his five-year career. Milt had scattered two thefts over a dozen years. One came when he was with Houston in 1975; he lumbered in on the back end of a double steal when the catcher tried for the runner at third. His second came six years later when he was going on the hit-and-run, and the batter swung and missed. The catcher, hyperventilating at the prospect of throwing someone out by twenty feet, threw a strike—but to the center fielder.

The speed revolution in baseball had diminished the value of catchers like Milt May, men who were good hitters and decent receivers but didn't have much of an arm. Managers were looking for bazookas, and Milt only had a mortar. He had led the Giants in hitting in 1981 with a .310 average and felt good behind the plate: "I think I help my pitchers—I think they like to throw to me." But opposing teams had pilfered an average of 1.01 bases a game against him in 1981—the third-worst record in the league. And he only threw out an average of .51 runners a game—fourth-worst in the league.

On top of everything he was coming off an injury. Earlier in the spring he had tripped and thrown a ball off-balance, injuring his arm seriously enough to sideline him for several games.

The aforementioned Steve Boros, Expo, B.A., a student of the game, had noticed that May hadn't been throwing the ball hard during infield practice. He'd also noticed that the Giants' pitcher, Greg "Moon Man" Minton, who'd already had three runners at first since coming in in the eighth, hadn't shown much of a pick-off throw to first.

But then, as May was later to say, "Give me a pitcher who can get the ball to the plate quickly over a guy with a great pick-off move any day." Catchers always say that. Any time they have to make a throw they get blamed for a steal, even when there's no hope of getting the runner because the banana-head on the mound was so sluggish about getting the ball to the plate.

If that makes catchers sick, Boros was sick of two things. The first was his supposed prodigy's so-so start on the basepaths. After twenty-six games Raines, the man who'd been billed as the fastest in the game, had only ten steals. Rickey Henderson, Raines' arch-rival at Oakland, already had thirty-five.

But mostly Boros was sick of losing, and saw victory staring at him from the basepaths. "When you've got the best base stealer in the National League and a catcher who isn't throwing well, you've got a weapon you don't stick in your pocket," he was later to say, thoughtfully.

In the dugout, Jim Fanning was sending telepathic messages to Raines. "If you go," he transmitted in a mutter, "you'd better be sure you've got it." The air was crackling with thought waves.

In the Expos' broadcast booth, Dave Van Horne didn't even bother alerting his listeners to the possibility of a steal because he didn't think there was a possibility; it wasn't a steal situation. His partner, Duke Snider, noticed that the infield was playing fairly deep, meaning they'd give up a run to get the double play. "Good," he said to himself, sure the run would score.

On the mound, Minton, one of the best relief pitchers in baseball when he's on, was worried about his fastball. A few years earlier it had picked up a magical sinking movement after he'd dived for a ball in spring training and shattered his knee in forty pieces. When the knee healed he had a new pitch.

But just recently it hadn't been sinking so much, and on this particular evening it hadn't even been moving very quickly. At its best Minton's fastball went at around 92 mph, but tonight the radar gun was clocking it at 87. All four hits he'd given up facing five batters had been off fastballs. He decided to stick with sliders.

And his thoughts turned to Tim Raines, a man he regarded as being blessed with talent but not that smart a baserunner—not yet. In his rookie year, Raines had stolen third several times before coming to San Francisco, where the Giant pitchers had figured out a legal way to look like they were throwing to the plate but come across to third instead. They had nipped Raines right there, 90 feet short of counting for anything.

Minton guessed that Raines probably wasn't much more educated yet. Now Milt wanted to try a pitch-out on the first pitch. Usually when you try to get the ball up there quickly on the pitch-out you have to disguise what you're up to by doing a bit of a leg kick. Not as high as normal because every bit of motion slows you down, but enough that the runner won't pick up the obvious change in your motion and stay at first. If he does, you'll have wasted the pitch-out and be behind 1–0 on the count. Then you'll have to come in with a good pitch or you'll get too far behind. But if you come in with too good a pitch, you'll have Jerry White up there, and he'll probably hit it somewhere you don't want him to, like four of the last five batters have done. But Raines stole on a pitch-out last night, and desperate times call for desperate measures. Life's a gamble, no?

The time was 10:36. The game was three hours old. Around the donut hole leading to the starless sky 1,076 2-kilowatt mercury vapour lights were burning. It was a chilly high noon. The gentlemen checked their weapons: it was showdown time.

White stepped into the batter's box, hitting left-handed against the right-handed Minton. By hitting from the left side he blocked May's vision of first base a touch, giving the National League's best baserunner a slight edge.

May splatted a stream of Beech Nut tobacco juice into the dust off to his left, wiped his bristly red moustache with the back of his freckled throwing hand, squatted into position, and went through the motions of signalling for the pitch-out they had already agreed upon.

Raines edged off first, creeping furtively 13 feet, 14 feet, 15 feet out, until his right foot was on the Astro-turf. In his head, the game was won. All of a sudden, Minton was at the top of his stretch, and there was a scurrying off first. Less than 1.15 seconds later—as fast as you can snap your fingers—the ball was in Milt May's mitt, then into his right hand, and there were two men caught under the lights of high noon. One was an apparition two long strides out in front of the plate, holding a baseball like Exhibit A. The other was a dead man, looking for a grave.

Someone snapped their fingers again and the ball was in the glove of Johnnie LeMaster, the shortstop. It had been Milt May's best throw, better than his best throw—hard and low on the bag at second. Holding the ball like a spear, LeMaster went after the league's most talented baserunner who was now wriggling, squirming, and dodging, looking pleadingly toward third, hoping against hope Phillips might be dancing there, threatening to score, diverting attention . . . anything.

But Phillips had pitched a tent and settled in. If Boros wanted to attach his name to reckless forays, third-base coach Billy DeMars did not. Phillips, under instructions, closed his ears to the screams of the dead.

LeMaster scuttled crab-like toward his victim, and snapped the ball into the glove of first baseman Darrell Evans just as Raines hurtled back toward Sodom. The ball was there to greet him, the trap door opened, and he was gone.

"I didn't kick my leg at all," Minton was to say later. "The more I thought about it the more I realized there just wasn't time. We had to take a chance he wouldn't notice."

May shook his balding head and smiled at the irony. "So Steve Boros noticed I wasn't throwing hard during infield practice. I like that guy—he's smart, he notices everything.

"The funny thing is that when I don't throw well during infield it doesn't mean my arm's in trouble—in fact it usually means the opposite. When my arm doesn't feel strong I throw hard in practice to try to get it going again. If it feels good I rest it—I flip the ball. I guess that's what he saw. It was nice to get Raines."

Jerry White ended up popping out to third baseman Tom O'Malley deep behind the bag, just in fair territory. O'Malley had to lunge to make the catch, and fell clutching the ball. But instead of tagging up, Phillips had moved a few steps down the line on the off-chance the ball would fall in—having no idea O'Malley would fall down catching it, giving him a chance to score.

At 10:41 Andre Dawson hit a routine fly to center, off a Greg Minton slider. By 10:42 the booing had stopped, and witnesses were draining from the stands. By 10:44 Milt May was in the visitors' dressing room, piling several slices of salami on a piece of rye bread.

Jim Fanning had worried about Tim Raines in spring training. To most people Raines seemed relaxed. To Fanning he seemed lackadaisical.

He was a hero, a handsome young man who decorated the sports magazines, which were full of stories about his prowess as a baserunner. Some of the stories linked him with Rickey Henderson, who had stolen 100 bases away back in 1980. But the emphasis was on Raines, who had stolen 71 in 88 games in 1981, while Henderson had 56 in 108 games.

At the root of the interest was the possibility that this little man—Raines is 5′8″ and 180 pounds—might be larger than the game. It had always been assumed that baseball's geometry was one of life's rare perfections—that the measurements were just right to separate the gifted from the not-so-gifted in subtle enough ways to keep the contest interesting and not entirely predictable. But Steve Boros had been suggesting that with Raines on first looking to second, there was only a freak possibility that mere mortals could do anything to stop him from getting there.

The formula was simple. Boros had been dedicated to bringing science to baseball since his days at the Kansas City Royals' Academy of Baseball. He used his ever-present stop-watch to determine that only 20 per cent of the pitchers in the National

117

League could deliver the ball to the catcher's mitt in 1.3 seconds or less; and only 20 per cent of the catchers in the league could pull it out of the mitt and whip it down to second in 2.0 seconds or less: total 3.3 seconds, if you got a fine 16-to-1 combination.

But Raines could get from first to second in 3.2 seconds with his normal jump—0.3 seconds quicker than your average runner. The odds against him being confronted with laser beams bouncing from the mound to home to second were remote. Before catcher Alex Trevino was traded from the Mets to the Reds, Boros determined that he (1.9) in combination with relief pitcher Neil Allen (1.1) could turn the trick in 3.0 seconds if the throw was perfect. An unlikely possibility, involving the best from the best.

But in the vast majority of cases, science showed there was no problem. Raines had been picked off first by pitchers seven times in his rookie year 1981, before he'd had time to study the pitchers' motions carefully. But he had only been thrown out by a catcher four times in 75 attempts—a 95 per cent success ratio against all the Milt Mays out there.

Boros is a school-of-life optimist about self-improvement. He was a mediocre third baseman with the Detroit Tigers between 1957 and 1962. When he was traded to the Cubs in 1963, he discovered how to be an aggressive fielder by watching Ron Santo from the bench. In 1964, at Cincinnati, he set the Reds' record for third basemen by playing fifty straight errorless games. If he could do that with his modest skills, the sky was the limit for Raines.

Still, Fanning was worried, even though he would pronounce hopefully on Raines' intelligence and diligence. "Tim works at his base stealing," he told Earl McRae of *Today Magazine*. "He has devised his own technique and strategy based on his knowledge of the opposing pitchers and catchers—in fact, of all the opponents who come into play on a steal—and his innate sense of the nuances of the game. It ain't just run and pray." But by August, Fanning would be directing Raines to abandon his innate sense of the nuances and just run and pray.

Fanning told reporters at spring training that he'd had his eye on Raines and had tried to counsel him. "I told him that things would be tougher than last year. Never before in the history of the game has a runner intimidated pitchers, catchers, and infielders as he did. He has to be ready for a new challenge.

"That's one of the reasons that his relationship with Andre

Dawson is so important. He can be inspired by Dawson. He can draw from Dawson—we all can. If Tim Raines were a puppy dog he'd do well to tag along with Dawson. He'd be in good hands. He'd never stray."

The comparison of Raines to a puppy dog was an unfortunate one and may have been counter-productive. It's hard to find a 22-year-old black superstar who will gobble up a 54-year-old white journeyman's advice if it's predicated on behaving like a puppy dog. But Fanning's intentions were good. He had seen enough to know that baseball in the majors can occasionally be played by boys, but only if they have the mental toughness of men will they excel. Young chaps with talent who have never failed at anything should beware, he knew, because no matter how good they were they wouldn't go unchallenged by men intent upon survival.

Under the puffy white clouds of West Palm Beach, mock-wrestling with friends in the early afternoon sun, Raines pooh-poohed the messenger from the world of the earnest word. They'd tried their special plays last year, he pointed out. Where had it got them? Indeed, added Warren Cromartie, celebrating the sun in anticipation of the gloom of Olympic Stadium. You had to relax to play baseball, he chided. You couldn't play it if you took it too seriously.

But a few hundred feet away, standing in the shade, Andre Dawson said he could see Fanning's point. He was serious about baseball himself, and didn't apologize for it. Ellis Valentine had had great talent and let it fritter away.

Ah! But who could say Raines was frittering? He hit .386 in spring training and went 9-for-10 on the bases. And if they wanted to try to get him, well let them come; but in fairness they should know what they were in for:

"I shouldn't give away secrets like this," he says with a small chuckle, "but I guess it's not so much how you do it as who does it, right?"

"Right."

"Main thing is that I have lots of strength. My legs. They're very strong and muscled. Like the rest of me. That's why they call me Rock . . . I'm basically a sprinter, see? I run like a sprinter. Head down. You can't get drive and momentum with your head up."

He floats his arms out from his side, leans forward on the balls of his feet, legs spread, feet about shoulder width. "Another main thing is to have your weight neutral. Don't favor one side or the other when you take your lead-off. Keep the pitcher guessing. And being that I'm *fast*, I take a good lead-off. And I never *talk* out there. The first basemen, often they'll talk to me to try to break my concentration, but I don't hear *nuthin'*, man, I just look at that pitcher."

"What are you looking for?"

A rueful smile. "That I ain't sayin'. Let's just say certain signals, certain little things that give away when they're going for home or when they're gonna try and pick me off. I have a book on those guys. That's top secret. But when I get that signal that he's going for home I take off. I have the green light to steal all the time. It's up to me. Big thing is the jump. It's gotta be split second."

Then, in mock slow motion, he pivots to his right bringing his back leg—his left leg—over and in front. His body is crouched, his head is down, his arms frozen in a driving position. "Now, here's a big key. You'll notice I start running with my *left* leg. Not my right, which seems the natural way and which most guys do. I cross my left leg over. You get better drive and traction that way. Man, I hope I'm not saying *too* much. Anyway, then I take off, right. Man, I'm *gone*."

—Earl McRae
Today Magazine

The young players we get aren't like the young players we got ten or fifteen years ago. How prepared are they to accept the great disappointments and discouragements of professional baseball? Most of them haven't done a day's work in their lives. Most of them . . . I shouldn't use the word spoiled, but now, all of a sudden, they've come into a man's game.
—Jim Fanning
Philadelphia
August 2, 1982

For a fast man, Raines' season started slowly. After 5 games he had 2 singles in 21 times at bat—an .095 average. He had one stolen base, tied with Gary Carter and Warren Cromartie. Rickey Henderson had 9. By the time Raines had 4, Henderson had 19.

And when Lou Brock dropped into town toward the end of May, the Expos were 4 games back of the Cardinals, as usual, and Raines had 15 stolen bases. Henderson had 49.

Now grey in the sideburns, eight years after stealing 118 bases to break Maurice Morning Wills' major-league record, Brock marvelled at Raines' skills.

"Because all the attention is paid to his base stealing people don't realize he's one of the finest hitters in baseball. He's got split-second timing. His front foot doesn't make a move until the pitcher's arm comes up. That final split second is the most critical moment of hitting, and he's got it timed."

As for his base stealing said Brook, it was a matter of him "adjusting to the mechanics of the game."

"He's waiting for the perfect moment, and there is no perfect moment. He has to make that perfect moment. Fear of failure holds back a lot of good runners. It's a real animal. Disaster is right there behind you.

"What he needs I call baserunning arrogance. The ones who have it are highly successful. Their will to win is incredible. They have a passion for it, and they're consumed by it."

But the only thing Raines seemed consumed with was uncertainty. Going back on balls in left field he was often unsure which way to turn. On the bases he seemed as desperate to stay as to go. "Last year he had a tremendous instinct for when to go," recalled Boros. "When he went he had the jump. When he stopped, he didn't. This year he often stops when he has the jump and keeps going when he doesn't."

Even his hitting tore him in two directions. No matter which side of the plate he was batting from, he went after the ball like a pretzel. Working from a closed, pigeon-toed stance, posed like a statue in the farthest back corner of the batter's box, he'd step toward the plate with his front foot, and whip his hands and upper body away from the plate—pushing with his bottom half and pulling with his top. It was a hopelessly twisted motion, saved from a .196 average by reflexes alone.

In the end, simply because of his raw talent, he was not humiliated. He stole 78 bases, 52 fewer than Henderson, but good enough to lead the National League. He hit .277, down from .304, but not an embarrassment. But if you looked more closely, it was a long drop off the mountain.

Take Raines' Total Average. Total Average was designed by Thomas Boswell as a quick, clear measure of a player's offensive production. It assumes the business of a batter is to swallow up bases like Pac-Man, and gives him credit for every 90 feet he achieves—through singles, doubles, triples, home runs, walks, stealing bases, and being hit by pitches. It also penalizes him for every 90 feet he loses—being thrown out on the basepaths, hitting into a double play (double jeopardy), or just making an out. The number of bases gained are divided by the number of bases lost, to come up with a ratio.

In all of baseball history, only 17 players have had a lifetime total average of over 1.000—that is, more bases gained than lost. Babe Ruth was first with 1.432. The legendary Ty Cobb was eighth with 1.062.

In his rookie year, Raines was on the right track. He had a total average of 1.081, higher than Cobb's lifetime mark and second only to Mike Schmidt (1.243) among active players.

In 1982 he dropped to .804—the mark of a decent offensive outfielder, but not much more. Raines had become, in a word, ordinary.

The most serious breach of a player's contract is for him to make himself unavailable for a game. There's no telling what one game can mean, what one game might have meant during any of the past three seasons. One game simply can't be dismissed. That is not fair to the franchise, the fans, everyone.
—John McHale, commenting on the release of Bill Lee
   May 8, 1982

Once a month, for three months in the heart of the Expos' season, distress flags were raised; something was very wrong with Tim Raines.

At 7:25 on Tuesday, June 29, five minutes before the Expos were scheduled to play the New York Mets at Olympic Stadium, team publicist Richard Griffin advised reporters to alter their line-ups. Jerry White would replace Tim Raines in left field.

A few minutes later Griffin stated that Raines was not at the park; that he had talked to Jim Fanning and had been advised to stay home; that Raines had said he had tried to make contact with Fanning much earlier but had been unable to get through by phone; and that Dr. Robert Brodrick, the team physician, had been sent to see Raines because he said he was sick.

After the game Fanning appeared muddled about how Raines had finally managed to get his message through, impatiently reminding reporters they had received the official explanation in the press box. He said the phone on his desk was often very busy. Anyone who spent any time in his office knew it was often not very busy at all. In any case, if Raines, who was supposed to have been at the park by 4:30, had called the Expos switchboard and relayed his urgent message during the afternoon, it would have been given to Fanning immediately.

The more furtive Expo management got in protecting Raines, the more suspicious the press and the public became that this wasn't your ordinary case of food poisoning.

On Sunday, August 1, "Camera Day," he showed up two hours late for an afternoon game, arriving while his team-mates were out on the field getting their pictures taken by fans. He didn't start the game because of what was described as an upset stomach, but he was later sent in, and managed to get a base hit and to throw out a runner.

On Wednesday, September 1, he appeared just before game time and was assessed a fine. How much, Fanning refused to say. Asked whether Raines had been in shape to play when he showed up, Fanning said he resented the question. "If you know something, print it."

What everybody knew, off the top, was that they were dealing with a dozey, bleary kid who was playing at half throttle and who liked to sleep in the late afternoon. He seemed always to have a cold.

The symptoms screamed cocaine, a drug that produces a euphoric but short high and leaves the user craving more, often at the expense of sleep.

McHale, in an August discussion, acknowledged that there had been drug problems on the Expos. "We've had some cases and spent a lot of time on it in the last two months around here. I've gotten involved in it myself, personally. And I see some progress. I think we've turned a couple of guys around."

McHale certainly was involved, to the point that he was abandoning his president's chair twice a week to drive Raines to sessions with Dr. Alan M. Mann, psychiatrist-in-chief at the Montreal General Hospital. But at the time McHale was talking, Raines had yet to be turned around.

He snorted cocaine right up until the last week of the season, although—he later told *Gazette* columnist Michael Farber—not with the frequency he'd been using it earlier in the season. But it would have been all but impossible to match that frequency; snorting up at night with friends, in his car when he got to the ball park, and even between innings in the clubhouse.

Within nine months he managed to spend $40,000 on the white powder. Even when he was undergoing therapy, any upset was an excuse for more.

When Fanning came back from his migraine attack in September he was greeted by a spate of printed quotes from players saying he wasn't the man to manage. Some of them were from Raines, whom he'd prided himself on supporting through difficult times.

It was decided that Fanning should go to the various players involved and talk to them "man-to-man." When he got to Raines, he waved him over to the dugout and chewed him out for fifteen minutes, apparently satisfied at the end that his wayward prodigy has been suitably chastised.

But Raines walked away fuming. "The man's a mental case," he muttered. That night he started back on cocaine, fueled by the "bad feeling" Fanning had left him with by berating him before he could open his mouth.

Throughout the summer, Raines had blamed his performance on other things. He slept in the afternoon, he said, because of mental fatigue. But was it mental fatigue when he fell asleep on the bench during a game he didn't start and had to be wakened by a team-mate when Fanning wanted him to pinch hit?

He was lonely. He was depressed. He was a superstar with a $200,000 salary; he was a kid whose favourite uncle had just died; and he was a husband whose wife had just had a miscarriage. Once he had been able to do anything he wanted to on the baseball field without thinking about it. Now he couldn't seem to do anything.

Of course it was harder when you sometimes couldn't see the ball. And when your mind, as he was later to admit, was "lost for a while."

It was a hard year to be blurry. The pitchers and catchers had worked on new moves to hold him close to the bases and to fake him into running when they had a play on. At the plate he was seeing a lot more curve balls, and getting jammed inside where his pretzel swing wouldn't work.

He enjoyed going to bars and wasn't particular about who he sat with, as long as he wasn't alone. He had married his wife Virginia three weeks after he turned twenty. Sometimes she was a comfort to him, but they had their differences—particularly over all the money he was shelling out to strange people in the bathroom for what he said was "jewelry"—gems she never saw.

What she did see was white powder, and she flushed it down the toilet. He started staying away from their downtown apartment. Sometimes she would leave him, and that would make it worse.

"I feel more support when she's here, when my little boy's here. I feel more secure. I have somebody to talk to. Then I don't have to worry about going out and looking for somebody to talk to."

Andre Dawson tried to help; but Dawson was a serious person, and not at all 22. "You see people abusing their bodies by drinking or whatever, and you try to talk to them, and they don't listen or they tend to hear what they want, and I guess you sort of draw away from them. It seems like they're in their own world—that they have a mind of their own and they're going to do what they want to do."

There are limits to sympathy for Tim Raines. He wasn't stricken with cancer as a young man. He didn't land at Dieppe when he was 18. And he wasn't a .200 hitter like Rodney Scott. If he were, he would have been gone.

"As a human being we are terribly interested in Tim Raines, as we are in all our people," McHale said in December. If that didn't seem to include people like Scott, well, you couldn't say Scott was as much of an asset as Raines was, nor did he seem to want to change his ways.

"The Expos will go as far for a player as he is willing to go to help himself," said McHale. McHale always seemed to know Raines was willing to help himself, even when he was still snorting three months after he had admitted his addiction and McHale had begun his chauffeuring missions.

Despite the booing toward the end and Fanning's lecture, people were nice to the boy with the talent. Nicer than they had seemed at spring training, when they were warning him that his second season wasn't going to be easy.

"Yeah—I remember Fanning saying it was going to be tough, but I didn't really think that it was. And when it was, I panicked. I guess maybe I was mistaken all along."

On October 11, 1982, the Expos announced that Raines had checked into a San Diego medical clinic for treatment of drug abuse. After four weeks of treatment, he emerged and began working out in Florida, starting very early to get ready for the new season.

"My goal is to report to spring training ready to give my best effort every day of the 1983 season," he said. "I realize I've had a problem for some time now. I just want to solve it once and for all, and put it behind me."

He was a nice kid, who liked to laugh. And unlike Lot's wife, he would get a second chance.

The Dog Days

*We've got to get more offence from that second-base
position.*
—Jim Fanning
  March 22, 1982

You've gotta have defence at that position.
—John McHale
  August 3, 1982

*And what you say in the spring and what happens in August
aren't necessarily the same thing.*
—ibid.

The All-Star Game came and went, only this time in the Expos'
own back yard, with their own players everywhere. How they had
progressed! In 1973—the year the team finished 3½ games out of
first place—the Expos had been represented by one token player,
Ron Fairly, as required by the rules. In 1982—when the team
would finish 6 games back—there were five Expo All-Stars and
not one a token: Gary Carter, Andre Dawson, Tim Raines, Steve
Rogers, and Al Oliver.

Jeff Reardon had better numbers than most of the pitchers
chosen by Dodger manager Tommy Lasorda, but who was going
to quibble when the field was already full of Expos?

Not a one of them embarrassed anybody. Rogers won the game,
which ended 4-1 for the Nationals. He wasn't brilliant, but he
hung in and gave up only one run as the starter, leaving after three
innings with a 3-1 lead.

Oliver went 2-for-2, Carter was 1-for-3 with an RBI, Dawson was
1-for-4, and Raines walked and stole a base.

Jim Fanning, a coach, was booed. Duke Snider, a captain, was
not. It was the eleventh straight win for the Nationals and the
twentieth in the last twenty-one games.

The game itself was a bit of a yawner; but if you had to pick
three highlights they might have been these:

1. Five intrepid fans who somehow worked their way into the lip of the Big O's toilet-seat roof, about half a mile above Andre Dawson's head, where they watched in sun-soaked ecstasy for several innings;

2. Dave Concepcion's two-run homer in the second, eliminating the traditional American League lead and any hope of an upset;

3. Hundreds of tons of shrubbery brought in to relieve the gloom on the other side of the outfield fence, an area that resembled a burned-out set from West Side Story before and after the shrubbery, which wasn't around long enough to water.

If it was a time to celebrate Montreal's bounty of talent, it also offered a pause to mourn past heroes.

Jackie Robinson had been dead for a decade, his fire extinguished at 53. And Jean-Guy Black had died a few weeks before the All-Star Game, stricken with a heart attack at 46. They weren't at all similar, but they were both integral parts of Montreal's baseball history.

Robinson, of course, was the man who broke baseball's colour barrier. Branch Rickey, president of the Brooklyn Dodgers, selected Robinson for his skills and intelligence, asking only that he dissociate his temper from his pride long enough to make the transition successful.

The Montreal Royals served as Robinson's last stepping stone to the majors. When his apprentice year was over, fans at Delormier Stadium serenaded him with "*Il a gagné ses epaulettes*," and later chased him down Ontario Street as he raced to catch a plane. As a reporter from the American South was later to write, "It's probably the first time a white mob of rioters ever chased a Negro down the streets in love rather than hate."

There is a bronze plaque that's easy to miss in the main lobby at Olympic Stadium. It features a relief of Robinson and something he said in 1946: "This is the city for me. This is paradise."

His elegant wife Rachel was introduced on the field prior to the 1982 All-Star Game, and the crowd cheered in emotional waves. It was a good moment in a summer when some Montreal taxi companies were refusing to hire blacks because customers were asking for white drivers.

Jean-Guy Black wasn't mentioned in the ceremonies, but *The Sunday Express*, having missed his death earlier, used the occasion

Raines

Oliver

Carter

Cromartie

Dawson

Mills

Wallach

Francona

Flynn

Speier

Tito and Terry Francona

Rogers

Fryman

The Spaceman

Scott on Opening Day

to pay tribute to a little guy who made people smile before anybody ever thought of Youppi:

Jean-Guy Black had the distinction of being Montreal's most celebrated peanut vendor.

Since the Expos' inception and even before that, selling peanuts in the stands was all Jean-Guy knew. He enjoyed what he did and made an art of his trade by throwing bags of peanuts to his customers, with them tossing back the money.

At first this was a rather easy task, seeing that a bag was only 25 cents. But as inflation took its toll, Jean-Guy's job became all the more difficult. When the Expos and Als moved to the Big O the price of peanuts had risen to 50 cents. Now it stands at 65.

Jean-Guy met the challenge in style. His arm seemed to improve with age, and last year, during the National League championship series against Los Angeles, Mr. Peanut accomplished what many believed to be impossible.

A fan from the 600 level screamed at Black, who was selling in the 300 level. Jean-Guy looked up, aimed, and fired. The bag landed right in the fan's hand. He in turn dropped three quarters down in Jean-Guys direction, hollering "keep the tip."

Jean-Guy was truly a sports-vendor legend.

All of this was true, although the fan *couldn't* have been any higher than the 500 level. *Poetic licence.* The guy was uncanny, and deserves a spot in the archives with "The Dancer" and "The Guy-Who-Brought-His-Duck-to-the-Game." Guerrilla fighters in the concrete/plastic jungle.

For that slim majority of Expos who didn't make the All-Star team the game meant three days rest after having dropped 15 of their last 20 games. They were 43–42, 4 games back of the Phillies and the Cardinals, and a game and a half behind Pittsburgh.

Jim Fanning hadn't wanted a break. "We don't need three days to think about the last three weeks," he sighed.

What should have been taken as a clear managerial warning against thinking during the 72-hour period eluded Chris Speier, who had gone home to Ste-Adèle, north of Montreal, for the duration.

Speier said he expected that Fanning would be fired if the team continued to struggle in its upcoming tour of the West Coast. "If we don't do well, changes will be made," Speier said. "That's only common sense."

In a later telephone interview Speier said there was a "lack of unity" on the club. "That's going to happen on any club. When you have losses on the field, the backbiting becomes more prevalent."

Al Oliver defended Fanning, but on the backhand. "I almost feel sorry for Jim Fanning. I think he's too good of a person, if anything, to be a manager."

So who needed a break? But four days later there was John McHale saying "The three-day rest at the All-Star break is the best thing that could happen to my ball club. We should give them three more days rest at the start of September."

The Expos came out of the second-half chute like gangbusters, sweeping 4 straight from the Padres with great pitching and timely hitting. The Expos scored 23 runs to the Padres' 8. "I'm glad we're through with you," muttered Dick Williams blackly.

Mike Gates was hitting .281 and Dave Van Horne was referring to him, almost imploringly, as "the dandy second baseman" because he was turning double plays. The Expos seemed to have got their second wind. They were 3 games back.

An old man brought them back to reality. Vicente Romo was a refugee from the Mexican League; he hadn't won a major-league game in eight years, and hadn't won as a starter since April 27, 1970. Romo shut the Expos down on three hits over seven innings, and the Dodgers went on to win 2-1. Romo attributed the victory to his wife's advice that he throw more fastballs.

The next day the Dodgers went on to bomb the Expos 10-1, knocking Charlie Lea out with a tender shoulder.

The Expos won the finale 4-1 in 11 innings on superb pitching by Steve Rogers and a home run by Tim Wallach, but the fun was over. In San Diego it had looked as though the second half might be magical, but all the old flaws were re-emerging. Three of the five hits off Rogers were ground balls that Speier couldn't make plays on. Raines was still trying to operate from the far distant corner of the batting box, and Dawson was still trying to pull outside pitches, in or out of the strike zone. And the bench stunk—the pinch hitters were 1-for-their-last-25. Other teams had experience on the bench. The Expos had kids who looked uncertain about their roles. Office, Milner, and Scott were being missed.

130

The Expos snuck in a win in the opener against the Giants when Raines hit a home run in the thirteenth. They had been leading 7–2 and won 8–7.

The next day Speier and Frank Taveras took turns making crucial errors at shortstop to account for the difference in a 5–2 loss.

But the team saved their *pièce de résistance* for the rubber match on Sunday. Scott Sanderson coasted into the eighth inning with a 1–0 lead on a three-hitter that should have been a no-hitter. The first hit had been off Oliver's glove, the second under Oliver's glove, and the third a ground ball through second that Gates was slow diving for.

In the eighth, Sanderson got the first batter on a hard liner to Taveras at short, but then walked pinch-hitter Champ Summers. Max Venable was the second out on a tapper to second, but then Duane Kuiper hit a routine grounder to short, where Taveras bobbled and booted it.

Chili Davis, who'd been ready to leave for the clubhouse on what should have been the third out, came to the plate instead and lined to right field to score the tying run.

Jack Clark then smacked another liner to the glove of Gates, who dropped the ball, picked it up, and threw wildly toward home, past Gary Carter.

Jeff Reardon, who had taken over for Sanderson and had given up the single to Davis, backed up the play at the plate, and fired the ball to third in an attempt to get Davis. Tim Wallach stabbed at the ball to make a quick tag, but failed to hold on to it. He was charged with the second Expo error of the game. There should have been six.

Final score, after an Andre Dawson home run in the ninth: Giants 3, Expos 2.

Jim Fanning, who had said "Errors are part of the game" after Saturday's loss, this time said, "What you saw in that eighth doesn't happen very often." Neither, of course, do mass murders or ship wrecks.

The Expos led the league in ERA and home runs, and they were third in batting average. But they were last in double plays and second-worst in giving up unearned runs—not to mention the earned runs that scored on mediocre fielding.

But life went on. The Expos won two from the Cubs, the first on

Rogers' thirteenth victory and the second saved on a wonderful catch by Dawson.

They were five games back, but sixteen of their next nineteen games were against the Cardinals and the Phillies. It was comeback time once more.

Everything started well again. The Expos took three of four from the Cardinals at Olympic Stadium in a series that drew 190,472 despite a transit strike. And to rub it in, they did it even though they were outscored 21–15 on the series—winning by a single run in each of their victories and getting blown out 10–1 in the loss.

In each win they came from behind, as was not their wont. Dawson set the tone in the first game by whirling all the way to third when Willie McGee threw behind him, scoring on a sacrifice fly to win it in the tenth.

In the second game he doubled in the eleventh to drive in Tim Raines with the winner. The Cards bombed Ray Burris in the third game; but in the fourth game Raines threw out a runner at the plate (after entering the game late because he was late arriving at the ball park), and Al Oliver drove in the winning run in the seventh.

Despite all the unconscionable losses, the Expos were 11–5 since the All-Star break. Optimism permeated the concrete.

It was off to Philadelphia, where the Phillies turned the tables— despite a last-ditch cavalry charge led by John McHale.

McHale had already made the latest in a series of internal shifts at the beginning of the Cardinal series, bringing up shortstop/second baseman Bryan Little from Wichita and sending infielder Chris Smith back down.

Smith himself had been called up at the break to replace third-string catcher Brad Gulden, and had barely had time to go 0-for-2 and make a perfunctory appearance on Duke Snider's post-game show. "This is a good organization," he told The Duke. "It's been good to me." He wasn't heard from again.

That was the fourteenth roster change McHale had made since the season had opened, and he wasn't finished.

The cocky, swaggering Little became the Expos' sixth second baseman of the year, replacing the slumping Gates, who was benched. And although it was too early to tell, Little looked right at home.

But McHale was on the prowl. He had talked to Paul Richards, an adviser to the Texas Rangers, who said the Rangers would be pleased to get rid of Doug Flynn and his $375,000-a-year salary, guaranteed for 4½ years.

Flynn, a second baseman, was best known for his decent fielding and terrible hitting. His fielding statistics when he played with the Mets in 1981 were marginally better than Rodney Scott's. He was seventh in the league in range; Scott was ninth. He was sixth in fielding percentage; Scott was seventh. Flynn was seventh in double plays turned, playing with Frank Taveras; Scott was tenth, playing with Chris Speier. Both were pretty good second basemen. If you ranked Tommy Herr, Manny Trillo, and Juan Bonilla as 9s on a scale of 1 to 10, you'd rank Scott and Flynn between 7½ and 8.

Scott, of course, had a bad name as a batter because of his .205 batting average in 1981. But Flynn's average was only .222.

Moreover, at the end of the 1980 season, baseball guru Thomas Boswell had singled out Flynn as "the most inoffensive player in baseball"—the worst batter. Boswell's system of Total Average, remember, ranks players on the number of bases they achieve through hits, walks, steals, and being hit by pitches, and deducts for all kinds of outs, with double penalties for hitting into double plays, and deductions for getting caught stealing.

By this yardstick Flynn—a slugfoot on the bases who rarely coaxed a walk at the plate or managed anything more than a single—was the worst.

By 1981 Boswell had upgraded him to *one* of the worst, judging that Bill Russell had beaten him out of the title of Worst Middle-Infielder in Baseball because, although Flynn's hitting was deplorable, Russell's fielding was even worse.

Scott, on the other hand, ranked seventh in the National League in Total Average among second basemen, almost tied for sixth with the respected Phil Garner.

The Expos were picking up in Flynn almost exactly what they had dumped in Scott four months and five second basemen earlier —and were paying both salaries.

It must be acknowledged that Flynn had a more promising lifestyle and a cheerier attitude than had Scott. He certainly had a cheerier attitude than Mike Gates, who departed when Flynn arrived.

The lobby of the Franklin Plaza Hotel in Philadelphia is cool and modern, as much like an art gallery as a hotel. Its brown, baked-enamelled doors do not revolve, but if the Expos are going to continue to make it their Philadelphia home, they should insist that they do.

Just before two in the afternoon on August 3, 1982, Mike Gates stood inside the non-revolving doors leading to his taxi, leading to his plane to Montreal and his wife Eydie, leading to another plane and Wichita.

Hard and lean, in a khaki shirt, with lively blue eyes, long front teeth, and a relentless nose, he refused to go quietly as tradition demands.

He had been to see Jim Fanning. "They're panicking," he said. "You don't got a team out there right now. You've got guys coming and going. When I saw Jim Fanning I wanted to tell him how I felt, and give him a piece of my mind.

"It seems to me they were telling me I wasn't doing a job, but he said I was. He said it was a numbers game. I just don't understand why.

"Jim said it was experience. Experience isn't going to make Flynn a better hitter than he was in the past, and that's what they keep saying they want—offence.

"I'm just going to go down and have fun. Up here it was nerve-wracking and a lot of pressure. I've seen what they do. They bring people in and send them out, bring them in and send them out.

"I didn't think I was doing anything wrong. I thought if anybody would get sent down it would be Bryan, because he was the last called up.

"I'm upset because I don't want to go back down. It gets to the point where you say forget it. You can't play under pressure. You've got enough pressure as it is. It wasn't pressure from my family. It was pressure from my team."

He carried a scruffy leather satchel and a new blue suitcase embossed with the Expos insignia. He had a high blow-dried, puffed-up hairdo and wore lizard cowboy boots. And he was gone.

Half an hour later Doug Flynn arrived, wearing jeans, a diamond bracelet, and ostrich cowboy boots.

He had his mother, father, and breathtaking wife in tow.

He met John McHale and Jim Fanning at the elevator, and they all laughed when he said what he was happiest about was that he'd be playing with his boyhood idol, Woodie Fryman. He went to his room.

"You know," said John McHale, "it's been a funny year for planning. It's not as offensive a league as it's been in other years."

The next evening Joel Youngblood showed up. He'd been the starting centerfielder for the Mets in Chicago that afternoon, driving in the winning run early in the game, and leaving it in the fourth when he found out he'd been traded. He set out for Philadelphia, where he arrived in the third inning and stepped into an Expos uniform.

Expos equipment manager John Silverman, inordinately proud of never having been caught without a uniform for a player, was forced to drive deep into the suburbs of Philadelphia, where a local glove-salesman's secretary had a sewing machine.

When Youngblood entered the game in the seventh inning, the Silverman triumph shouted out from across the back: YOUNGBLOOD, 25.

Little did he know there was an Expos initiation rite that he would not experience for another two weeks. Flynn got his over with in his first game.

It involved going to the exact spot in short right-center field, "the Bermuda triangle," where it is difficult, but possible, for any one of three people to catch a ball: the second baseman, the right-fielder, or the centerfielder.

In his first game with the Expos, Flynn went there, camped under a ball, waved for it, and had it slammed out of his glove by Warren Cromartie, who was either over-hustling or exercising his territorial imperative.

The error—awarded to Flynn—loaded the bases for the Phillies, who were trailing 2–0 with one out in the sixth. Bo Diaz then hit a high chopper to Wallach at third, who threw to first to get the second out.

One runner naturally scored from third; but Gary Matthews, knowing Oliver's shoulder injury hampered his throw to the plate, also scored from second as Oliver watched sadly.

The Phillies won 3–2, after taking the opener 2–1 coming back from a 1–0 deficit on a Bo Diaz homer and a Bo Diaz sacrifice fly.

And the Phillies won the third game 5–4 after trailing 3–2, when

Dawson and Youngblood tried the experiment of getting as far away from each other as they could with Pete Rose up. It didn't work. With Dawson in left-center field and Youngblood playing on the line in right, Rose, incredulous and batting left-handed, smacked the ball between them, driving in the tying run. "How could they play me there?" he asked later, almost insulted at his opponents' inattention.

The Expos came back to take the final game 9–2 as Tim Wallach hit a grand-slam home run; but the Phillies had done to the Expos exactly what the Expos had done to the Cardinals in the previous series. The Phils were outscored (16–12), but won three one-run games, all comebacks. The Expos were 6 games down to the Phillies, 4 to the Cardinals, and 1½ to the annoyingly competitive Pirates.

It was off to St. Louis, which was not only a more pleasant city, but quieter. Warren Cromartie, whose last public pronouncement had been a less than elegant reaction to the acquisition of Youngblood, had taken a vow of silence, appointing publicist Rich Griffin as his spokesman. "He says he'll talk when he's traded," said Griffin.

St. Louis was a treat. Steve Rogers waited through a 37-minute rain delay with 2 strikes on Expo-killer Dane Iorg, who was hitting .481 against Montreal at the time. He struck him out on a sinker, and went on to win the game when Jeff Reardon shut down an eighth-inning Cardinal rally. Expos 5, Cards 3.

The Cards won the second game 9–5 by mauling Bill Gullickson, Dan Schatzeder, and Bryn Smith; but then Woodie Fryman pitched 3⅔ innings of one-hit relief to save a 2–1 game for David Palmer (6–4), who was thought to have tired in the heat. Considering the condition of his elbow, it was no wonder he tired. It was to be his last win of the year. In the previous 10 days Fryman had pitched 10⅔ innings against the Cardinals, winning 2 games and saving 2 others without allowing a run.

The Phillies had been swept in a three-game series against the Cubs. The Expos were four games back yet again—it was a niche that felt like home. But there was hope. The stage was set for a five-game series at home against the Phillies, after three warm-up games against the Cubs.

Except the Cubs won two of them. Fergie Jenkins, the big Canadian who's always been considered burned out by the Canadian-based teams when he's come available, won the first one 9–2 en route to a 14–15 season that would have been 19–10 with most teams.

The Cubs won the second game 5–3 on a Jody Davis bloop triple that eluded Joel Youngblood, playing center field in place of sore-wristed Andre Dawson. But the Expos salvaged the third 3–0 on a four-hitter shared by Charlie Lea, Woodie Fryman, and Jeff Reardon.

Now 5½ games back, the Expos would have to take 4 or 5 from the Phillies to threaten the leaders.

It was a series no Expo fan will ever forget, but who remembers the first three games—all Expo victories?

On Thursday, August 12, the Expos swept a double-header from the Phillies, 6–3 and 8–7, before 55,097 jubilant fans. The Montreal *Gazette* proclaimed, "There's a brand new pennant race in the National League East today . . ." What that meant was that the Expos were four games back again, with the Cards in front and the Phillies half a game behind.

Warren Cromartie, who had been benched in favour of Youngblood for four of the five games on the home stand, slammed a two-out pinch single in the bottom of the ninth to win the nightcap and perhaps save his life.

So strongly had the fans turned against him that McHale's acquisition of Youngblood—who ended up batting a mediocre .200 —may have been the best deal he made all year. It allowed Cromartie to regroup on the bench, which was exactly where the customers wanted him for the moment.

If Cromartie had started in right field after the Expos had returned from the road trip the fans might well have undone the splendid image Montreal had built up when that mob of white rioters chased Jackie Robinson down the street in love, rather than hate. Cromartie wasn't as fast as Robinson, but he'd have had to run harder.

Strangely, Cromartie wasn't having as bad a year as it appeared, despite an apparent loss of confidence in the field and confusion at the plate. He was leading the club in game-winning RBIs—never his forte—and a number of them had come in the ninth or extra innings.

On Friday, August 13, in the thirteenth game of Dave Palmer's comeback, the Expos won the third game of the series.

The good part was that Doug Flynn hit a chalk-line triple into shallow right field to drive in two runs, and Al Oliver singled in another as the Expos parlayed three hits into three runs to win 3–2.

The bad part was that Palmer, who'd spent two years trying to nurse his elbow back into shape after it was operated on, called Gary Carter out to the mound after striking out Mike Krukow and throwing two balls to Pete Rose.

"There was nothing on those last two pitches, was there?" he asked Carter.

Carter hesitated. "Not really," he finally replied.

"My elbow's killing me," said Palmer.

Carter called for the manager.

Palmer stood waiting, his arms crossed, his jaw set in its usual determined way, staring at the plate as though in a dream. It was the way he'd dreamed over the winter, in Cordova, Tennessee, thinking about striking out Mike Schmidt when he got back to the majors.

Not that there had been that much hope of him making it back, except in his own mind. He had been the only professional pitcher with an ERA of infinity in 1981: he threw to one batter who walked and later scored when he was convalescing with the Memphis Chicks in August. "Something in my elbow snapped on the fifth pitch, to make it three and two. I tried to throw another one, and bounced it half way to the plate to walk him."

His arm had already been operated on the previous November, and it was too early to cut again. So he worked on a tension machine all winter, gradually trying to build up his strength with exercise.

In the spring he pitched well. After striking out two batters to cap two scoreless innings of relief against the Baltimore Orioles at West Palm, his eyes welled up with tears.

He had come back. A reporter congratulated him, saying that nobody would have bet on his recovery. "People who thought I wouldn't come back," he said with his jaw set firmly, "don't know me."

He was sent to the minors again to work himself slowly back into shape. On Tuesday, May 25 he started his first game with the Expos since October 1980, giving up only two hits but six walks in a six-inning performance against the Astros. It got him the win, 6–1.

The comeback continued. He finally caught up with Mike Schmidt on August 3 in Philadelphia, and struck him out on three curve balls—"about three of the best I've thrown."

Ten days later it was over. He had gone 6–4, with a 3.18 ERA, on an arm that was still unravelling. They operated in September.

It was supposed to be minor, just bone chips. "When they got in there," he says, his bright-blue eyes clouding over, "the tendon and the muscle just kind of fell right in their laps."

They took a ligament out of his wrist to replace the damaged tendon in his elbow, re-attached another ligament, and moved his funny bone into his forearm. Only one pitcher has come back from similar surgery to pitch successfully in the majors—Tommy John. Nobody else. Thousands hadn't.

They said it would be a full year before he could do any serious pitching. The glory seemed more and more evasive. Everything he'd done had been right. He had been 24–13 with a 2.89 ERA since he'd broken in. The kind of thing nobody would remember, if he was finished.

He had worked hard, never quit, and wasn't going to now. "I'm going to stay in good shape and I'm going to work hard on my arm, and I know it's just a matter of time."

But he thought he might look at a real-estate licence. If his arm had held up he'd have been making half a million dollars a year by now, with more to come. Instead he'll have to make do on $100,000 a year for the next few years and then look for something else if things don't work out.

No problem. When he was growing up, in Glens Falls, New York, his father had been a prison guard. There were six kids to feed, and vacations came once every year or two.

If worse came to worst, he'd just learn another trade. Things would be all right. He had known this since one day late in August, when he'd been hanging around waiting for them to decide about his operation.

"Someone came up to me and said, 'Would you go by and say hello to that little girl down there. She's fifteen years old, and at the end of the week she's going to have her leg amputated for cancer.'

"And I did. And that's when I knew I didn't have a problem. I'd give a lot to go out there and pitch again. And I will give a lot, trying. But if I don't ever pitch again I don't have a problem."

Saturday August 14 and Sunday August 15 were hard on pitchers, too. Up to a point, Saturday was particularly hard on Steve Carlton, the Phillies' ace.

The scene: A rainy day at the Big O. The Expos were just three games back of the league-leading Cardinals, and two and a half behind the Phillies, whom they'd just beaten three straight.

It was the bottom of the seventh, and the Phillies had just come back to even the score at 4–4. But Bryn Smith had come on with the bases loaded and nobody out, and had retired the side, popping out Schmidt, striking out Diaz, and getting Garry Maddox on a bouncer to first.

Smith was the first batter scheduled in the eighth, but since he was pitching so well, Jim Fanning didn't put in a pinch hitter for him. Smith got on on an error, and by the end of the inning the Expos had racked up an 8–4 lead.

Before sending Smith out to bat Fanning had asked him how his arm was feeling, since he'd been used several times in recent weeks. Smith said his arm felt a little tight but that he'd be okay. If Fanning was worried about Smith's arm, this was the time to remove him from the game and put in a hitter who might help break the 4–4 tie.

But Fanning waited until after Smith had batted to take him out of the game, obviously deciding that keeping an effective pitcher in the ball game was more important than worrying about a middle reliever's arm when the score was 4–4. The arm was suddenly worth saving when the score was 8–4 in his favour.

It's the kind of decision hundreds of managers have made over the years. At crucial moments, managers—and players—have to wrestle with whether to take a chance on playing somebody hurt. Smith would have made it easier for Fanning if he'd either said he was fine or said he was hurting. But he didn't, so Fanning decided to take a chance with him, and then reversed himself when he got a healthy lead.

If it wasn't a great decision, it fell considerably short of being a terrible one. Until the Phillies scored nine runs off his four other relievers—Fryman, Reardon, Burris, and Schatzeder—in the eighth, going on to win 15–11.

As usual, Fanning played the martyr, accepting the blame while phrasing himself carefully enough to indicate it wasn't all his fault, but that he was man enough to be the lightning rod.

"I didn't manage the eighth very well. You can pin that loss on me. It will make your stories easier."

Easier than pinning it on everybody who could have prevented it—not just Fanning, but his entire five-man bullpen.

It was going to be a bad weekend for Gentleman Jim.

Sunday was better only because it was sunny. A crowd of 57,694 showed up, a single-game record. Total attendance for the four-game series was 211,600—third-biggest total for four dates in the major leagues, topped only by two Giants-at-L.A. series twenty years earlier.

The Expos took a 1–0 lead in the second inning, when Al Oliver scored after Manny Trillo threw wildly to first on a double-play attempt.

Steve Rogers, who'd pitched with only three days' rest in his previous start against the Cubs so he would be available for this game, nursed a shutout until Garry Maddox smacked a homer to left to lead off the eighth.

The inevitable Pete Rose led off the ninth with a single, and was sacrificed to second. One out. Gary Matthews popped up. Two out.

Muscular Mike Schmidt entered the batter's box. Rogers had dominated Schmidt over the past two seasons, holding him to a .083 batting average and 1 RBI in 24 at-bats. He had also struck him out swinging twice that afternoon—in the second and the fifth.

They had dueled in the eighth to a smattering of rhythmic clapping, with Schmidt fouling off three pitches and forcing Rogers to 3–2 before popping a ball up a foot foul in behind first base, taken by Doug Flynn in the sun. Two of the pitches Schmidt fouled off skipped straight back into the netting: if Rogers had fooled him slightly on location, there hadn't been any problem with Schmidt's timing.

Now a good chunk of the crowd chanted, "Walk him, walk him!" But it wasn't their decision. It belonged to Jim Fanning, who abdicated, sending pitching coach Galen Cisco to the mound to tell Rogers it was up to him. Pitch to Schmidt, or walk him and go to George Vukovich, batting fifth and hitting .276 with 4 home runs and 30 RBIs. Schmidt had entered the game at .289 with 25 home runs and 60 RBIs.

Rogers chose Schmidt. In fact there was no decison. Good ballplayers live as much off their egos as their talent. Great ballplayers duel with one another. It was Rogers, the best ERA pitcher in the National League, against Schmidt, the best power hitter. "I decided to pitch to him," Rogers was later to say, "because I'll pitch to anyone I'm given a choice to pitch to." He didn't usually have that decision in this kind of situation, he said. It normally came from the bench.

Rogers threw Schmidt two good pitches, the first one catching the corner for a strike. The second one was a sinker, low and inside in the strike zone, the perfect pitch. "I put it exactly where I wanted to," said Rogers.

Schmidt smote the ball on a line to dead right field: in the complete opposite direction from where his greatest power lay, in the complete opposite direction from where any right-handed hitter should be able to put an inside pitch—over the 99 m marker into the stands. Duke Snider, who with Dave Van Horne had been begging over the air waves for an intentional walk, turned off his microphone and said fuck.

Bob Dernier, hitting for Vukovich, popped out to short to end the inning. Ten minutes later, the game was over.

"He's a very strong human being," Phillies manager Pat Corrales said of Schmidt.

"I can't believe he put that pitch in the air," said Gary Carter. It was a moment for awe in the wake of a great duel between great players. But it was a moment for second-guessing as well.

"I don't want to create any controversy," said Carter, "but that was a decision that had to be made beforehand and not left up to Steve Rogers."

"Managers are paid to make decisions like this—nobody else," said columnist Red Fisher.

Rogers himself wouldn't quite say that, after a decade of castigating management for not treating players with enough respect. If there was one thing Fanning was consistent at over the year, it was giving Steve Rogers every chance—and perhaps one he shouldn't have—to prove himself great.

Schmidt thought it wasn't a bad decision, but then he would. "Let's face it—the homer is a very low percentage play. I think they thought George was more of a threat to hit a single and beat them."

Beat them? Who could be more of a threat to beat anybody than the one and only Mike Schmidt?

"I see that they're not going to walk him and that makes me happy," said the man who might have had the best insights on the subject, Pat Corrales. "Who would you rather have hitting—Mike Schmidt or George Vukovich? I'm not knocking George, but Mike Schmidt is paid a lot of money to do exactly what he did."

Five-and-a-half games back, with 46 left to play. The shadows were getting long as summer slipped away. But the odds were getting longer.

A trip to Atlanta offered a glimmer of hope, with the Braves mired in a horrific, soul-destroying slump. They'd been 9 games ahead of the Padres and 10½ ahead of the Dodgers on July 30. By August 15, they were tied with San Diego and 2½ games back of the first-place Dodgers. They'd lost 17 of 19 while the Dodgers were winning 14 of 18.

The slump hadn't ended: The Expos scored 8 unearned runs on 5 Atlanta errors in the opener of a four-game series and won 13-7. They took the second game on an Oliver RBI single in the ninth, tying the game, and a Cromartie RBI single in the tenth, winning it. Oliver had been 9-for-16 with 10 RBIs in the Phillies series.

Andre Dawson had two home runs and a single, and Bill Gullickson pitched a six-hitter as the Expos took the third game 12-2. The Braves were now 2-19 in their last 21 games.

The slump ended in the fourth game when their young pitcher, Pascual Perez, obtained his driver's licence and attempted to drive to the ball park, where he was scheduled to start the game. Luckily for the Braves he got lost, and Phil Niekro had to start in his place. Niekro won, 5-4.

Scott Sanderson, winless in 10 starts, left the game after 6 with a 4-3 lead, complaining of dizziness. A win would have brought him around more quickly than smelling salts, but Woodie Fryman and Jeff Reardon couldn't hold the lead.

A Houston paper claimed John McHale had talked to Bill Virdon, deposed manager of the Astros, about taking over as the Expos' skipper at more than $200,000 a year. McHale and Virdon were said to be friends.

McHale dismissed the report, saying, "I am not going to dignify that story with a denial." It was much the same indignity he had shown in West Palm Beach when a radio station created an outrageous story saying Al Oliver and Larry Parrish were going to trade uniforms. One man standing alone against irresponsible journalism.

August went out with a whimper.

The Expos visited Houston, where they dropped two out of three. Joel Youngblood was finally initiated into the Bermuda Triangle, bumping with Dawson on a fly ball to hand the Astros a 4–3 win and prolong Steve Rogers' quest for his fifteenth victory.

They next dropped in on Cincinnati, where they also lost two out of three, and met Brad Lesley, the rookie Red pitcher who snarled and growled at batters after disposing of them. The Expos bad-mouthed his foolishness, but he mowed down Dawson, Oliver, and Carter in the ninth to save a 1–0 win for Bob Shirley. Rogers lost a four-hitter.

The Expos jerked back to life again in Montreal, coming from behind to beat Houston twice; they lost the third game as Joe Niekro outdueled Charlie Lea; and they won the finale 5–3 as Bryan Little showed off his baserunning.

The Reds came to town for the last two games of the month and each team took one. Rogers finally won his fifteenth, 3–1, as Raines and Dawson stole two bases each.

But Paul Householder, the weak-hitting Cincinnati outfielder, responded in the best tradition of other underachievers like Ron Gardenhire, Alan Fowlkes, and Alan Knicely—all overachievers against the Expos. His single dropped in to right field in the fourteenth inning when Warren Cromartie, who had thrown out a runner at the plate in the thirteenth, hesitated on his approach to the ball.

The Expos had played 27–20 baseball since the All-Star break, which wasn't bad. Prorated over a season, it would give a team 93 wins—enough to win any division in 1982 baseball except the American League East.

But they'd been four games back of Philadelphia at the break. Now they were six games back of the Cardinals. Teams that were supposed to fold hadn't. Pitching that was supposed to collapse— both in St. Louis and Philadelphia—had come on strong.

And of the 16 crucial games they'd played against the Cardinals and Phillies, the Expos were 9–7. Nice. But not good enough.

Even for a team that loved September, time was getting short.

Nicknames Other Than "The Kid"

If the Expos needed poetic inspiration—which they did—all they had to do was look to the broadcast booth, where Edwin Snider sat in silver-haired splendour, wrapped in one of the great nicknames of baseball.

Edwin himself doesn't know why his father started calling him "Duke" as a young boy. Whatever the reason, you had to give him credit for prescience. He must have seen young Edwin was going to have the proper bearing to wear a title comfortably. Others tried, and withered.

Leon "Duke" Carmel came to the St. Louis Cardinals in 1959 while Snider was still playing. He was later traded to the Yankees to see if the pinstripes would help, and ended a four-year career as an outfielder with a .211 batting average and 4 home runs.

Catcher Duane "Duke" Sims came up with Cleveland in 1964 and played for 5 teams over the next 11 years, winding it up with a .239 average. Who knows. Maybe either one of these men could have hit .240 unhampered by the pressure of being called "Duke."

But the name was just right for a man with a lot of swagger, who could play the field gracefully and slam tape-measure home runs in the clutch; and, in the end, it was the kind of name that, attached to the right guy, was impossible to keep out of the Hall of Fame. It's short, elegant, memorable, distinguished, powerful, and became a legend just by putting "The" in front of it. And as The Duke himself says, "It's a hell of a lot better than Edwin."

As perfect as some nicknames are, many are too heavy for mortal men to carry, and should be retired, like uniforms. You'd have to be larger than baseball itself to want to be called "Babe," no matter what your mother called you. What chance did Rene Valdes have after he started calling himself "The Whip" when he came up with the Brooklyn Dodgers in 1957? None. Ewell Blackwell had been "The Whip," and at 6'6" with a crackling fast ball he could carry it. Valdes pitched in five games, accumulated a 5.54 ERA, and was gone. If he hadn't tried to steal a name that wasn't right for him he might have won 300 games instead of one.

Some guys, like Valdes, would be better off without a nickname. Warren Spahn never had a nickname, and he won 363 games. And there were thousands of others who used their own names and were as happy as office workers. Jim Fanning was just Jim.

Some could have done better. Sanford "Sandy" Koufax should have been "The Sandman." Every kid knew The Sandman; he was the one who came around to sprinkle your eyes and put you to sleep. Which is just what Koufax did to batters, even if he wasn't as gentle about it.

Some were just lucky. Wilmer "Vinegar Bend" Mizell was from Vinegar Bend, Mississippi; that made it easy. On the other hand, Wilmer Dean "Fat" Chance didn't have much of one, did he? They were bound to call him that. Nor did Mordecai Peter Centennial "Three-Finger" Brown, even with all other options available.

Some turned clay into gold. When Steven Norman Carlton came into the National League, he shared a nickname with thousands of his contemporaries and predecessors. Nearly every left-handed ballplayer, at one point or another in his career, is called Lefty. Now only Carlton is. As the ill-fated Clint Hurdle once said, "When you call a pitcher 'Lefty' and everybody in both leagues knows who you mean, he must be pretty good."

In this sophisticated, non-romantic era of businesslike, briefcase-carrying ballplayers, some people think nicknames are outdated. Charles (The Outrageous) Finley knew better, and we have Jim "Catfish" Hunter because of it.

If baseball is recorded elegance, nicknames turn statistics into poetry. Edward William Brown died in Vallejo, California, in 1956; he probably would have wanted to be remembered for his .303 batting average over seven major-league seasons. Instead he is remembered as "Glass Arm Eddie" Brown, and baseball is probably the better for it.

Reading *The Baseball Encyclopedia* is one way of getting a feel for the game over the decades. But so is reading William "Sugar" Wallace's poem *Anthem*:

Catfish, Mudcat, Ducky, Coot.
The Babe, The Barber, The Blade, The Brat.
Windy, Dummy, Gabby, Hoot.
Big Train, Big Six, Bid Ed, Fat.

146

Greasy, Sandy, Muddy, Rocky.
Bunions, Twinkletoes, Footsie. The Hat.
Fuzzy, Dizzy, Buddy, Cocky.
The Bull, The Stork, The Weasel, The Cat.
    Schoolboy, Sheriff,
    Rajah, Duke,
    General, Major,
    Spaceman, Spook.

The Georgia Peach, The Fordham Flash,
The Flying Dutchman. Cot.
The People's Cherce, The Blazer. Crash.
The Staten Island Scot.
    Skeeter, Scooter,
    Pepper, Duster,
    Ebba, Bama, Boomer, Buster.

The Little Professor, The Iron Horse. Cap.
Iron Man, Iron Mike, Iron Hands. Hutch.
Jap, The Mad Russian, Irish, Swede, Nap.
Germany, Frenchy, Big Serb, Dutch,
        Turk. Tuck, Tug, Twig.
        Spider, Birdie, Rabbit, Pig.

Fat Jack, Black Jack, Zeke, Zack. Bloop.
Peanuts, Candy, Chewing Gum, Pop.
Chicken, Cracker, Hot Potato, Soup.
        Ding, Bingo.
        Hippity-Hopp.

Three-Finger, No-Neck, The Knuck, The Lip.
Casey, Gavvy, Pumpsie, Zim.
Flit, Bad Henry. Fat Freddie, Flip.
Jolly Cholly, Sunny Jim.
    Shag, Schnozz,
    King Kong, Klu.
    Boog, Buzz,
    Boots, Bump, Boo.

King Carl, The Count. The Rope, The Whip.
Wee Willie, Wild Bill, Gloomy Gus. Cy.
Bobo, Bombo, Bozo. Skip.
Coco, Kiki, Yo-yo. Pie.
    Dinty. Dooley,
    Stuffy, Snuffy,
    Stubby, Dazzy,
    Daffy, Duffy.

Baby Doll. Angel Sleeves, Pep, Sliding Billy,
Buttercup. Bollicky, Boileryard, Juice.
Colby Jack, Dauntless Dave, Cheese, Gentle Willie,
Trolley Line, Wagon Tongue, Rough, What's the Use.

    Ee-yah,
    Poosh 'Em Up,
    Skoonj, Slats, Ski.
    Ding Dong,
    Ding-a-Ling,
    Dim Dom, Dee.

Famous Amos. Rosy, Rusty.
Handsome Ransom. Home Run, Huck.
Rapid Robert. Cactus, Dusty.
Rowdy Richard. Hot Rod, Truck.
    Jo-Jo, Jumping Joe,
    Little Looie,
    Muggsy, Moe.

Old Folks, Old Pard, Oom Paul. Yaz.
Cowboy, Indian Bob, Chief, Ozark Ike.
Rawhide, Reindeer Bill. Motormouth. Maz.
Pistol Pete, Jungle Jim, Wahoo Sam. Spike.
    The Mad Hungarian.
    Mickey, Minnie.
    Kitten, Bunny.
    Big Dan, Moose.
    Jumbo, Pee Wee; Chubby, Skinny.
    Little Poison.
    Crow, Hawk, Goose.

Marvelous Marv.
 Oisk, Oats, Tookie.
Vinegar Bend.
 Suds, Hooks, Hug.
Hammerin' Hank.
 Cooch, Cod, Cookie.
Harry the Horse.
 Speed, Stretch, Slug.

The Splendid Splinter. Pruschka. Sparky.
Chico, Choo Choo, Cha-Cha, Chub.
Dr. Strangeglove. Deacon. Arky.
Abba Dabba. Supersub.

Bubbles, Dimples, Cuddles, Pinky.
Poison Ivy, Vulture, Stinky.
 Jigger, Jabbo
 Jolting Joe
 Blue Moon
 Boom Boom
 Bubba
 Bo.

Despite their short history the Expos have a proud tradition of nicknames, which has begun to show a distressing tendency toward limpness in recent years.

They inherited Jose "Coco" Laboy, Dick "The Monster" Radatz, Bob "Beetles" Bailey, and Mack "The Knife" Jones. These men brought their nicknames with them, although Jones solidified his label in Montreal by pulling a blade on a sportswriter. Rodney Scott was dubbed "Cool Breeze" by John Mayberry when he was in Kansas City; Scott always regretted that Mayberry hadn't just gone with "Breeze." That would have suggested "a nice thing coming through," he thought. He attributed a lot of his problems with management to them thinking that "Cool Breeze" meant that he thought he was so cool nobody could talk to him or teach him anything. Which might have been true.

"Boots" (Charles Frederick) Day and "Bombo" (Jesus Torres) Rivera had nicknames so indelible when they came out of the farm system that few people knew what their real names were.

Tim "Crazy Horse" Foli earned his nickname with bouts of temper and by sleeping overnight at second base after making three errors during a game in the minors. Bill "Spaceman" Lee was self-explanatory. Steve "Cy" Rogers, alias Steve "Sigh" Rogers, was compared to the immortal Cy Young by team-mates who were impressed by his incredible 1973 debut and amused by his presumption. John "The Hammer" Milner hit just the way it sounded, if not every time.

Al "Scoop" Oliver was named by a broadcaster while he was in the minors, when he was a first-class first baseman. Chris "Waxo" Speier was dubbed by a room mate in San Francisco for no apparent reason. But Waxo seems a bit wacky, and Speier does like a practical joke. Ray "The Beast" Burris looks like one when his hair is allowed to go to seed, even if he is a gentle soul.

"The Hawk" is the right music for Andre Dawson. True, Ken Harrelson, the first baseman/outfielder/golfer, was called "Hawk"; but he was named for his nose, not his wings. There's nothing wrong with Tim "Rock" Raines, even if it suggests muscle from head to toe. And it leaves his son, Tim Jr., with a name charged with black history—"Little Rock" Raines, of course.

But if Woodie Fryman is "Goat," so is every ballplayer over 40. And if Terry Francona is "Tito," what was his illustrious father?

It gets worse. Take a look at this partial list of Expos' nicknames —*sobriquets des Expos*—set out in the club's official 1981 press guide. There was no mention of "Cool Breeze" or "The Beast"; there was no poetry at all:

Elias Sosa: "Sose"
Bryn Smith: "Smitty"
Larry Parrish: "LP"
Brad Mills: "Millsy"
Dave Hostetler: "Hoss"
Warren Cromartie: "Cro"
Tom Gorman: "Gorms"
Stan Bahnsen: "Bonce"
David Palmer: "Palmball"
Tom Weighaus: "Wiggy"
Bill Gullickson: "Gully"

Which isn't even to mention Scott "Sandy" Sanderson. If

"Glass Arm Eddie" Brown had been alive and playing for the Expos, he'd surely have been known as "Brownie."

Luckily enough a small rebellion was starting to grow in the Expo club house toward the end of the season. It got off to a false start when Dan Schatzeder asked to have the nickname on the back of his chair taped over. But it turned out that he only wanted to go from "Schatzey" to "Schatzy," and even then the tape fell off.

But Jeff Reardon, who had been tagged with "Yak-Yak" by Warren Cromartie because he hadn't talked very much when he came over from the Mets, held a small but important press conference with a reporter outside the training room one day.

"No, I don't like Yak-Yak that much," he revealed. "In New York I was called 'X.' I prefer that." You could see how he would. "X" is a sharp, mean letter, reminiscent of X-ray, which is, of course, in itself reminiscent of a quickly pitched ball.

Then Brad Mills, sick to death of "Millsy," allowed that he almost preferred the name a few guys had been calling him— "Sap." After Ronnie Milsap, the singer. Now a man who doesn't mind Brad "Sap" Mills is a man who understands the "Glass Arm Eddie" Brown tradition.

The movement was taking on momentum. Bryn Smith, who had languished for eight years in the minors before learning how to throw a palm ball, was bored with "Smitty"—a minor-league nickname if there ever was one.

At 6'2" and 200-odd pounds Smith is a hefty, shaggy, shambly kind of guy who is rather mild and friendly, but likes to challenge a hitter and wouldn't mind a more aggressive image.

Bryn (The Bear) Smith was suggested. He put his hand on his muzzle for a moment, pondering. "I could go for that," he said finally. Not long afterward he was seen autographing a baseball in exactly that manner, making little growling noises as his paw pushed his pen across the ball.

"The Kid" Himself

I've always been named The Kid, and then when I went to my first big-league spring training in '73 I was a vivacious and enthusiastic young kid that had great strives of wanting to get to the major leagues. And so they nicknamed me the young, 18-year-old kid. And the tag has just stayed on ever since. And until the day I die I'll be nicknamed The Kid.
—Gary Carter
  1982

At his first spring training in 1973 a bunch of us older guys were sitting around drinking beer in a bar one night and he came in and asked us what we were having. So we told him and he kept ordering rounds, only each time he'd order a zombie for himself. After a while he got sick and then he passed out with his head on the table. We left him there and they sent him back down.
—Ron Hunt
  1982

Gary "The Kid" Carter. Kid Carter, for short. It's the kind of nickname you dreamed about when you were really a kid lying awake in bed, your games played, your papers delivered, the chores done, your homework finished. Some day your picture would be in all those newspapers, and your name would be magic wherever you went.

SEATTLE (AP)–Dave Parker and Kid Carter combined to snuff out an American League rally yesterday as the National League won its eighth straight All-Star Game, 7–6.

The game, televised on ABC, was watched by an estimated 60 million viewers.

CLEVELAND (UPI)–Kid Carter banged two home runs in front of 72,086 screaming fans yesterday as the National League won its eighteenth All-Star Game in its last 19 tries, 5–4.

NEW YORK (AP)–Kid Carter, who hit two home runs and was named Most Valuable Player in last year's All-Star Game, has amassed 2,785,407 votes from fans around the major leagues to lead all players in the balloting for this year's game.

Kid Carter sounded so good. Like a combination of Kid Gavilan, the fighter, and Kit Carson, the cowboy. And if ever any kid deserved to make it to where the crowds would go crazy for him, it was Gary Edmund Carter, born April 8, 1954, in Culver City, California.

He remembers having the dream, he says, from the time he was about five. He would be a major-league ballplayer, and he would do everything possible to get there.

But if he was a driven little guy, crazy about baseball, he didn't fit the California pattern of easy days in the sun. Baseball . . . hang around . . . baseball . . . go to the beach . . . baseball . . . whadya wanna do now?

These were easy, laid-back days for most kids, even if they lived in a ghetto. Eisenhower was just out, Kennedy was in, Dr. Spock was popular, the economy was as good as it was going to get. It was a time to relax and enjoy growing up.

But not for Gary Carter. For a start it was his nature to be busy. His parents—his dad was an aerospace worker—taught him to be responsible. And necessity did the rest.

When he was 12, his mother died of leukemia.

"That's probably what changed my life around, because I became very independent. My parents always taught me the value of a dollar. I had odd jobs when I was seven, eight years old. I cut lawns. I had a paper route for 4½ years. I hustled to get money. And what I bought—like a set of drums or a trumpet—I took very good care of.

"Even today, I'm very organized, very meticulous. You see, after my mother passed away if I didn't make my bed and keep my room neat, nobody else was going to. My father wasn't going to come in and clean it up. Neither was my brother.

His words spill out like a volcano erupting, tumbling over each other.

"My father didn't have to kick our butts to do this stuff. We kind of took it upon ourselves. We became kind of a team then.

"And if my father was late from work, we'd have dinner started when he got home. And if the vacuuming needed to be done, I'd do the vacuuming. If the table needed to be set, I did that. If the washing needed to be done, I'd do that. Cutting the lawn and keeping up around the house. We always had our chores. We were never given an allowance or anything like that. We had to earn that outside the house."

The Kid was not only busy. He was ambitious.

"That's something that has been a great motive for me throughout my life has been ambition. Because if everybody puts their mind to it they can really achieve what they want to achieve, I feel.

"Like the good Lord blessed me with the ability to play baseball. I realized that he had granted me with that kind of talent, and I realized it at a very young age. So athletics were a large part of my life very early.

"I was very ambitious about my subjects at school. I was on the honour society every year and I always wanted to achieve good grades. To get into major colleges you had to have good grades."

As much as Gary Carter loves his nickname, there's some question as to whether it's the right one. For a start, it had an owner, and a combative one at that. Ted (The Splendid Splinter) Williams called himself The Kid when he came up. (In his magnificent story about saying good-bye to the retiring Williams, "Hub Fans Bid Kid Adieu," John Updike remembers Williams' "determined designation of himself as 'The Kid.'")

But more important, how much of a "kid" is dimple-chinned Gary Carter? Or has he ever been?

There's no doubt he thinks he qualifies. "I'm friendly, I'm outgoing, I'm energetic, enthusiastic, congenial, and warm—loving."

Which nobody can deny. He also has a boyish smile, enjoys childish pranks, and plays baseball with gusto and enthusiasm. The name seems to fit.

But if the boyish smile comes naturally enough, you see more of it on the field than you do in the clubhouse. To a degree, at least, the smile is part of a performance, the day's work of an entertainer in the center ring.

"This is a source of entertainment," he says of the game. "These people love to see a smile on your face, and that brings a smile from them. And I feel that I can oblige. Just a little 'hi' or a wink or a smile will bring them back to the ball park."

154

He's thought about extending his entertainment career once his playing days are over. "I've been involved in some commercials and I have an ambition to get involved in some motion pictures, but that's a long-time ambition, and away up the road."

He admires movie stars who play tough guys or villains, but doesn't see that as his niche. "I don't think so, because of the type of person that I am. I think I would be more the fun-loving type of guy—the kind of guy the fans look at and go—'Wow! I'd like to meet him!'—or something like that. That's the way I've been looked at here, so why change? If promoted in the correct way—I think it's important to find out what role is best suited for the individual."

Beyond the smile, there's no question about the gusto and enthusiasm. Nobody plays harder than Carter. The fans want performance, and he delivers. It's more than his numbers, although they were his best ever last year: .293, 29 home runs, 97 RBIs at the plate, and the most runners thrown out from behind it.

It's his drive, his hustle. On September 5, as the Expos were making their next-to-last run at catching the Cardinals, Carter came to bat with two out in the bottom of the ninth and the score tied 1–1 against the Braves.

He hit a routine ball to Rafael Ramirez at short, so routine that many batters would be half way back to the dugout before the put-out was made at first. But Carter ran it, flat out; Ramirez bobbled the ball, and the game was over. "Carter just hit a routine ball to their shortstop, but his hustle won the ball game," said Jim Fanning. The Expos had been held to one hit.

Hustle is Carter's business. "I know that my mind has to be working and attentive and alert at all times. In Little League all you have to think about is getting out there and having fun and playing the game. But this is a business. You're out there to produce wins."

When the Expos dragged themselves out of bed at 6 a.m. and flew to Toronto for their exhibition Pearson Cup game against the Toronto Blue Jays, Carter wasn't keen on going. It was the beginning of the Expos' hoped-for September pennant drive, and Carter had been given virtually no rest all season. The fatigue was starting to show.

But when he got there he performed, hitting a double, stealing third, and scoring before he was taken out of the game. Stealing third? In an exhibition game, after a hard season? "I like to give them their money's worth," he said.

The smile and the hustle that bring in the customers belong to The Kid. The Kid is not one, but two corporations: Kid 8 Inc. handles Canadian ventures, and Kid 8 (Worldwide) Inc. handles the States, Japan, and the rest.

Both occupy a lot of their president's time, just as his paper route did. Not only does he like the world of business and promotion—"I can operate on their turf"—it's his nature to keep himself busy.

"I don't feel like my day is filled unless I do something. I can't sit around the house and watch TV. I can't waste my time that way because there are too many things that are important.

"I keep busy around the house doing odd jobs. Then I go to my office and there are phone calls to make and business appointments and interviews and different things like that. I'm on the phone quite a bit during the day. I keep up with all the accounting because I write all the cheques, and I keep up two corporations and I do all kinds of different things."

His endorsements include SSK of Japan (baseball gloves), Pony Sporting Goods Ltd. (shoes), Seven-Up (soft drinks), Dominion Textiles (bed sheets and sporting clothes), Gillette (razor blades), and Adam Brands (chewing gum). The Kid corps. received and digested more than $400,000 from endorsements in 1982.

Business is helped by the smiles and phone calls, but primarily it's good because this is a pretty fair country ballplayer. He's built like the number he wears—8—with big shoulders, big thighs and buttocks, chunks of muscle everywhere, propelled by some special energy cell buried deep within his body where science can't see it, immune to everything except pink eye. It drives his football body through this slender, subtle game, 215 pounds craving fastballs to drive deep into the left-field blue, 215 pounds springing up like a guard dog from behind the plate and snapping to second for the put-out.

Not only does he swallow the game whole, he plays smart baseball. The Expos pitching staff had the second-lowest ERA in the major leagues in 1982, partially because of Carter's photographic memory for batters' weaknesses. And when his bludgeon of a bat isn't working he'll lay down a bunt for a hit, moving all that body like a great big missile hurtling toward first.

Dick Williams, ex-manager of the Expos and now with the Padres, told the Ottawa *Citizen*'s Bob Elliott that if he were starting a new franchise tomorrow, "the first person I'd want would be Gary Carter." He figures Carter, at 28, has another 10 years left in him.

These were strong words coming from Williams. His own catcher, Terry Kennedy, is considered one of the bright new stars in the game, and Kennedy's hitting statistics last year were almost identical to Carter's.

If Carter does have another decade left in him and can continue to improve his hitting consistency the way he did in 1982, might he not rank as the best catcher ever?

"That very well could be true," Carter responds with a nod instead of a smile. "That would be a very nice tag to leave this game with."

There are a few obstacles.

Johnny Bench, for one. Not much of a third baseman, but the best catcher of the 60s and the 70s. A man of nonchalant backhands, cat-like quickness, and whistling throws, the effortless Bench was rookie-of-the-year in 1968 and MVP in 1970 and 1972. Six times he drove in more than 100 runs in a season.

Roy Campanella of the Dodgers and Yogi Berra of the Yankees were the catchers of the 50s. Campanella was MVP three times before he was cut down in an auto accident. Berra, his cross-town rival, hit 358 home runs and drove in 1430 runs over a nineteen-year career. Carter has 161 homers and 609 RBIs after nine years, so he'd need superb seasons at the plate to match Berra offensively.

Bill Dickey of the Yankees stood out in the 30s and early 40s, before passing the torch to Berra. Big, clean cut, and easy smiling, Dickey hit an outstanding .313 over 17 seasons, with 202 home runs and 1209 RBIs. "He made catching look easy," said Detroit second baseman Charlie Gehringer, who never said anything unless he had something to say.

In the 20s and 30s the standouts were rotund Gabby Hartnett of the Cubs and big-eared Mickey Cochrane of the A's and, later, the Tigers.

Hartnett hit the famous "home run in the gloamin'" at dusk on September 28, 1938, to break the Pirates' backs and lead the Cubs to a pennant. He averaged .297 over a twenty-year career, with 236 homers and 1179 RBIs.

Mickey Cochrane may have been the best of all of them, despite his trouble with Pepper Martin—"the Wild Horse of the Osage"—in the 1931 Series. Cochrane, whose career ended in a near-fatal beaning, averaged .320 over 13 years, with 119 home runs and 832 RBIs. He is remembered as being fast, fierce, and a natural leader.

Natural leaders were in short supply on the Expos last year, and some people, including Woodie Fryman, thought it was a problem. "When you don't get your leadership from the manager, you've got to get it from players everybody respects. Dawson's not a leader. Neither is Carter, or Oliver. Dawson and Carter are maybe three or four years away from being true leaders. We haven't got anybody like a Willie Stargell or a Mike Schmidt or a Pete Rose."

It's a moot question as to whether the leadership qualities of particular players have much to do with winning ball games. Nobody in particular leads at Los Angeles, yet the Dodgers seem to win a lot. Whitey Herzog leads at St. Louis, not Keith Hernandez. Being a good referee was more important than being a leader when the Oakland A's fought their way to three straight World Series victories.

But Fryman is right about one thing. If a leader does emerge from the Expos' ranks it isn't likely to be Carter, at least not in the foreseeable future.

"Too many of them are jealous of him," says Fryman. "It's not just the money. It's that they all came up together, stepping over one another. And the feeling is that the Expos gave him everything—he was the favourite."

In one corner of the dressing room you'll find Ray Burris, the most fervently religious Expo, drafting for a reporter a list of the team's most committed Christians. Carter, who often leads the team's prayer sessions, isn't on it. Chris Speier says he should be, but Burris won't include him, saying he doesn't want to go into why.

In another corner you have Andre Dawson, who makes approximately half Carter's salary and spends half his on-field life watching his catcher attentively from center field, trying to pick up what pitch might be coming and where he should play the batter.

"Even now," says Dawson, "I feel that management is trying to build the team around Gary Carter. It's been trying to do that since I've been here."

Dawson feels Carter has manoeuvred himself into the position where he can do or say what he wants—that management treats him with kid gloves, as it were—and that Carter has the support of the press and the fans.

"You see one thing about Gary. He knows how to promote himself. He knows how to sell himself."

And what's wrong with that? Reggie Jackson knows how to sell himself. Babe Ruth knew how to sell himself. "A man ought to get all he can earn," said The Babe. "A man who knows he's making money for other people ought to get some of the profit he brings in. Don't make any difference if it's baseball or a bank or a vaudeville show."

Jackson and Ruth knew how to promote themselves so well that they named candy bars after them. Nobody complains about Warren Cromartie knowing how to promote himself.

There are other grievances. Carter was needling Tim Wallach at the batting cage late in the season, and Wallach retaliated by imitating The Kid.

"Who am I?" he asked the other starters. And then, in a high voice, he squeaked, "Hey, why can't I have a day off? How'm I gonna hit if I have to play every day?"

Carter's smile faded, and his face froze. "That's pretty weak," he admonished. "That's really weak."

Since 1977 Carter has caught in 94 per cent of the games the Expos have played. In 1982 the team finally acquired a competent back-up catcher, Tim Blackwell; but Carter still caught 153 games. Of the nine he missed, five were due to an eye infection. He was given four real days off, lots fewer than any other major-league catcher. He felt he was overworked and that the Expos should go to Blackwell more often if only to protect their investment in him. But Fanning said Carter was being paid a lot of money and was going to play a lot of games.

"When a guy makes two million a year and comes in after the game and is bitching because he's in the line-up for the following day's game, then you don't know how to react," says Dawson. "You're lost for words. When you've got other guys who are busting their behinds every day trying to win, and you've got other guys who expect to be playing and aren't, it sort of creates an ill feeling."

If it does, it shouldn't. Catching takes ten times as much energy as any position except pitching, and pitchers get a lot of days off.

"I know there are some jealousies of me on the ball club," says Carter, slowing the avalanche for a second. "Maybe they're saying 'he gets everything,' or whatever. But I worked very, very hard for those things.

"I've always put out. And the fans like that better than when a guy doesn't show up at the ball park, or whatever. I'm not trying to name names, but things happen and pop up in the news, and something negative is written, and that's why fans get down on guys."

Carter gets annoyed. He worked hard on the field and had his best year, but was somehow not considered to be quite the team-man he might be. Tim Raines disappeared into his own cloud for a year and was forgiven.

There is no question that some of the edge of resentment about Carter is based on petty jealousies and is dismissible. But something lingers, an impression that the underlying grievance among grumbling team-mates is that he's out for himself, that the team is incidental.

Any ballplayer who says he isn't out for himself is a liar or just going through the traditional locker-room banalities. It's a short-term profession, and an essentially lonely one. Nobody takes up collections when a player is released, whether or not he was the best "team" player on the club.

"I think we're all aware of our stats," says Al Oliver. "We have to be, because that's how we make a living. Let me go out and hit .200 and it doesn't matter if the team goes all the way. I'm gone."

They all know what Oliver is talking about. Deep down, they're all alone. But the mythology holds that the team that goes for glory will most likely be the one that is more than a collection of individuals. It will be the team that has a spirit transcending all the professionalism, the loneliness, and finally, the devotion to self that has dragged these men to the top.

There is no question that The Kid puts out for this team on the field. Perhaps this should be enough—after all, Oliver defines a team player as "a guy who does his job." There is also no question that Carter tries, in his way, to go beyond that. Who bought all the chairs in the dressing room, with everybody's nickname on them? "Nobody wants to be liked more than Gary," said Larry Parrish before he was exiled to Texas.

Steve Rogers gets annoyed when team-mates are cool about Carter. "He doesn't run around with $25,000 bills hanging out of his pockets. He runs around with the same meal money as the rest of us. If there had been any kind of negative atmosphere [about Carter this year] I'd have been teed off at the guys more than anything. Gary hasn't taken a single penny out of any of our pockets."

But there was something in the air.

When somebody commented that Carter had looked slow on a pitch that skipped off his glove and that he was probably tired, why would a pitcher reply, "It's more likely because he was 0-for-3 and his average dipped under .300?"

In the middle of talking about Carter, why would Dawson say, "There are some players who don't mind winning, but who put their personal stats first"—and then stop himself and say, "But I'm not saying that about him." Of course not.

Human nature? The gloom of a losing season? When you lose, fingers are pointed everywhere but in the mirror.

Black-white hostility? Maybe a touch. Carter grew up going to a high school with only one black student and doesn't have much of a feel for black culture. His jive talk around the batting cage is awkward and unnecessary. But he tries.

But maybe most of the problem goes back to the odd jobs, the paper route, the lawn cutting. Baseball, someone once said, is meant to be savoured, not gulped. Even when Gary Carter's grandest dream was to be a major-league player, baseball wasn't enough to occupy his time. There's an edge of contempt about him for people who don't have anything better to do than linger around a ball park—which a lot of his team-mates do. And even if they did have something better to do, many of them would still linger; there is no nicer time at a ball park than between three and four in the afternoon, before everything begins to bustle in preparation for that night's game.

The Kid doesn't usually arrive until sign-in time or sometimes a little later. And even then there's business to take care of—dozens of letters a day, each one to be answered with a signature. He is busy. He is ambitious. And he doesn't apologize.

"Everybody has personal pride in themselves—they all want to excel. I've always had a great theory that nobody remembers number two and everybody remembers number one, so I've always strived to be the best at what I do.

"Now I'm acknowledged to be the best catcher in baseball. Well, I want to live up to that. I want to go out there and do the best I can. I want to make the plays in the field. I hate to make an error. I want to catch every ball. I want to throw everybody out. I want to do everything I possibly can behind the plate. But, all in all, it's also contributing to the team."

What if the team needs more from him?

"I think that there's twenty-five leaders. I don't really think that there's one leader. I think that each player is looked at in a different capacity. . . . I think that players recognize and understand what I go through during the course of the year—especially catching, which is such a demanding job.

"And I have so many other outside activities. I mean I'm showing up at functions and I'm doing this and I'm doing that, and my time is very busy. And my time is very limited.

"And a lot of these guys, I hear, that live at the Chateau Lincoln and all, have got so much time on their hands they don't know what to do with it. And all they do is look forward to coming to the ball park.

"But if I had that kind of time, I don't know what I would do with it. You know—that's why I think some of them are looking at me and saying, 'God, this guy's got so much going on and he's doing so many other outside activities and all and look what he's still doing on the baseball field.' "

Some of them do say that.

And the others? Maybe what they expect, from a guy who's being paid $15 million to play on their team, is less of The Kid Inc., and a little more of the kid.

And maybe there isn't one.

Perhaps what we've got here is a businessman, with a lot of hustle and a great smile. But even if that's all there is, there's one thing for sure.

He's got one hell of a product to sell.

Scoop and a Half

I don't see how anybody can criticize a player of my ability and attitude.
—Al Oliver

The inexorable confidence of Al Oliver is not at issue here. Oliver is a surprisingly quiet man with genuine dignity. He is that very rare person who can sit stark naked and hunched over in a dressing room eating a Polish sausage with his fingers and somehow make it seem genteel, as though he were in the dining room of the Ritz Carlton.

Side by side with his dignity is this confidence. Oliver glows with confidence. It makes you smile because it casts such a pleasant aura. Unlike its ugly cousins brash confidence, false confidence, and over-confidence. There is nothing selfish about Oliver's confidence—he'd like everybody to try it on, get the feel of it, enjoy it. It's made him both successful and nice, and Lord knows the world needs successful niceness.

There are those who find it outlandishly smothered in ego, but these are the terminally grumpy—writers, mainly, from newspapers in Texas and Pennsylvania. He played well for the Rangers and well for the Pirates, and what did he get? Nice fans, he says. But grumpy, grumpy writers. Cynics who saw him as self-centered and conceited.

He ran from their gloom, arriving in Montreal by accident when the Yankees failed to get him because Oscar Gamble refused to be used for barter. Oliver had insisted on being traded because he was sick of losing, sick of the writers, and sure he was underpaid. Texas chose Larry Parrish and Dave Hostetler over an unhappy 35-year-old man with a large contract; and the deal was made a week before the season opened. Little did he know how warmly he would be embraced in the Great White North. *"Expos get left-handed punch by stealing Rangers' Al Oliver,"* read one headline. *"Yesterday McHale won the NL East,"* bannered a column assessing the deal. The writers were on-side, and so was management. McHale immediately began renegotiating his $325,000-a-year salary, settling on $900,000 a year for four years. And he, Fanning, and other Expo executives made it clear they were tickled they had acquired him.

"Montreal took me away from a lot of negatives that I didn't want to be part of. When I came here management didn't necessarily talk that much about my ability on the field. They talked about the person—the man—which has never been talked about before. Jim Fanning said I was one of the nicest people he'd met since he'd been in baseball. Now I'd never heard that before."

Confidence piled on confidence. The previous October, on his thirty-fifth birthday, Oliver decided he was too fat. He was confident that he had the self-discipline to lose a lot of weight—and he did, dropping from 220 lbs. to 192 lbs. by eating Caesar salads and not much else while continuing to sweat it out at the racquetball court.

"When I got on that scale and weighed 192 there wasn't anything in the world I didn't figure I could do. Except swimming, maybe."

The closest Al Oliver comes to swimming is the five or six showers he takes every day. "I've always been a personal-hygiene freak." Everyone who came from his home town of Portsmouth, Ohio, was an athlete, he says. "Not only an athlete, but a super athlete." Gene Tenace. Larry Hisle, Chuck Ealey. Before them, Branch Rickey and Del Rice. And others who didn't make the big time. The black ones were generally best at all sports, he thinks, with the exception of swimming. "The reason we couldn't swim is that we weren't allowed in the city pools."

There is no bitterness in his voice when he says this. In fact, he guffaws at the idea that he'll probably never join Terry Francona in diving into puddles during rain delays. "Actually it's nice to know I have one little flaw. I guess it means I am human after all." He guffaws again, beaming at the thought of such a tiny-flawed person being him.

Portsmouth was a smokestack town of steel mills, brick plants, and shoe factories when he grew up there. His mother died when he was 11. His father was a deacon at Beulah Baptist Church. A fastidious man, he pulled on his pants in the morning standing on the bed, so the cuffs didn't touch the floor. But he worked at the brick factory, and his lungs were full of dust. He died of silicosis the day his twenty-year-old son signed his first pro contract.

There was a younger brother and a younger sister, and the house was full of harmony. "My mother and father were the most positive people I've ever met. We never heard them argue. I was born an optimist, and they reinforced it. They more or less told us there was nothing we couldn't do if we set our minds to it."

They were taught, above all, to be honest. "If you lied in our house you got whipped for it.

"I was marble champion in our neighbourhood. I had thousands of marbles. One day my friend, Jimmy Parker, was riding his bike to the store, and I knew why he was going there. To steal some boaters—they were the great big marbles. I found myself in there with him, and all of a sudden I was stealing. The guy knew we had something, but we said we didn't, and ran for our bikes. Jimmy rode off, but I had to stop. I knew I was wrong.

"The guys still tease me today. They were standing in this park in our neighbourhood approximately half a mile from our house, and they heard me crying and yelling from my father whipping me. Ever since then I haven't even thought about lying and stealing."

If there were also lessons about modesty and humility, they didn't sink in. Besides, confidence seemed a better ally than humility when you were a crack sprinter, a broad jumper, a forward on the basketball team, the quarterback on the football team, and getting into baseball.

His favourite sport was basketball, but he claims he chose baseball because it promised a longer career. The dubious may wonder how much future a 6'0" forward would have had in professional basketball, but Oliver does not. When baseball players first talked of striking, he considered playing for the Dallas Mavericks. "There's no doubt I could have done it, because basketball is my game."

Nevertheless, he showed more aptitude for baseball than, say, Danny Ainge. He came up to stay with Pittsburgh in 1969 and, despite being bounced around from first base to various outfield positions, he had made himself into a .300 hitter by 1972 and has dipped below that only twice since. His averages from 1972 to 1982: .312, .292, .321, .280, .323, .308, .324, .323, .319, .309, and in 1982, .331. During that eleven-year stretch only Rod Carew hit for a higher average. If you take just the last decade, Carew, George Brett, and Bill Madlock have hit higher than Oliver. Rose, Dave Parker, Steve Garvey, Ken Griffey, Bill Buckner, and several hundred other players have not.

After 14 years in the majors, Oliver has a .305 lifetime batting average, 206 home runs, 1163 RBIs, and 2362 hits; he's shooting for 3,000. "The only reason I want 3000 is that it should get me into the Hall of Fame. I'm the kind of guy who could get 2999 and not make it."

Oliver at the plate is stone-faced majesty, the kind of natural, pure hitter the Expos had been missing, a perfect left-handed counterweight to bat between Dawson and Carter. Every batter has a different facial expression at the moment of truth, when the ball leaves the pitcher's hand and starts hissing toward him. Dawson glowers, Carter snarls. Oliver stands there deadpan, as though he's escaped from a wax museum.

Steve Carlton blanks out the batter when he pitches. Oliver blanks out the pitcher when he bats, except to pick up the blur of the delivery beginning. This signals him to lift his right foot into a stride forward, a stride that will give him the momentum to shift his weight from his back to his front foot. Some batters stride with a lurch; Oliver's stride is smooth and rhythmic: it is designed to set that right front foot down with either haste or leisure, depending on the speed of the pitch, and to throttle the shift in weight from back to front at precisely the moment the hands, arms, and shoulders want support in flinging the head of the bat forward to drive the ball.

The hands are the essence of the motion. Many batters move them too quickly in an attempt to be quick on a pitch, to pull it. The shoulder flies out, the neck twists, the head flies up, the eyes come off the ball and the batter lunges, guessing where the ball is. If it isn't where he suspected it would be, there's not much he can do about it because he's committed himself early and his eyes are lifting off the ball anyway. Larry Parrish (1974–1982).

Oliver does not guess. He is looking for the ball and he tries not to care whether it's high, low, inside, or outside, as long as it's hittable. His magic word is "wait."

Feel loose in the batter's box; keep the hands back until the last possible micro-second, which will give you the best view of the ball and force you to maximize your bat speed; and hit the ball where it's pitched. Drive forward into the ball with a short, quick, powerful stroke, trying neither to pull it in one direction nor place it in the other. Infinitesimally small errors in timing will take care of directing the ball; your job is to aim it up the middle, and to hit it as quickly and hard as you can.

And nobody hits the ball harder, more consistently, than Al Oliver. He swings down on the ball so the bat head is positioned to drive the ball it meets instead of lifting it. Swinging down while keeping the hands back eliminates long loopy swings that have large holes in them against good pitching. When Dave Kingman times a pitch perfectly he can whomp it a mile; but if he's the tiniest fraction off in his timing he gets nothing, because the ball found the loop in his swing. Oliver's bat, coming at the ball straight, is in the contact alley longer.

Or, as Oliver told Tim Wallach when he asked for hitting advice in spring training, "See the ball and hit it." He chortles again when he thinks of saying that. He has been thinking of becoming a hitting instructor when he's through playing, but after he talked to Wallach he realized he was going to have to get a little more analytical.

But all the analysis in the world doesn't alter the fact that the best batters have the quickest reflexes. And behind all the muscles, this slowly aging man still has them. When Oliver was playing with Pittsburgh, a doctor used to treating athletes told him he had the best hand-eye co-ordination he'd ever seen. And perfect vision. A head start.

"Lots of guys have great hand-eye co-ordination," he says modestly. "But for one reason or another they don't have the confidence. That's the difference." The inexorable confidence of Al Oliver was tested all spring and summer and found whole.

Professional baseball is riddled with false confidence, simply because it's such a fragile existence. The egos of home-town heroes have been nurtured all their young lives on the splendour of their arms, bats, or gloves, which look less like gold and more like clay the closer they get to the top. Most of the young men who come to the major leagues today have never failed at anything, Jim Fanning points out. "All of a sudden they come into a man's game. How prepared are they to accept the great discouragements and disappointments of major-league baseball?"

The terror of failure is never far below the surface of a game in which the average player lasts four years, then disappears. Clubhouses are full of religious fervour now. Some believe deeply, some are clutching. In one prayer session held in the trainer's room in the Expos' clubhouse last July, every member of the team's starting line-up was present. Except Al Oliver.

"You couldn't get more religious then we were," he says, remembering his childhood. And he still considers himself religious—he reads the Bible—but religion isn't at the core of his confidence. Whatever is at that heart was sorely tested in and around first base in 1982.

When the young Oliver played first base for the Pirates, he was one of the best in the game. "Me and Wes Parker of the Dodgers —they compared us as the best." He was nicknamed "Scoop" by a radio announcer in North Carolina while he was in the minors, for his prowess around the bag.

But that was many years ago: before he developed the bone spur in his throwing shoulder that stabbed him with pain when he had to throw quickly; before Texas turned him into a designated hitter and his fielding skills began to atrophy. Before he turned 35.

By the All-Star break Oliver had fourteen errors, three more than any other player named to the National League All-Star Team, and seven more than any other first baseman on either squad.

And it wasn't just the errors. There were countless base hits "under Al Oliver's glove" or "just past Al Oliver." And throws to home he'd make badly or not at all. Opposition runners soon had their instructions: if you're on second and there's a play at first, keep going when you get to third.

Oliver carried his affliction with dignity. Nobody ran harder on pop-ups near the stands or in the stands, to the point of risking injury. Nobody came off the bag with more flair upon completing a successful play, even if he sometimes came off a touch early. That Al Oliver played in the league without designated hitters spoke of foolishness. It also spoke of courage and desire. But it hurt, physically and emotionally.

Toward the end of the year he thought that on a scale of 1 to 10, his arm might have come back to about a 6. "At the start of the season I would say it was a 2.

"After the first few throws I said 'O Lord!' It's a sharp pain on certain throws. If I get in position it's all right, but if I have to hurry my throw, I'm in trouble."

So bad was his arm that he thinks there were balls that he didn't want to catch. "Because, I said, when I field the ball, then what am I going to do with it? Then I didn't field the ball. When you don't field the ball, you don't have to worry about throwing it. I admit it—for the first month of the season I was out on the field hoping they wouldn't hit a ball to me."

He snorts, chuckles, and shakes his head. "I've had to swallow a lot of pride this year. I've always had as much pride in my defence as my offence. It's those easy errors— they're what really bother me. Balls I just used to suck up. But in my mind I know it's not an ability problem. It's an adjustment problem. It's timing.

"What really helped me was that the fans were patient. That really took a lot of pressure off me. Because if they hadn't have been, I wouldn't be having the kind of offensive year I'm having now. I'm very appreciative for that."

Has he ever thought about what kind of speech he'd give if he were elected to the Hall of Fame?

"I've definitely thought about it. When the time comes I've got a pretty good idea of what I'm going to say." There is a pause in the conversation. It will be a glorious moment, and there's no sense in giving away the script now. "All I can say is the tone won't be bitter. I'm going to rise above it; and the ones who criticized me way back when, they're the ones who are going to feel bad. I think what always bothers them is that I'm so sure of myself and they're not. They can't handle it."

His father whipped him for being dishonest. The press has whipped him for being honest. He thinks his father was right.

Perhaps Canada was the right place for him to come. Perhaps Canadians, generally a self-effacing bunch, are sick of modesty and false humility and happy to see a man who feels good about himself.

He isn't sure. "All I know is that it's very self-satisfying for me to be able to be Al Oliver, and for the first time in my career feel accepted." The sportswriters named him the Expos' Most Valuable Player.

And when he's through playing baseball?

"I'd like to be a hitting instructor. But maybe not just with one team. I'd like to be a major-league hitting instructor, going around from team to team and teaching hitting, not so much from the physical aspect as the mental aspect."

There is another pause. He tugs at an All-Star ring, and ponders. Suddenly his confidence slips forward into still another gear. We're in hyperspace.

"What I would really enjoy doing is going around the world

speaking, talking about life. I think that I have something to offer—various philosophies on life that I think are very important to people. That if they would acquire these philosophies there wouldn't be any problems in the world."

He is the Norman Vincent Peale of baseball. Of course he is. He smiles. "I didn't have to work at it. It just happens to be me."

Gentleman Jim Revisited

If you understand your business and your players give you credit for understanding your business and you never lose your enthusiasm for what you're doing, and you have just a normal amount of smarts, you can manage.
—Gene Mauch

The fact that the 1982 Expos turned belly-up and died shortly after Jim Fanning was incapacitated by a migraine headache was never treated as anything more than a coincidence by anyone.

The day before the migraine shattered Fanning, leaving him delirious and out of action for 4⅓ games, the Expos had lost a game to the Mets after having won five in a row.

It had been a serious loss with only seventeen games to go, but they were still in the race. They had a three-game series coming up against the lowly Cubs, whom they'd pasted in a three-game series a week earlier. The league-leading Cardinals were playing a five-game series against the unpredictable Mets, beginning with a double-header that evening.

"If everything goes right," said Fanning before the opener with the Cubs, "we'll be just one game out of first after tonight."

Six innings later, with the score tied 1–1 at Olympic Stadium, Fanning left the game in obvious pain. Within minutes he was grey, alternating moans with gulps for air. Aides took him to his apartment and put him to bed. "Where am I?" he asked. In his apartment, he was told.

"Can't be, can't be. Where was I?"

In the dugout, he was told.

"Why?" he asked.

Because he was manager, they told him.

"I'm not the manager. I'm the general manager."

They rushed him to Queen Elizabeth Hospital, where he was placed in intensive care in the fear that he was suffering a stroke.

Vern Rapp took over as manager when Fanning left the game. Cubs' rookie Pat Tabler scored in the seventh on a Jody Davis sacrifice fly and in the ninth on a Davis single to give the Cubs a

3–1 win. The Cards, meanwhile, swept their double-header with the Mets.

By the time Fanning returned to the dugout the following week the Cards had won five straight; the Expos had dropped four out of five. St. Louis had a seven-game lead, and for the first time there was no doubt: the season was over.

If Whitey Herzog, Joe Torre, or Gene Mauch had been felled in battle and his team had collapsed without him, somebody would surely have made the connection.

In Montreal, nobody did.

When John McHale asked Jim Fanning to take over as manager of the Montreal Expos in the middle of the 1981 pennant race Fanning was exhilarated. "If I had an electrocardiogram on now," he told his old friend McHale, "I'd break the machine."

His enthusiasm radiated at the beginning, when he was as much a cheerleader as a director of men. And there were still traces of it at the end. A week before he would announce that he was giving the job up, a reporter in Philadelphia asked him whether he wanted to continue as manager.

He was non-committal about what he intended to do, but not about what he thought of the job. It was exciting, he said. It was challenging. He pointed to a Phillies coach. "I can see why guys like Dave Bristol there, who has managed different places, would jump up and down like a little boy if the opportunity came along for him to manage again."

For Jim Fanning the chance had lasted a little over a year, and was unlikely ever to come again.

He'd been hired as what McHale had called a "caretaker manager"—hardly the label you'd slap on somebody you intended to keep in the position. But McHale wasn't worried about the year 2000. He was looking at the 1981 World Series, and he didn't think Dick Williams could get his team there. He thought the Expos had the talent, but that Williams, for all his tactical skills, had gone flat. Williams was not only caustic about the players to the press, but he was proving to be a fraud as a disciplinarian. He talked tough, but he was soft on players who were more worried about a life-style than a team. He drank. He was, as far as management was concerned, getting lazy. His line-ups were repetitive and boring. Out.

Enter Jim Fanning. An example. A hard worker who would protect his players rather than savage them. An enthusiast for the game who wasn't afraid to show it. The kind of guy who might provide inspiration, at least in the short term. Who'd let the players play, and show what they could do. And who was loyal to McHale and wouldn't thwart him at every turn, as the tempestuous Williams had.

It nearly worked. Operating with a forty-man roster and what seemed like a lifetime supply of luck and inspiration, Fanning came within a pitch of the Fall Classic. When it ended, he'd done his job.

But wait. Who else was available who was going to do any better? Hadn't he earned a full chance? If he'd done that well without any notice, what could he do with a winter's preparation? And, other things being equal, where were you going to get a guy as willing to comply with your front office as someone who was from your front office?

Re-enter Jim Fanning.

He thought he could do it. Not the way he'd like to—the old way, where you did what you were told and produced or got out. You couldn't kick them around like that any more. The new generation was not only slow to obey, it was expensive. Players cost a lot to develop, their contracts were enormous, and they cost a lot to get rid of.

Never mind. He'd play their game, and they'd play his. Williams was gruff and treated them like chattels, except for his favourites. Fanning would be warm, thoughtful, and a gentleman with everyone. Williams was uncommunicative. Fanning would encourage players to come to him if they had problems. Williams tore strips off them for reporters. Fanning would shoulder the blame himself.

In return, he thought, the players would look up to him and learn to share his reverence for values that had made the game great in the 50s.

If Williams had become boozy and lazy, Fanning was decent, intense, earnest, patient, courteous, and diligent. They could at least learn to be diligent.

Some, like Rodney Scott and Bill Lee, would never understand his formula, of course. But both were close enough to the fringe to dispose of when the time came. The rest he would treat honourably. They, in turn, would see him as a man of honour, and produce for him.

By the All-Star break, we all knew it wasn't working.

A lot of people—including some of his players—said it didn't work because Fanning was too nice a guy. It was an easy catch-phrase, but it probably wasn't true. He was unusually courteous and polite for the semi-civilized world of baseball; but it wasn't immediately evident that those traditional qualities were spillovers from any vast, underground well of niceness. Maybe, maybe not.

Others said he was too meek. He didn't get thrown out of ball games. He wasn't macho enough. McHale made sure everybody knew the story about Jim beating up a couple of toughs outside a restaurant at spring training one year, but the image persisted.

There is no evidence that Fanning was the least bit nervous about arguing with umpires. He may have seen these dust-ups as frivolous at best and counter-productive at worst. Who was to say you couldn't get a little better treatment from the officials if you treated them with more dignity than the other guy?

It might have worked, but his image suffered; and by the end of the year he was out there fuming and swearing as much as any other manager, although he was still unable to get thrown out of a game.

The more frivolous thought the fact that Fanning didn't spit had something to do with his failure as a manager. If he didn't do it because he found it impolite and a disgusting habit, the argument went, he was looking down his nose at the manly habits of his entire trade. If he didn't do it because he thought he'd get the tobacco juice on his uniform, well, that was worse.

In the end, none of these things mattered much. What mattered was that, in addition to being decent, earnest, diligent, patient, courteous, and all the rest, he was also awkward, tense, and sometimes ponderous.

To have been a quick and incisive tactician might have been enough—Williams' mind without Williams' abusiveness. But whether it was lack of managerial experience or lack of managerial instincts, it wasn't there.

To have been relaxed might have been enough. It was enough

for Harvey Kuenn at Milwaukee. The game is easier to play when you're relaxed. It wasn't all Fanning's fault. He was placed in a situation in which the odds were 100-to-1 against him from lack of experience alone, and he foundered. If John McHale wanted to re-establish control of his baseball team, he would have been better to take to the field himself, the way Whitey Herzog did.

In the end, as Mauch said, your players have to give you credit. They have to respect you. In the end, Fanning couldn't bully them, charm them, bribe them, scare them, impress them, inspire them, cajole them, motivate them, amuse them, or make them love or respect him. He made them numb.

It was partially their fault. For all their talent, many of them hadn't mastered the simple fundamentals of the game—things like bunting, baserunning, and making the right play. There's not much use in being a master tactician if your players can't execute.

But Jim Fanning wasn't a master tactician. And he wasn't quick on his feet. When Al Oliver came over from Texas, some-body—preferably the manager who had been in charge of the farm clubs—had to know whether Wallace Johnson could play beside him without destroying the right-hand side of the infield. Jim Fanning should have known. He didn't.

In the end, he managed like he played. He had been a second-string catcher with determination but without the God-given gifts. There was no shame—and much to praise—in that.

But for the manager of the Expos, in the year that was to be their glory, it just wasn't good enough.

September

They think they know how to win, and maybe that's right.
But they still have to prove it to baseball.
—Mike Schmidt
   April 11, 1982

Maybe the Cards will hit a dry spell.
—Andre Dawson
   September 1, 1982

These were the Boys of Autumn, and their time had finally come. Late August had been cruel, so cold that maple trees had turned red and dropped their leaves a month ahead of time.

But September was warm, and a warm World Series at Olympic Stadium wasn't out of the question. September had always been the Expos' month. Nobody was sure why, but for a team that had little aptitude for coming back in the late innings of ball games, they were deadly at winning games late in the season.

Bill James, the analyst and statistician, attributed it to latitude, contending that the Expos aren't withered by the heat as are those who play in the doldrums. As evidence he cited the Chicago Cubs, a team that plays all its home games in the heat of the sun and is notorious for being useless in September.

"Exactly what is implausible about the notion that playing baseball in the heat drains a man?" asked James. "Did you ever put in 162 working days between April 10 and October 1?"

Whatever the reason, the Expos had always been stretch runners, no matter how many lengths they'd fallen behind. Over their history they had amassed a 212–195 record in September for a .521 mark—remarkable, considering they'd played over .500 for only three of their thirteen years in the league.

Between 1979 and 1981 they'd gone 64–37 after September 1 for a .634 average, the best in baseball.

1982 looked even more promising. Pitching was supposed to be crucial in the stretch, and the Expos were nip-and-tuck with the Dodgers as to who had the best staff in baseball. The bullpen was blooming. Jeff Reardon already had 7 wins and 20 saves, and Woodie Fryman had recovered through July and August. Bryn Smith had emerged as a strong third reliever, with a 1.23 ERA in his last eight appearances.

The starting core of Rogers, Lea, Gullickson, and Sanderson was still strong, even if Gullickson and Sanderson were giving up too many home runs.

The hitting had been spotty in recent days, but the batters were still third in the league in average (.264), fourth in home runs, and fifth in RBIs.

Even the fielding had improved a bit. Flynn was making the double play at second, and Oliver was approaching respectability at first.

And for the icing, seventeen of the Expos thirty remaining games were at home, where they'd been playing like their old selves during the second half.

On September 1 the surge began. Fryman and Reardon struck out the side in a dramatic ninth-inning downpour to preserve a 2–1 win for Randy Lerch over Cincinnati. Lerch had been picked up from Milwaukee, where he'd been abysmal, giving up 123 hits in 108 innings and walking 53 with only 33 strikeouts.

Never mind. He knew where he was in September.

The chaps spent September 2 in Toronto, catching a little sun on a pleasant afternoon and winning the Pearson Cup 7–3. Darren Dilks and Mark Schuler, both up from Memphis, threw five no-hit innings between them.

Nobody had bothered to tell the players what a Pearson was, so most of them didn't know.

"Who was Pearson?" asked Dan Norman.

"I don't know anything about it," said Jeff Reardon.

"What is this, anyway?" asked Bryan Little.

Bill Gullickson knew. "I heard it on the radio this morning. It's named after the late premier or whatever."

Chris Speier, an unpredictable type who makes his year-round home in Quebec, and whose daughter would sing the Canadian national anthem in French at Olympic Stadium, bitched. "This thing is a farce—it's a joke. We're busy in the middle of the season. When you're down in the midde of a pennant race, this is the last thing you need."

The game drew an enthusiastic crowd of 23,102 at Exhibition

Stadium; many of the fans rooted for the Expos. It also raised more than $100,000 for amateur baseball in Canada.

The next day, back at the Big O, somebody lost a page of the script for September, and the Atlanta Braves took advantage, winning 4–3 on Claudell Washington's three-run homer and boosting Phil Niekro's record to 14–3.

But the Expos came back with a 4–1 victory as Warren Cromartie hit a home run and went 3-for-4. Astonishingly enough, one of the Expos' runs came on a squeeze bunt by Doug Flynn—a leaf from the Cardinals' play book. The Expos would complete two successful squeezes in 162 games.

Those same Cardinals lost three in a row to the red-hot Giants, leaving the Expos only 3½ games behind on the eve of a three-game series in St. Louis.

It was another must series, and the Expos' hopes of drawing first blood in the opener looked like they'd be realized when Chris Speier singled in the second inning, and Flynn smashed a ball past Willie McGee into deep center. Speier was on his way home and Flynn was rounding second. But wait—the ball had bounced into the stands for a ground-rule double; Speier stayed at third. Bill Gullickson struck out. No score.

Gullickson and Joaquin Andujar settled into a pitchers' duel. The Expos threatened again in the seventh, when Al Oliver beat out an infield hit, Gary Carter sacrificed him to second, and Tim Wallach drove a base hit into left field.

But Billy DeMars held Oliver up at third at the very moment Lonnie Smith was lofting a high marshmallow throw toward the plate. Oliver likely could have scored—even after hesitating—but held up. Wallach didn't see how hopeless the throw was, held up, and was soon trapped in a double play when Speier tapped back to the pitcher. The inning was over.

In the ninth, Ken Oberkfell singled for the Cardinals, took second when Keith Hernandez singled, and came home when a seeing-eye grounder off the bat of George Hendrick scampered to freedom in center field.

The game was over. United Press International transmitted a fine picture of Gary Carter staring toward the outfield as the winning run scored. The photographer didn't have to be quick. Carter stood staring for a long time.

The Expos came back to win the second game 7–4 on two-run

homers by Andre Dawson and Tim Wallach. But in the crunch, it was the Cardinals. In the finale, Bob Forsch handed the Expos their fourth shutout loss in 14 games. The score was again 1–0. Hernandez tripled in the third with two out to drive in Willie McGee, who had walked.

The Expos were 4½ games back, with 23 to go. Once again they pulled themselves together and set out for the top.

They swung into Chicago and swept three straight from the Cubs, who seemed dutifully exhausted from all that heat. The scores were 7–2, 10–6, and 11–3; the bats were rumbling again. Even Scott Sanderson hit his first major-league home run, a wind-swept grand slam.

Then it was back to Montreal, where Warren Cromartie made two fine catches to save a 3–1 victory over the Mets, with Al Oliver driving in two runs. They were two games back. After all the disasters, they were on the threshold.

They beat the Mets again the next night, as Speier hit a bad-hop double to turn a 4–2 deficit into a 5–4 lead that ended in a 6–5 win.

The Cards won, too, but no problem. The Expos, on a five-game roll, were 9–3 in September (all three losses by one run) and were playing 11 of their next 13 games at Olympic Stadium, where they'd been 16–7 since the All-Star break.

Their next six games were against the Mets, with whom they were 10–5 on the year, and the Cubs, with whom they were 12–3. They were 14 games over .500 and had been two games better than any other team in the East since the break. Now was the time.

But the Mets turned obnoxious and won the third game of the series, 9–4. Bryn (The Bear) Smith, a rising star for the past month, gave up five runs on five hits in the seventh.

And worse lay ahead. For, unbeknownst to all but a few ancient historians, it was vendetta time. The Cubs came to town and seemed bitter. Larry Bowa muttered something about humiliation and settling grudges, and most people thought he was talking about the way the Expos had whomped the Cubs throughout the season. It was the kind of talk you'd expect from a tired person.

But 1982 was the least of it. What the Expos were up against were the ghosts of 1969: Ernie Banks. Billy Williams. Don Kessinger. Randy Hundley. Bill Hands. And yes, The Great Canadian, Ferguson Jenkins—the modern-day Cubs' last link with their hopes for glory.

Leo Durocher's Cubs had been coasting along with a 4½-game lead over the Mets on September 1, 1969, and were 40½ up on the brand new, but mostly elderly, Expos. They had been leading the league all year and were well on their way to their first pennant since 1945. But by September 9 the Mets had whittled down that lead to half a game. What the Cubs needed then was what the Expos would need thirteen years later—a little help from the league doormats. Over the next two weeks the Expos found themselves at the eye of history, facing the Mets five times and the Cubs four.

Some claim it would be stretching it to say the Expos killed the Cubs that year—the Cubs themselves were either exhausted from the heat or suicidal. But the Expos helped. The day the Mets first tasted first place—a sunny September 10 in New York—it was because they had just taken a double-header from the Expos. The Expos lost all five games to the Mets.

There was no such generosity for the Cubs. The Expos split their four games with them, beating the Cubs 8–2 on September 15 as sore-armed Mike Wegener fought his way to a three-hitter, and again on September 23, when Ron Fairly and Rusty Staub hammered homers off Ken Holtzman.

"It's great to win," said Gene Mauch, the Little Spoiler. "I so much wanted to end the season well."

The next day the Mets clinched the pennant in New York. Ten thousand fans stormed the field, chanting "Goodbye Leo!"

Leo hung on for another two years; but the Cubs fire turned to ashes, and they never came close again. Banks, Williams, and the rest would end their careers never having played in a World Series—object of pity to their peers. Vengeance belonged to their successors, thirteen years later.

On Thursday, September 16, 1982 at 7:45 p.m., the Expos were two games back of the Cardinals. On Sunday, September 19, at 4:35 p.m., they were 6½ games behind.

During that period the Cardinals won five straight games from the Mets, who seemed unappreciative of everything the Expos had done for them in 1969. The Expos, meanwhile, played the Cubs.

Jenkins, who wasn't scheduled, and Williams, in his last year as a batting instructor, stood back and watched the carnage. The Cubs won the first game 3–1 behind the pitching of Randy Martz, who entered the game with a 4.38 ERA and had given up seven runs in three innings in his previous start.

Just before Jim Fanning left in the sixth inning, suffering from his migraine, Gary Carter came churning around second and was tagged out heading for third, a base already occupied by Al Oliver. Instead of bases loaded it was the end of the inning.

The Expos leaped to a 7–0 lead in the second game, clubbing Doug (The Fidrych) Bird for 8 hits in 4 innings. The rejuvenated Randy Lerch shut the Cubs out for five innings, but they broke through for three runs in the sixth to make it 7–3.

They then proceeded to send ten batters to the plate in the eighth against relievers Ray Burris (two singles and a homer), Bryn Smith (walk, fielder's choice), and Woodie Fryman (triple, pop-up, walk, home run).

Final score: 10–7 for the Cubs. After weeks of near infallibility, the Expo bullpen was crumbling.

And then the Cubs got Rogers. Ten hits and five runs in 5⅓ innings. When he left, the game was tied 5–5. Smith, his magic eluding him now, gave up two runs in 2⅓ innings to lose it, 7–5.

The Expos dropped the first game of a double-header against the Mets the next day and, suddenly, the season was over. They had a dozen games left to spit out the butt ends of their days.

Of all those throngs of forecasters, only the people at *Sport Magazine* had guessed the Cardinals. And the people at *Sport* had been right.

The Cards were a dandy team. They seemed to enjoy being together and playing baseball. Their manager, Whitey Herzog, had gone up to head office for long enough to build the team he wanted and then come back down to manage it. So deft was he in trading for ballplayers, that any one of three of his acquisitions—Lonnie Smith, Bruce Sutter, and Ozzie Smith—could have worn the MVP crown without discomfort.

If his players enjoyed playing the game, Herzog—with a face like an apple doll set under a blond early Beatles' cut—enjoyed managing. Managing and bass fishing. On most days he did both.

The theory at Olympic Stadium was that to inspire players, a manager had to be seen to work long and hard. Herzog's theory was that fishing relaxed you, and so should baseball; and it would if you did what he said.

There were complaints in Montreal—from fans, players, and writers—that the Expos didn't have a leader. Carter, Dawson, and

Oliver had failed to emerge as latter-day Willie Stargells or Pete Roses. The problem didn't arise in St. Louis. "Who is your leader?" Herzog was asked one lazy day in his dugout. "Me," he replied without blinking.

Here was a man who loved the little game—the hit-and-run, the suicide squeeze, hitting to the right side to move the runner over—and he had acquired the players who could make it work.

The Cardinals couldn't hit the ball off the tee the way the Expos could—the Expos had nearly double the Card's home-run total, 133 to 67. But in a season in which the Expos couldn't find anybody with enough bat control to hit second after Terry Francona was injured, the Cardinals had a line-up full of people who could place the ball.

But they didn't win the pennant at the plate. And they didn't win it on the mound, although their pitching did turn out to be gutsy and under-rated. Indeed, in the five games the Cardinals took from the Mets in their finishing kick to the divisional championship, eight pitchers—Forsch, Stuper, Sutter, Rasmussen, Mura, Kaat, Bair, and Lahti—took the mound, each putting in between three and $7\frac{1}{3}$ innings. Rasmussen gave up two runs. The rest gave up one or none. Sutter went a total of $4\frac{2}{3}$ innings, giving up no walks, no hits, and no runs. But they didn't win it on pitching.

And they didn't win it behind the plate. Darrell Porter might have been a deserving World Series hero; but he was booed unmercifully at home during the season, for both defensive and offensive failings.

To some extent they won it from the bench. Their pinch-hitters—guys like Dane Iorg and Gene Tenace—were old enough to know what they were doing. There was invariably somebody around to pinch run (including catcher Glenn Brummer), and Tito Landrum could bunt.

Jim Fanning, sat captive to a group of unripe graduates of his farm system (Norman, Mills, W. Johnson, R. Johnson, Gates, Little, etc.) and sometimes he seemed to freeze even when they could have been used to advantage. Wallace Johnson ran the bases like Rodney Scott when he was given the chance, Bryan Little might have been better than Speier at short and comparable to Flynn at second. Yet Fanning rarely inserted a pinch runner for Speier or Flynn when they got on base in the late innings.

Herzog wasn't perfect either. Sometimes he overdid it, like the night he sent Landrum in to bunt and pulled him out again after he'd fouled off two pitches and run up a two-strike count. Herzog let another batter swing away to complete the strikeout. It wasn't a move likely to give Landrum much confidence in his future as a major-league hitter.

But overdoing it beat underdoing it. Herzog never once called time and wandered on to the field at the exact moment his short-stop was trying to pull off the hidden ball trick. Jim Fanning did, and that was underdoing it.

But more than all this was the Cards' fielding and running. And of the fielders, you had to talk about Ozzie Smith separately. Ozzie Smith fielded like a snake with good hands.

Herzog claimed that Smith had saved him a hundred runs over the year. That seemed a terrible exaggeration at the time. St. Louis gave up the fewest runs in the league—609. The Chicago Cubs gave up the second-most—709.

Herzog was saying that if the Cardinals and Cubs traded short-stops—Smith for Larry Bowa—then the two clubs would be about even, since the Cubs (676) scored just about as many runs as the Cardinals (685) over the year. Which other player could change the Cubs into the Cardinals?

Herzog may have been exaggerating, but if he was, it wasn't by much. Almost once a game Smith stopped a ball from getting through the Cardinal infield that the league's imaginary average shortstop wouldn't have, even after taking into account that Card pitchers gave him some extra chances because they didn't strike out many batters. Over 162 games that would be a few shy of 162 bases; and since three total bases are statistically equal to a run, Smith probably saved Herzog at least fifty runs a year.

Which isn't a bad place to start, considering the rest of the defence was exceptional. Tommy Herr—the Sprite of St. Louis—ranked with the best second basemen in the league, even with a gimpy leg for most of the season. Keith Hernandez was the class of the league at first base, and Ken Oberkfell was fine at third.

Herr and Smith were both injured during the season, Smith during the crucial stretch drive, but Mike Ramsey took away the worry, playing like a regular whenever he was needed.

Behind the infield, in the vast chemical meadows of Busch Stadium, was speed. Lonnie Smith, Willie McGee, and David

Green could catch up with a ball on the warning track even when they played shallow; and George Hendrick could field and throw in right. With Dane Iorg, the hitter, the Cardinals had five gifted outfielders.

That the Cards could field better than the Expos shouldn't have come as a great shock. That they could run better did.

In 1981 the Expos had been known as the Quebec Track Team, with Tim Raines, Rodney Scott, and Andre Dawson dancing the diamond with gleeful abandon. The Expos stole 138 bases in 108 games, which would have come out to 207 over a full season. The Cardinals stole 88 in 102 games, which would have given them 140.

One year later the Expos stole 156 bases, fourth-best in the league and only eight better than the league average of 148. The Cardinals upped their total to 200 to lead everyone, even if they did get thrown out too often (91 times).

To watch the Cardinals was to watch pitchers fret as the bases whirled—with Lonnie Smith, Willie McGee, Tommy Herr, Ozzie Smith, and David Green. The Expos had two runners, Tim Raines and Andre Dawson. Their third-leading base stealer, Tim Wallach, had six, but was caught four times. Scott, who got to the plate twenty-five times in fourteen games before his departure, had five steals. He wasn't caught at all, but he was out.

The Cardinals were greatly inferior to the Expos in three important areas—pitching, catching, and power—but were nevertheless a more skilful team on the field, and were guided by a more skilful manager.

As for attitude, it probably didn't make that much difference. Attitude hasn't been considered the factor it once was since the fractious Oakland A's won all those championships in the 70s. But important or not, there was a difference in attitude.

Warren Cromartie and Darrell Porter, for instance, both suffered through difficult years at the plate. When the Cardinals came to town you could go to the ball park early and watch Porter hit baseballs while everyone else was still playing cards in the club house. You couldn't do that with Warren.

And when John McHale picked up Joel Youngblood to try out in right field when Cromartie was being jeered by impatient fans, Warren pouted his biggest pout. "It's getting like a fucking hotel around here with everybody coming and going," he snarled.

McHale's move turned out to be beneficial, although it may

turn out to be costly if Tom Gorman, the left-handed reliever traded for Youngblood, becomes more of a pitcher than the Expos thought he was. Youngblood didn't hit much, .200, in fact, but he took enough pressure off that Cromartie was able to pull himself together and play decently over the last two months. Decently and quietly.

A few days after Cromartie's hotel quote, Cardinal Lonnie Smith, sporting an average above .300 and fighting Raines for the league's base-stealing crown, was told to take a seat for a game so Herzog could get Expo-killer Dane Iorg into the line-up. Asked whether he resented the move, Smith laughed. "I don't mind sitting out when a guy's that good a hitter."

The same day the Cardinals recalled David Green from Louisville to help out in the outfield. It was hard enough to get playing time in St. Louis without one more outfielder. "That's great," said Smith with genuine enthusiasm. "We all thought it was time to bring him up. I think everybody's glad to see him."

And they were.

"It's just an example of the right mix of people," said Cardinal pitcher Dave LaPoint.

And it was.

The mixture gathered on Monday, September 27, in the visitors' dressing room at Olympic Stadium, following a 4–2 victory over the Expos.

"We did it! We did it!" they shouted, then showered in Spanish champagne.

A hundred yards to the East, the Expos dressing room was silent. "It's just an anti-climax," shrugged Steve Rogers. "We knew it was over."

The next day Jim Fanning said the team would go all out to finish second. "This team wants to finish second," he said. "*I* want to finish second," he added, poking the index finger of his right hand into his breastbone for emphasis.

In the interests of finishing second, Fanning played his veterans at their appointed positions: Chris Speier at short and Joel Youngblood/Warren Cromartie in right.

Bryan Little and Roy Johnson, unknown commodities in search of starting positions in 1983, were given three and two starts respectively to strut their stuff.

It might have been brighter to play them every inning, in the interests of finding out whether they could do the job. The more thorough the front office's assessment of them, the easier it would be to figure out who to trade over the winter.

But real baseball people probably have better ways of assessing players than putting them into the line-up and better ways of building up their confidence than getting them into games when the pressure is off.

Wallace Johnson, for instance, hardly touched the field when he was brought up in late 1981, because the Expos were in a pennant race. Yet enough was known about his fielding abilities in the spring of 1982 to start him at second base.

In the end, the Expos finished third—six games behind the Cardinals, three games back of the Philadelphia Phillies, and two games ahead of the Pittsburgh Pirates.

They were 16–14 in games played in September and October—17–14 if you counted the Pearson Cup.

Their performance in 1982 left them as the dominant team in the National League over the previous four years, with nothing but one divisional title to show for it. The standings, as prepared by Richard Griffin, the Expos' publicist:

Team (1979–82)	W	L	Pct.	GB
Expos	331	261	.559	—
Phillies	323	270	.545	– 8½
Dodgers	322	275	.539	–11½
Astros	320	277	.536	–13½
Pirates	311	277	.529	–18
Cardinals	311	277	.529	–18
Reds	306	287	.516	–25½

Each of the teams listed won a divisional title, as did the Braves, who were under .500 over the four years. The Cardinals, Phillies, Pirates, and Dodgers each went on to the World Series and became World Champions. The Expos may have been the class of the league, but had yet to disprove Mike Schmidt's suspicion that they didn't know how to win when it counted.

HITTING

There were a few chinks, but basically it was good. The team was fourth in the league in batting at .262, fourth in the league in home runs, with 133, and third to the Pirates in runs scored, which is what offence is all about.

Al Oliver won the batting title, hitting .331. He also led the league in doubles, with 40, in hits, with 204, and tied for the league lead in RBIs, with 109.

Gary Carter and Tim Wallach hit 29 and 28 home runs respectively, each driving in 97 runs. Carter raised his average from .251 to .293 and Wallach upped his from .236 to .268. Raines had an indifferent year at the plate but still led the league in stolen bases with 78.

The much-maligned Warren Cromartie fell far short of the .325 year he had been predicting (.254) but wasn't the offensive disaster he was made out to be. He drew 69 walks (a career high) hit 14 home runs (also a high); hit into fewer double plays than Carter, Wallach, Speier, and Oliver; and was second on the team to Dawson with 13 game-winning RBIs. He drove in 62 runs overall. In fact, because he boosted his walks and home runs and cut down on hitting into double plays, Cromartie's Total Average in 1982 (bases achieved divided by bases blown) was .769, up from the .735 he recorded in 1981.

Speier had a passable year at the plate, hitting .257 with 60 RBIs; but he hit .202 with runners in scoring position, .202 in September/October, and went 1-for-7 on the basepaths.

Dawson, hampered by wrist injuries, hit .301 to qualify as one of only seven batters in the league to hit .300, but drew only 34 walks and struck out 96 times in only a fair year for him.

Doug Flynn could not hit, walk, or run, but was somehow sent to the plate five times with the bases loaded, going 0-for-5 while pinch-hitters languished on the bench and Bryan Little waited to fill in at second.

The Expos batted .226 as a team with the bases loaded, coming up 124 times, collecting 28 hits, and driving in 61 runs—about 25 short of what might have been acceptable. The notables: Oliver 2-for-17; Carter 4-for-19; Dawson 6-for-16 (.375 with 12 RBIs); Raines 2-for-4; Cromartie 3-for-13; Wallach 4-for-20 (2 HRs, 15 RBIs); Speier 4-for-16; Blackwell 1-for-2; Norman 1-for-2.

Of the sixty-six times the team came out of the seventh inning behind, it went on to lose sixty times, managing to come from behind to overcome one-run deficits only four times and two-run deficits twice.

Of the seventy-four times they were leading coming out of the seventh inning, on the other hand, they blew eight games—twice after holding one-run leads, four times after two-run leads, and twice with four-run leads.

The bottom line: they scored eight runs to come back in six games and gave away eighteen runs to blow eight games.

But if the hitting wasn't always timely it was as good as anybody's. Other than Pittsburgh's.

PITCHING

The pitching was as good as the hitting. The staff was second to the Dodgers in ERA, second to the Reds in walk-to-strikeout ratio, and as formidable as any in the league.

True, Burris had a terrible year, and Gullickson and Sanderson marred what would have been fine records by giving up too many home runs. Gullickson, who had given up only three in shortened 1981, ballooned to twenty-five. Sanderson went from ten to twenty-four.

But Rogers had his best year ever, Lea made a miraculous comeback, and Reardon was one of the premier relief pitchers in the league, posting a 7-4 record with a 2.06 ERA. Throwing out five poor performances over the whole season would have left him with a 0.94 ERA in 70 other games. Fryman and Smith had decent years, and Palmer was valiant.

There was nothing much wrong with the pitching.

CATCHING

Carter remained the best. Defensively, he led the league in games played, put-outs, assists, and total chances. Only bazooka-armed Tony Peña of the Pirates was in his class. Peña edged Carter for the Eraser Rate Award for intimidating baserunners by throwing out 71 batters in 179 steal attempts (39.6 per cent), to Carter's 75 in 196 attempts (38.2 per cent). But Peña couldn't hit like Carter.

Padres catcher Terry Kennedy's offensive stats were similar to Carter's. But Kennedy couldn't catch like Carter.

FIELDING

It stunk, which shows how useless fielding averages are. The Expos tied for third at .980 and smelled like about ninth or tenth.

Carter and Dawson qualified as extraordinary—they were masterful at their positions.

Wallach, Flynn, and Cromartie qualified as ordinary.

Wallach played decent third base, making too many errors (24) but finishing seventh in range, handling an average of 2.69 chances a game compared to the league average of 2.55. Not bad for a rookie starter. But no lifesaver.

Flynn was the best of the Gang of Eight at second, performing well on the double play but handling only 5.03 chances a game, slightly below the league average of 5.09. Average fielding doesn't make up for terrible hitting, but these were desperate times.

Cromartie was sometimes marvelous and sometimes out to lunch. He did rack up ten assists—one of only eight outfielders in the league to get into double figures—and would at least go near the wall.

Raines, Speier, Oliver, and those who played second base for most of the season did not qualify as ordinary.

Raines made only two errors all season, and none in his last 86 games, but often didn't know where he, the ball, his glove, or the wall was. Or even the Astroturf. With his speed he may turn into a good fielder if he stays off the drugs, and if somebody ever takes the time to hit some balls to him. But he wasn't in 1982.

Oliver was a disaster during the first half of the season and a designated hitter with courage in the second. His hitting makes him worth it, but he shouldn't be playing in the same infield with Doug Flynn and Chris Speier. The web becomes too thin.

As ballplayers go, Speier is a decent fielder. As shortstops go, he has run out of gas. He finished tenth in the league in range, behind Johnnie LeMaster.

When you put it all together bad fielding dragged good hitting and fine pitching underwater, and they were never able to struggle to the surface.

When it was all over, Jim Fanning retired with carefully arranged dignity, returning to his role of vice-president of player development.

Bill Virdon was hired to replace him as manager. Virdon, who brought with him a reputation for demanding discipline and mastery of fundamentals, said, "The talent is here, or close to being here."

One or the other is true.

The People's Team

Steinbrenner sucks! Steinbrenner sucks! Steinbrenner sucks!
Steinbrenner sucks! Steinbrenner sucks!
—A sizable percentage of a crowd of 35,348 at Yankee
  Stadium one day in May 1982

You have to realize that the people come to the ball park
frustrated.
—George Steinbrenner
  The same day in May 1982

The Montreal Expos don't have a George Steinbrenner. Nor do they have fans who would yell, "Charles Bronfman sucks!" Or "John McHale sucks!" Or "Hugh Hallward sucks!"

There is some doubt as to whether Expo fans would even whisper such indignities. Or think them. But you never know. Who would have thought you'd ever hear Andre Dawson or Gary Carter booed in Montreal? It didn't happen very often, and it wasn't very loud, but it happened in 1982.

In the early days at Jarry Park you couldn't even work up a loud groan for that kind of thing. Those were the days of innocence, when lovers were treated with reverence even if they snored.

Of course you could always boo Gene Mauch, just as you could boo Jim Fanning. Managers are made for booing.

But "Steinbrenner sucks!"? A man would have to be uniquely offensive to qualify for that kind of abuse, you'd think, even in New York.

There's nothing most people would find offensive about Charles Bronfman, Hugh Hallward, or John McHale. Together they form the unofficial executive committee that makes important Expo decisions. Bronfman, the Seagram's heir and the richest owner in baseball, controls 45 per cent of the Expos' stock. Hallward, who made it big in construction and later in shopping centers, has 10 per cent, as does McHale, the baseball man.

Hallward, who got actively involved with the team after the disastrous 1976 season, calls the Expos decision-making process "rotating accountability."

191

"In baseball, as in life, everybody is responsible to somebody else. John McHale is not only a part owner, he's the general manager; and it's his job to make decisions." Who's John McHale responsible to? "To the Board of Directors, which basically boils down to Charles and me," Hallward says. "But we're accountable to the other directors, the other owners, and in turn to public opinion, the fans. That's rotating accountability.

"Minor trades, minor player moves—John does them. If it's a question of making a major trade he will discuss that trade with us first. I know of no case where we've tried to interfere. Occasionally we'll act as devil's advocates, questioning and probing. It's a question of consultation."

Bronfman thinks he has "a fair input into the decision-making process. I have more now than I had before."

Would he call it veto rights? "Yeah, I would say so. But I don't think I've ever said no."

He is careful in speaking about McHale's role, because McHale is proud of being a professional baseball man and would unlikely endure a situation in which he didn't have the final say, no matter how much Hallward and Bronfman might have turned themselves into knowledgeable amateurs on baseball.

With players, for instance, Bronfman is clear that "the buck stops at John McHale." Rodney Scott may have enjoyed his 1981 champagne-squirting bout with Bronfman in the dressing room after the Expos had knocked off the Phillies, for instance. But he could only wonder out loud where Bronfman was when McHale whizzed him in May.

Bronfman was nowhere around, and hasn't been since spring training in 1969, when Mack Jones tried to borrow $5,000 from him.

Bronfman had shelled out $4.5 million in pocket money and had himself a baseball team. He had only intended to kick in $1 million with ten other investors, but several had chickened out and in the end he was Owner Number One.

"I was awe-struck at this new thing that had happened in my life. I'd see Mack Jones every morning, and he used to call me 'Money'—that was his nickname for me. He'd say, 'Mornin', Money, how's it feel to have all that money in the bank.'

"And we'd kid back and forth. I remember one morning he broke three bats and I said, 'Hey Jones—that'll cost you fifteen dollars.' And he'd say, 'you cheap son-of-a-bitch'—you know.

"And then one day, all of a sudden, he said, 'Can you lend me five?' And I said, 'Five dollars—sure.' And he said, 'I'm not talking five dollars. I'm talking five thou.'

"And a bell went off right there in my head and I went running to John—literally—and said, John, I want rules right now. Because my partners were all down there, and I could see it was going to turn into a popularity contest. I'd say 'no' and one of the others would say 'yes,' or vice-versa, and they'd start playing us off against each other.

"I made John draw up a set of rules. And he thought it was great that we'd all go down to spring training and kibbitz with the players and do anything we wanted—play in the outfield, take batting practice. But then, once the season starts, it's the manager's team. If you're a player and you want to talk to anybody about anything you go to John McHale at the top—not anybody else.

"I remember when Rusty Staub was living in Montreal, I asked him to come to my office one day. And I said, 'Rusty, I would like to be a friend of yours, but there's something you've got to understand. I will never invite you to my house—ever.' And we had a real nice chat about it and I said, 'Please never invite me to your house.' And that was understood."

If both Bronfman and Hallward understand the importance of avoiding the Steinbrenner syndrome, still, there is the yearning of influential men to have influence, particularly when playing with their toys.

Bronfman, for instance, blames himself for Expo Tony Bernazard going to the Chicago White Sox in exchange for a left-handed pitcher named Richard Wortham, a hard thrower who lost what little control he had when he came to Montreal in 1981.

The trade never got the exposure of the horrendous Singleton/Torrez for McNally/Coggins deal of 1975, because Bernazard went off and hit .276 in 1981 and .256 in 1982—nice for a second baseman, but not automatic Hall of Fame. He did drive in runs, however (56 on 11 homers in 1982) and displayed the best range of any second baseman in baseball.

With Bernazard at second in 1982 the Expos might well have won the East. Wortham had to be released.

You'd think anyone anywhere near the Expos' head office would be denying having had the teensiest thing to do with this trade, but as an involved owner Bronfman claims a piece of it.

"I encouraged John on the bad side of things," says Bronfman, wistfully. "I said that Bernazard was never going to make my club. You do make these mistakes."

But McHale isn't about to surrender any of his territory, even if it's quicksand. He blames himself for Bernazard, "with all due respect" for other owners. "The directors of this club do have some opinions, and their opinions have greatly improved since Day One; but after all, they've been with professionals for fourteen years and you do see a lot of games.

"Bernazard was my fault."

Hallward doesn't claim to have given away any second basemen, but takes some credit for annointing the general manager who did. "I think one of my contributions to the ball club was in 1978—a very disappointing year. By August it was pretty obvious we weren't going anywhere. At that time, the decision was made that John McHale should become more involved—should become general manager. Charlie Fox was general manager at that time, but he was never really meant to be a general manager. [Fox had replaced Jim Fanning in 1977.] Dick Williams had to be controlled, and Charlie Fox didn't have any influence over Williams. John McHale was the only person capable of managing the manager, and Williams wasn't an easy manager to manage. I think I made a significant contribution to that decision."

The decision left McHale in firm control of the Expos. Perhaps not for life—as Hallward says, "nobody is immune" from the judgement of others. But certainly for now. With Bronfman at one shoulder and Hallward at the other, the ample, sad-eyed McHale, who married the owner's niece when he was a .193-hitting first baseman with Detroit during the war, has made the Expos what they are today.

He has assembled a staff, he says, to "present the game in an attractive way, and I'll stack up the result with anybody in the game."

What McHale and his people have done is indeed remarkable, and to a large extent intelligent. There is no team, other than the Toronto Blue Jays, more dependent on its farm system. American teams—particularly the West Coast teams—have a much easier time luring talented free agents to their bosoms than do Canadian teams. Americans simply don't want to leave America, especially for a chilly, French-speaking outpost without a lot of endorsement opportunities or career possibilities once they're out of the game.

So it's been important to bring players up through the Expos' own system, getting them acclimatized to Canada and maintaining a hold on them long enough to show them they can make a decent buck and live a decent life in a northern posting.

The Expos have been remarkably good at this, either through good management or good luck. At the end of the 1981 season, in which the team came within one game of making it to the World Series, Montreal had by far the largest percentage of home-grown talent in its division, and the lowest percentage of talent acquired through trade or free agency. Stars like Steve Rogers, Gary Carter, Andre Dawson, Warren Cromartie, Bill Gullickson, Scott Sanderson, and Tim Raines came up through the system. Blessed is the team that not only chooses the right young players to draft, but develops them so they play to the peak of their abilities when they arrive in the big leagues.

Why would anyone suggest that there might be an element of luck involved in putting together one of the best pools of baseball talent of the late 70s and probably all of the 80s?

Well, for a start there is always an element of luck, bad or good. There has to be some good luck involved in getting Andre Dawson as the 251st draft pick in his year. And there has to be some bad luck in having David Palmer come to look like he might be the best young pitcher in the league, only to have his arm fall apart.

But there is another question. How perfectly smart or capable can an organization's farm system be when the man in charge of that farm system takes over as manager, yet nobody seemed to know that Wallace Johnson could not play second base in the major leagues and that Tim Raines couldn't make the pivot on the double play?

Moreover, the 1982 Expos weren't exactly a showplace for baseball fundamentals—bunting, moving the runner over, throwing to the right base, etc.—and the farm system is where you're supposed to have these things ingrained in you.

Never mind. Nobody's perfect. A great pool of talent has been accumulated, and someone should be saluted for accumulating it. John McHale was named the major leagues' executive of the year in 1981, in a poll of owners and general managers. He obviously didn't win on the basis of clever acquisitions through trades or free agency. Or for wise money management. The Expos lost close to $3 million in 1982 despite attracting 2,318,671 fans and having the most lucrative television contract in the major leagues. More than

$1.3 million of that loss went to pay salaries of discarded players like Frank Taveras, Stan Bahnsen, Rowland Office, Bill Lee, and Rodney Scott. At the same time three players unlikely to field regularly for any major-league team two years from now (Chris Speier, Doug Flynn, and Al Oliver) were guaranteed lucrative contracts of between four and five years.

Nor was McHale acclaimed for overcoming the team's newness and building a franchise with character, traditions, and a romantic history. He didn't. The Expos undervalue that kind of thing. Other teams have coaches or veteran pinch-hitters that tie their teams to other generations, and special days when past heroes return for old-timers' games to have fun and rekindle waning memories. In the world of the Expos people like Woodie Fryman and Rusty Staub are too easily expendible. The club has a plastic soul.

Not that it's easy to build instant tradition. Bob Shirley pitched for the San Diego Padres—who came into being the same year as the Expos—before he was traded to the venerable St. Louis Cardinals. "Tradition in St. Louis," he marvelled, "is Stan Musial coming into the clubhouse and making his rounds. Tradition in San Diego is Nate Colbert coming into the clubhouse and trying to sell a used car."

What McHale has managed to do is take a good game, accumulate some good players to play it, and present it quite successfully to large numbers of receptive fans.

"We set up with the idea that it wasn't my team, and it wasn't my partners' team—that it was the people's team," says Bronfman.

"Right from the beginning that's how we wanted the team to be perceived and accepted by the people."

"We had . . . in normal business terms you'd call it a marketing concept. What we were selling was fun and amusement."

Average attendance in 1982 was 29,727, up from glorious 1981 when the average was 29,510. The fans were mostly from Montreal, of course—76 per cent of them. 15 per cent were from other parts of Quebec, 4.3 per cent from Ontario, 1.8 per cent from other parts of Canada and 2.2 per cent from the United States, according to a club survey conducted last summer.

Of those who came from Montreal, 83.5 per cent listed French as their mother tongue, 77.5 per cent were males, and a healthy 40.2 per cent were between the ages of 18 and 29.

Why did they come?

Because, in the overall scheme of things, they were still watching a pretty good ball club—a contender—whatever the year's disappointments. Because Youppi was funnier than most of the mascots around the league. Because baseball is fashionable in Montreal, unlike football cities like Pittsburgh. Because the hot dogs are good and the condiments are better than most. Because the Expos day-of-game bleacher tickets were the cheapest in the league—80 cents U.S. Because of the promotions—toques, jackets, scarves, etc.—even if the club wasn't smart enough to make sure every kid got one instead of the earliest to arrive.

They came despite things, too. Transit strikes, for one thing. And having a ball park with all the charm of a styrofoam cup. And Camera Day, when small children might have suffocated because nobody thought to organize access to the players.

And what were they like, as fans?

After the season was over, *Gazette* columnist Tim Burke charged they had turned into "obnoxious front-runners"—people who had lost all perspective about the game they were watching and who had begun to care only about whether their team was a winner.

Burke quoted relief pitcher Mike Marshall, an Expo in the early 70s, who said of Expo fans even then, "There has to be a great lack in a society that can get so high and so low about an event over which they have no control."

Expo broadcaster Dave Van Horne has been with the team since the beginning, and he's seen a change in the fans. "It's the nature of Expo fans to show their emotions in extremes. Extreme joy and extreme frustration.

"We've seen that right from the start. For the most part in 1969, we saw joy, day after day. It was a very special joy. Now, with a contending club, we still see great joy, but we also see extreme frustration. We see players booed. We see management booed."

In fairness, Montreal fans didn't just discover booing. Van Horne couldn't think of a single Expo player who had never been booed, with the exception of Rusty Staub.

But there was more of it in 1982, both when it was deserved—on stupid or uninspired play—and when frustrations were such that Gary Carter, who played hard all year and hit far better than anyone could have expected, was booed for striking out with a runner in scoring position.

Some of the players were bitter about it. Andre Dawson said publicly that Montreal fans had become spoiled. Al Oliver said he was shocked because he had heard the Expos had good fans.

"All it did was make us press more. I found myself saying 'I've got to get a hit or they might start booing me.' It came at a time when the team needed encouragement, not pressure."

Scott Sanderson was shocked when Expo fans went after relief pitcher Fred Norman when his skills began to desert him in 1980, after sixteen years in the majors.

"He must have been the nicest, most soft-spoken player in the league. I got goose bumps when I saw them boo him. It taught me a lesson—you can't let the fans get to you that much. They come to the ball park to vent their own frustrations. I think a doctor would say one of the healthiest things a fan can do is to cheer or boo. So it's something we have to accept."

John McHale certainly accepts it.

"They are very unusual fans. They have a terrible feeling of 'if we don't win it's our failure,' and they're so up to win that if a fly ball goes up in the air against us it's going to be a disaster, and when we don't knock a run in from third or second it's such a downer people boo, even when we're ahead a couple of runs.

"So expectations are high. Things have changed. When we first got here the fans would walk by and be very complimentary if we only lost by a few 'points'—like in hockey. But now—you've got to win now. There's a fear of not winning, an embarrassment of not winning that they don't want to be part of."

Does he look forward to the fans adopting a more mature attitude?

McHale, for all his hard-nosed piety and reverence for clean living and discipline, is one of the few people around the Expos with a droll sense of humour.

"I hope not," he smiles. "It all translates into attendance, you know. You can say all you want about how unpleasant it may be at times, but boy, they're here to express it, and that's pretty doggoned important. You'd rather have it that way than have them sitting at home unhappy."

Phyllis Roberts did a lot of sitting at home unhappy last year. Phyllis is 36, a Jamaican-born cleaning lady who belies the image of cleaning ladies.

Her stylish good looks and fashionable apartment on Decarie Boulevard do not suggest that for many years she liked to ride loudly through the streets of Montreal with Duke and Dave on the handlebars of her bicycle, but she did.

"People used to yell out at me, asking what the score was," she remembers with a laugh.

She came to Montreal in 1966, when she was 20—young and impressionable. She never thought much of the institution of marriage, but in 1969 she fell in love. At Jarry Park. With the Expos.

There were some tough years for both her and her team, but over the next decade they grew together. She saved her hard-earned money, never let the drudgery of cleaning other people's houses get her down, and built a comfortable and cheery life for herself.

Her apartment is tastefully furnished, with art nouveau lights, modern art, and street scenes from Paris. The ash trays are crystal. She insists upon quality, and if she can't afford to buy the best she'll wait until she can.

As the quality of her surroundings grew, so did the quality of her team. It was a dream romance. When she travelled—once to Jamaica and once to London—her employers would save her the sports pages so she could go through them when she returned.

Early in the 1982 season her radio slipped off her Raleigh ten-speed bike and broke. She hasn't had it fixed; but she still listens to Duke and Dave in the privacy of her own home, preferring not to go near the ball park anymore.

She is a knowledgeable, articulate, and passionate woman. On one evening in mid-August, with the Expos once again failing to give Steve Rogers much support, she spoke about her year, and why she hadn't bothered to get her radio fixed.

"Rogers—he going to go like Burris by the time they are finished, you know? Like tonight. We know you just have to give Rogers one or two runs, and if you have to scratch for those runs, then scratch for them. I mean Raines led off and stole second. Why didn't Dog Flynn sacrifice him to third so he will score when Dawson hits the fly? Why doesn't Fanning *try* something.

"Now Fanning, they all say he is such a gentleman, okay. He may be a gentleman, but as far as I'm concerned—me—I'm saying that if he was such a gentleman he could see at the All-Star break that the Expos wasn't going anywhere. Why don't he step down and go back to the front office, if he is such a gentleman?

"It's a good thing my neighbour next door is my friend. She don't mind me shouting. I shout like this because I was so frustrated, you know. I was never mad like this before. Usually I got nervous. But there's nothing to be nervous about the Expos this year. It's just frustration.

"I listen to Jeff Rumour and his phone-in show. And I get furious at Jeff Rumour. He say Jim Fanning don't have a bat—these players make a lot of money and why should Jim Fanning have to motivate them.

"Well I don't see it that way. Because if they didn't need a manager they would go out and play without a manager. The manager is there for a purpose.

"All the All-Star Game, they boo him. I mean I don't like that, okay? It's not nice. In all the years I only booed once, at Jarry Park. It was Joe Morgan and he was fighting with one of the Expo players. I think it was a Thursday in 1969. And when he came over at the bat I forgot and I boo. That's my first boo and my last one.

"I scream at my walls because the first thing they did wrong was to have Fanning as the manager. The guy was a terrible general manager, and eventually they kick him out. And he's been fantastic in development, okay? But what happened? Fanning and McHale, they are good friends, so now Fanning is the yes man. Whatever he say to Jim, Jim agree, okay? If Expos had a manager who said no, he wouldn't let Rodney Scott go until we have somebody to replace him. But there is no manager to stand up.

"The second most important mistake is Rodney Scott. I was not a Rodney Scott fan, okay, but you know that guy hit .220 but he go down and grind it out with just his fleet-footed alone. Scott wasn't as fast as that guy Raines, but he know how to run the bases.

"They say he had attitude problems. Let's face it—let's say you're going to have twenty-five kids in a class. Do you think you're going to have all twenty-five ladies and gentlemen? No, you know. One's going to come his own way, or her own way.

"Now they have twenty-five men there. Do they want twenty-five goodies? You're not going to get that. No way. So they release him. But why do they send him away before they can get someone else who can play the position?

"All the changes, and you know what. Now Fanning said if he had it all to do over again he would do it the same way. Now that is stupid. Nearly all the year spring training.

"I have never, never, since 1969 not liked a baseball player the Expos have. Because all the Expo players are my heroes, you know? All of them—before Andre Dawson I have never had an Expo that I could say he's my favourite player.

"Ken Singleton was okay. Rusty Staub, everybody liked. But Andre Dawson—somehow I liked that guy. He just did his work, you know, and he never complained, just go out and do his job.

"I could listen to the Expos twenty-four hours a day, you know. I would think when they play rotten games and Jim Fanning foul it up, I would say—oh, they're making me sick. But I can't turn it off.

"But Fanning. If things didn't change Fanning would be managing for the rest of this century and you'd never get in trouble by the umpire. I don't dig that. I mean I don't need Billy Martin here. But I need a guy that's going to throw the bat around, throw gloves around, when he gets mad.

"This man Zimmer, they call him Popeye. Because when this guy comes out of the dugout he's not going to fight, but you see him pop out—active. And if you are a player that stimulates you. This one in Baltimore—Earl Weaver—players need something like that to stimulate them.

"Gene Mauch—he was not one of my favourite managers. They said he was prejudiced, you know. But he got everything out of nothing. His brain was working, working, working.

"This team is dull, dull, dull, dull. Because they have a dull manager. Before, when the Expos win, I'd sit here and clap and clap. And I would call my friend, Gwen, and we would clap. And the other day I said, you know Gwen, even if the Expos win I don't think I could have that same amount of excitement in me that I had. It's terrible.

"When Neil Armstrong was landing on the moon, I was at Jarry Park, watching the Expos win, sweeping a double-header from the Mets.

"I remember the years—the Expos on the West Coast—I couldn't sleep. Turn off the radio, a big day tomorrow, and two minutes later it's back on and I'm listening. In England I listened to the All-Star Game on my father's short-wave radio and heard Carter hit his home runs.

"Now I listen to the game because I can't turn it off. It's like taking dope. I'm addicted to it.

"And you know what I'm going through now? Now I am in a slump. I can't get excited, so that's a terrible slump. I need motivation. They say why cannot the players motivate themselves? Well I cannot motivate myself.

"And I'm very, very angry. And I'm not angry at the Expos players. It's management. Because I know they ruin a good baseball team.

"I tell you something. If I have to manage these guys, I do a much better job."

She would tell all this to Bill Lee, now with Longeuil of the Quebec Senior League, when she found him working on his car on the street in Westmount on a sunny afternoon in August 1982, just after the Expos had blown another one to the Phils.

Speaking fan to fan, he had to agree.

Rotating accountability, on this, the People's Team.

Hard Core Support

My mother-in-law is a Senator's fan.
Even now—the team long moved,
The first to Minnesota
The second, Texas.
She'd root for anyone in Washington.

I watched her, years ago,
During a particularly long drought.
Once again an early lead blown
The pitcher wild,
Seemed planted in the mound.
She stomped across and stretched to reach the mantel
Switched off her small transistor:
"I can't stand listening to another
Mismanaged ball game!"

But every little while she'd stop—
Click it on, confirm and click it off

Then stalk away, red hair flying—
A bristling banty hen whose chicks
Persisted in their foolish straying.

—John E. Maxfield